Mr. & Mrs. Jonathan and
Martha Kent

Superman
For All Seasons

Strained Peas!

Jeph Loeb *writer* ~ Tim Sale *artist*

Bjarne Hansen *colorist* ~ Richard Starkings *letterer*

Superman created by Jerry Siegel and Joe Shuster

Shelby's Bath

Rusty's Naptime

Superman
For All Seasons

Fast Ball !

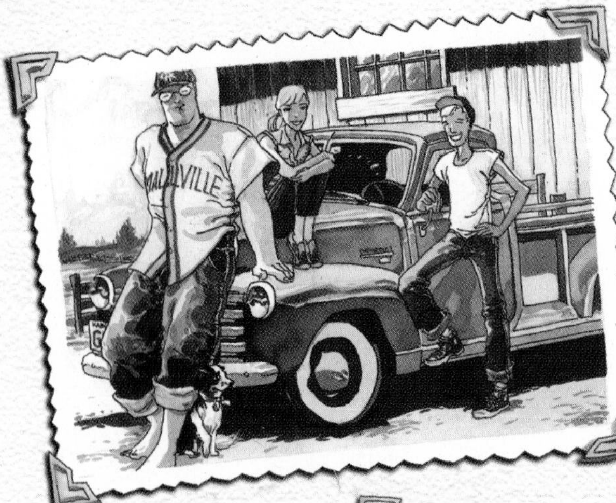

The Home Team

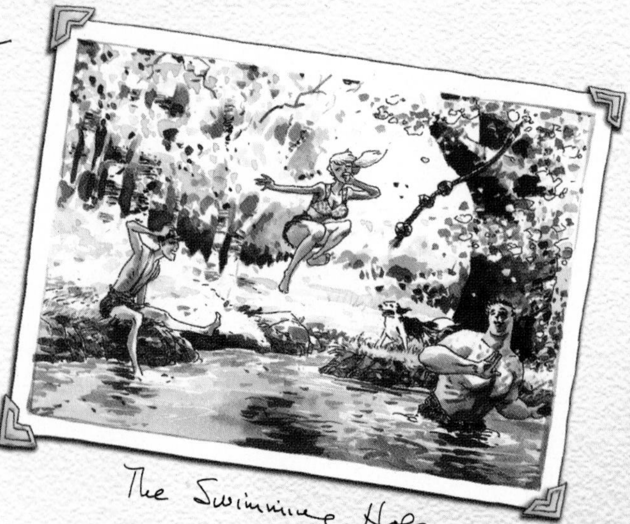

The Swimming Hole

Dan DiDio VP-Editorial   Joey Cavalieri Editor-original series
Maureen McTigue Assistant Editor-original series   Dale Crain Senior Editor-collected edition
Michael Wright Assistant Editor-collected edition   Georg Brewer VP-Design & Retail Product Development
Robbin Brosterman Senior Art Director   Paul Levitz President & Publisher
Richard Bruning Senior VP-Creative Director   Patrick Caldon Senior VP-Finance & Operations
Chris Caramalis VP-Finance   Terri Cunningham VP-Managing Editor
Alison Gill VP-Manufacturing   Rich Johnson VP-Book Trade Sales
Hank Kanalz VP-General Manager, WildStorm   Lillian Laserson Senior VP & General Counsel
Jim Lee Editorial Director-WildStorm   David McKillips VP-Advertising & Custom Publishing
John Nee VP-Business Development   Gregory Noveck Senior VP-Creative Affairs
Cheryl Rubin Senior VP-Brand Management   Bob Wayne VP-Sales & Marketing

SUPERMAN FOR ALL SEASONS

DC Comics, 1700 Broadway, New York, NY 10019
A Warner Bros. Entertainment Company
Printed in Canada. Third Printing. ISBN: 1-56389-529-3. ISBN 13: 978-1-56389-529-6.
Cover illustration by Tim Sale. Cover color by Bjarne Hansen.

The Back Forty

For my father who
would have loved this.
~ *Jeph Loeb*
Los Angeles 1999

For Norman Rockwell and his love of a
vision of Americana that resonates
through its limitations

Jane Burbank and her love
and appreciation of me and my work
with its inherent limitations

Trevor Burbank and his love of being
a kid despite its limitations.
~ *Tim Sale*
Seattle 1999

Good Morning

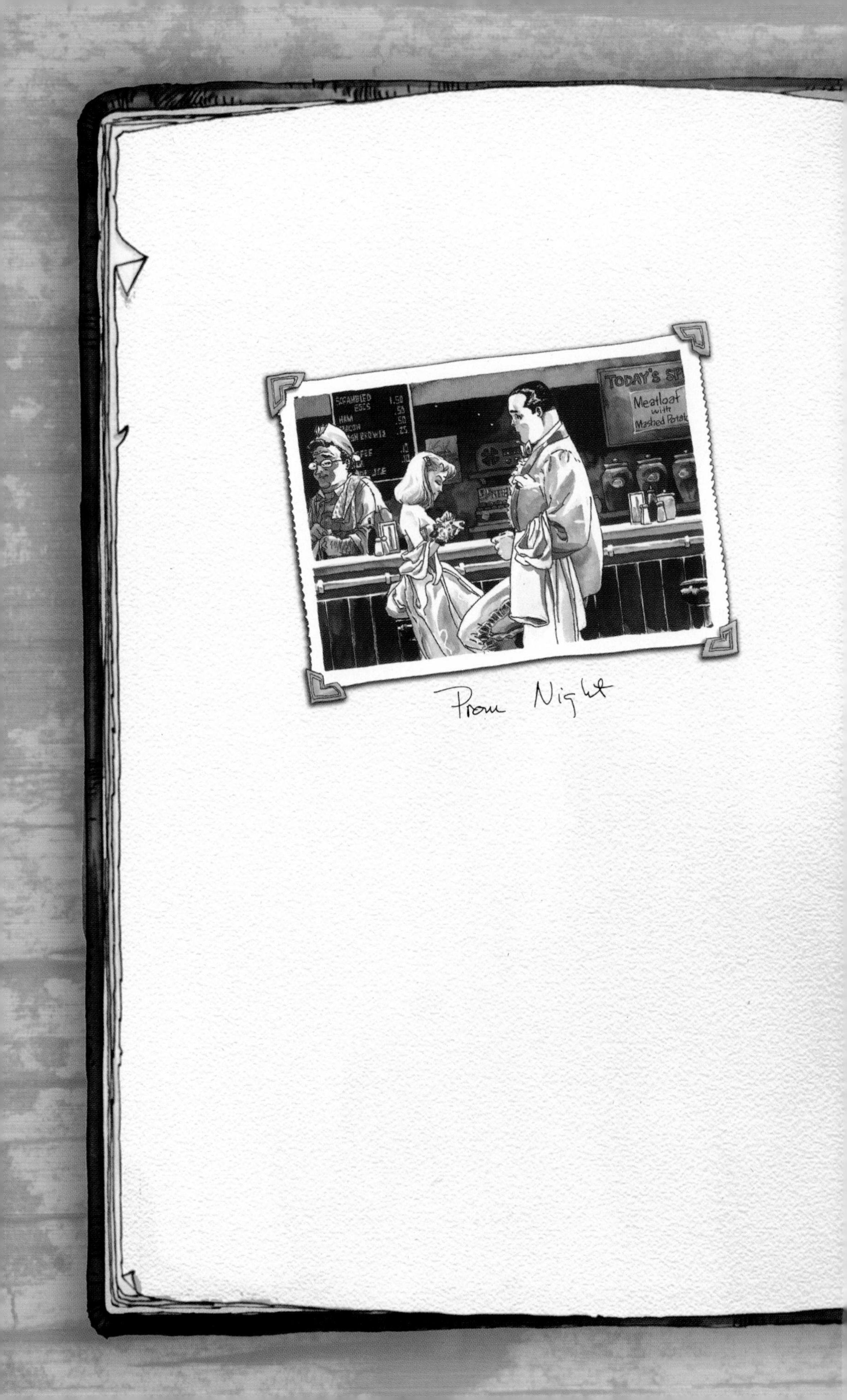

SCRAMBLED EGGS 1.50
HAM .50
BACON .50
TODAY'S SP
Meatloaf
with
Mashed Potat

Prom Night

Spring

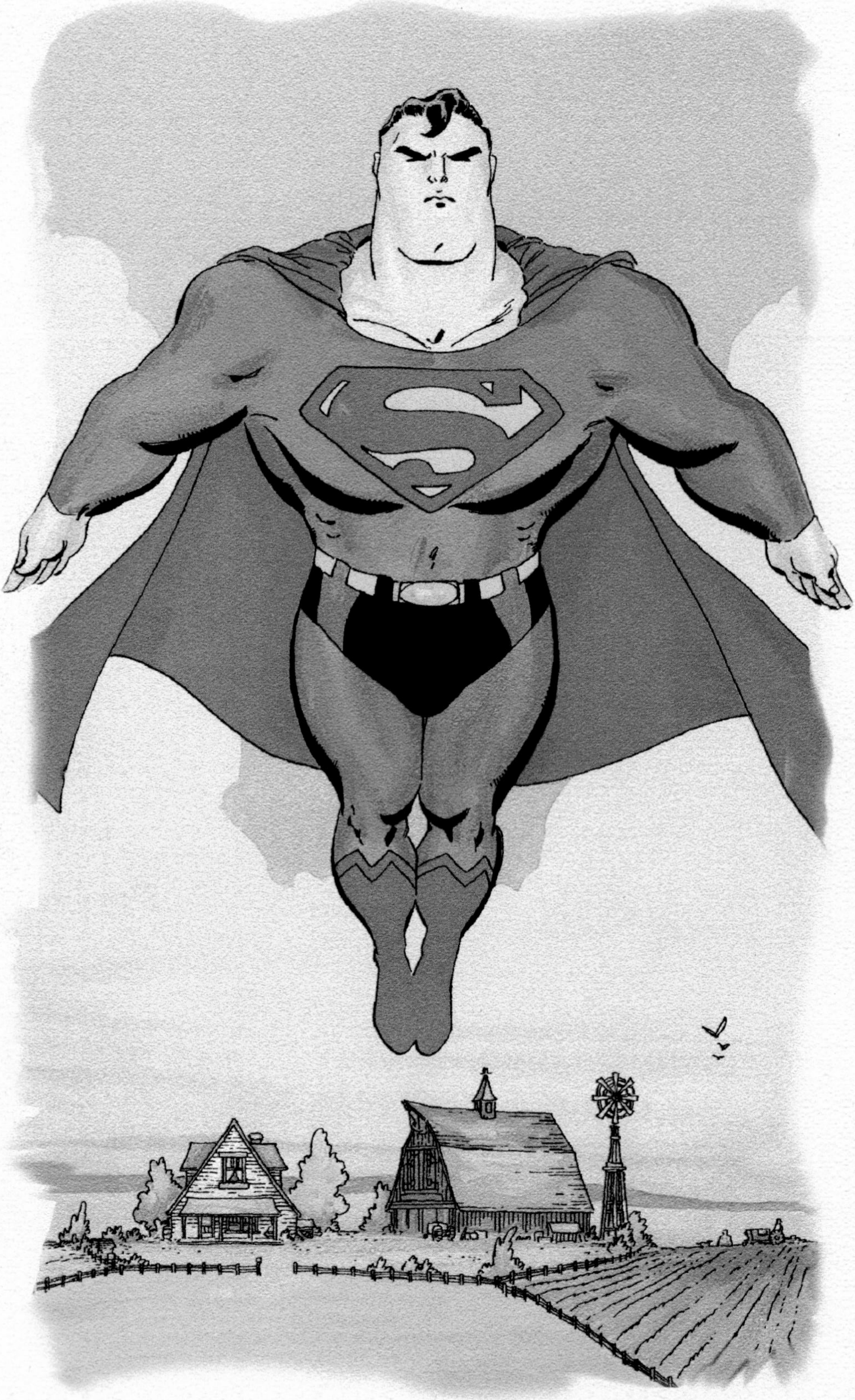

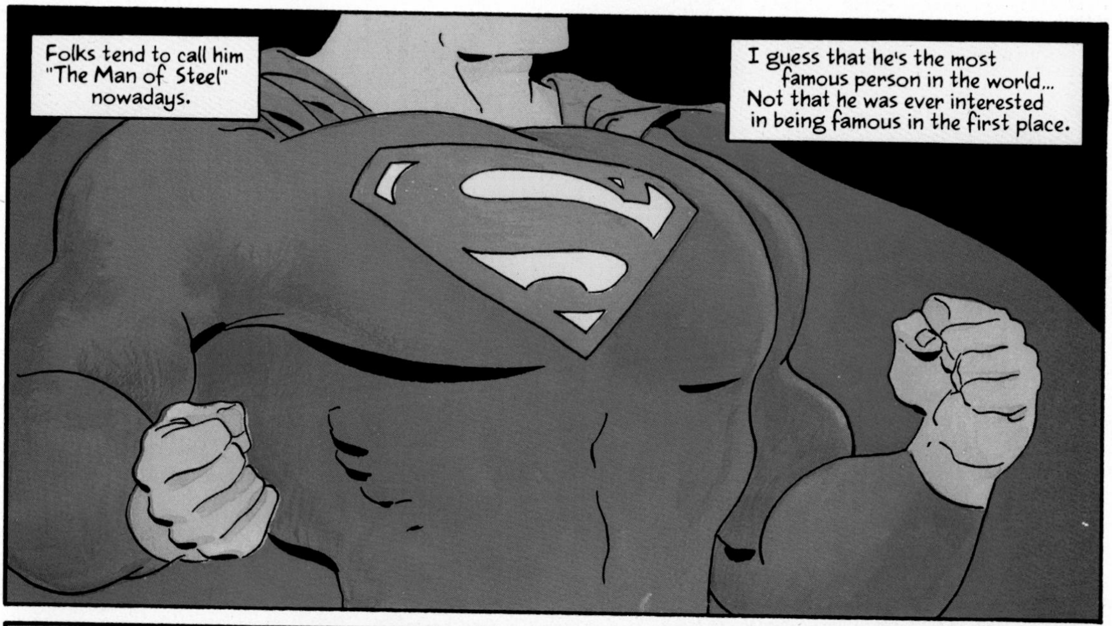
Folks tend to call him "The Man of Steel" nowadays.
I guess that he's the most famous person in the world... Not that he was ever interested in being famous in the first place.

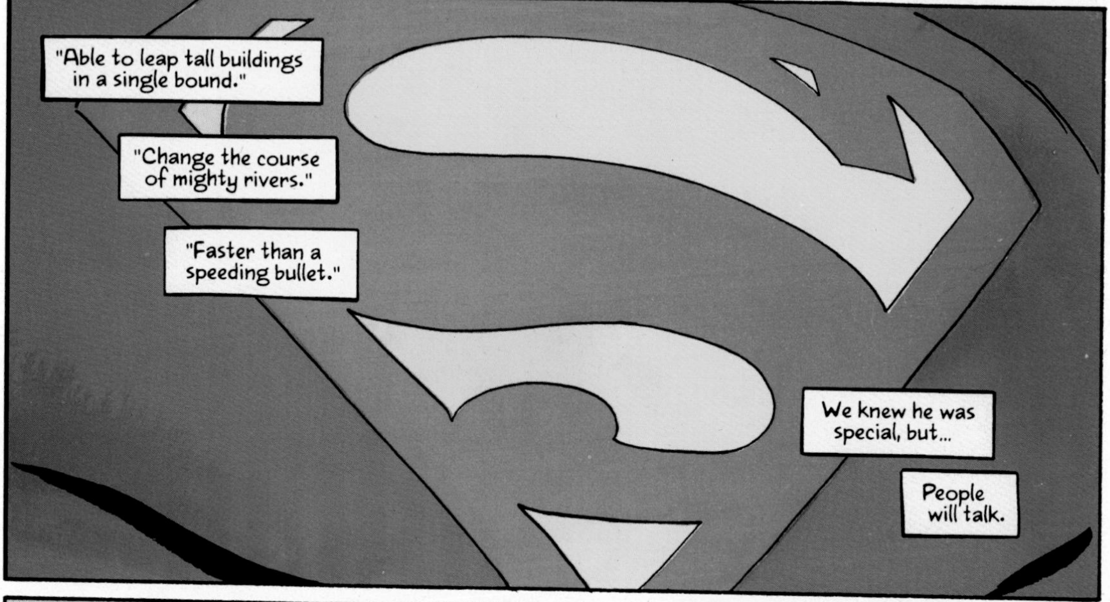
"Able to leap tall buildings in a single bound."
"Change the course of mighty rivers."
"Faster than a speeding bullet."
We knew he was special, but...
People will talk.

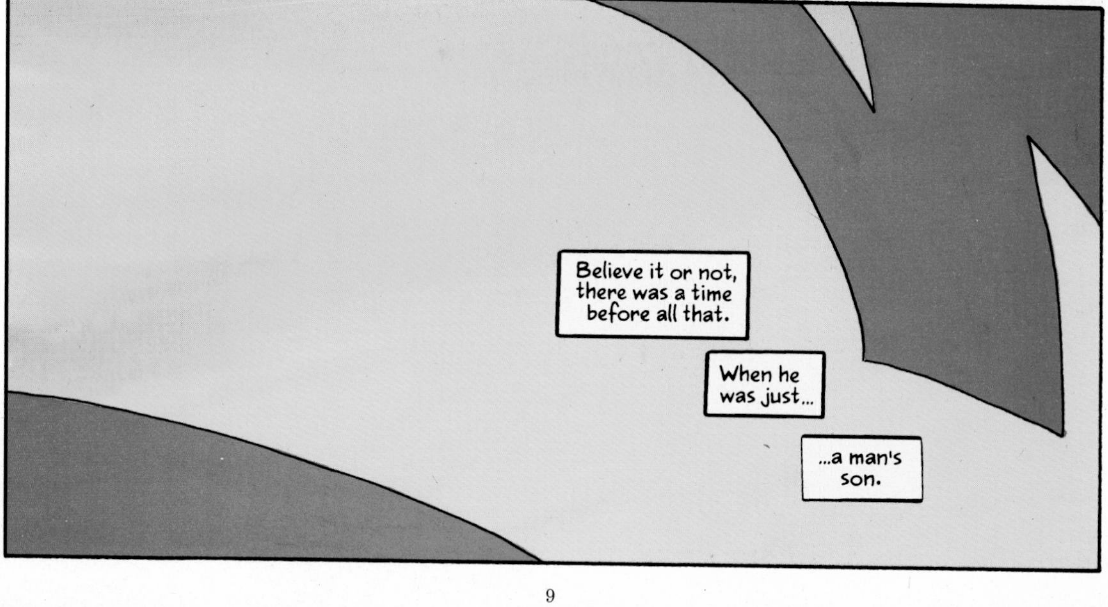
Believe it or not, there was a time before all that.
When he was just...
...a man's son.

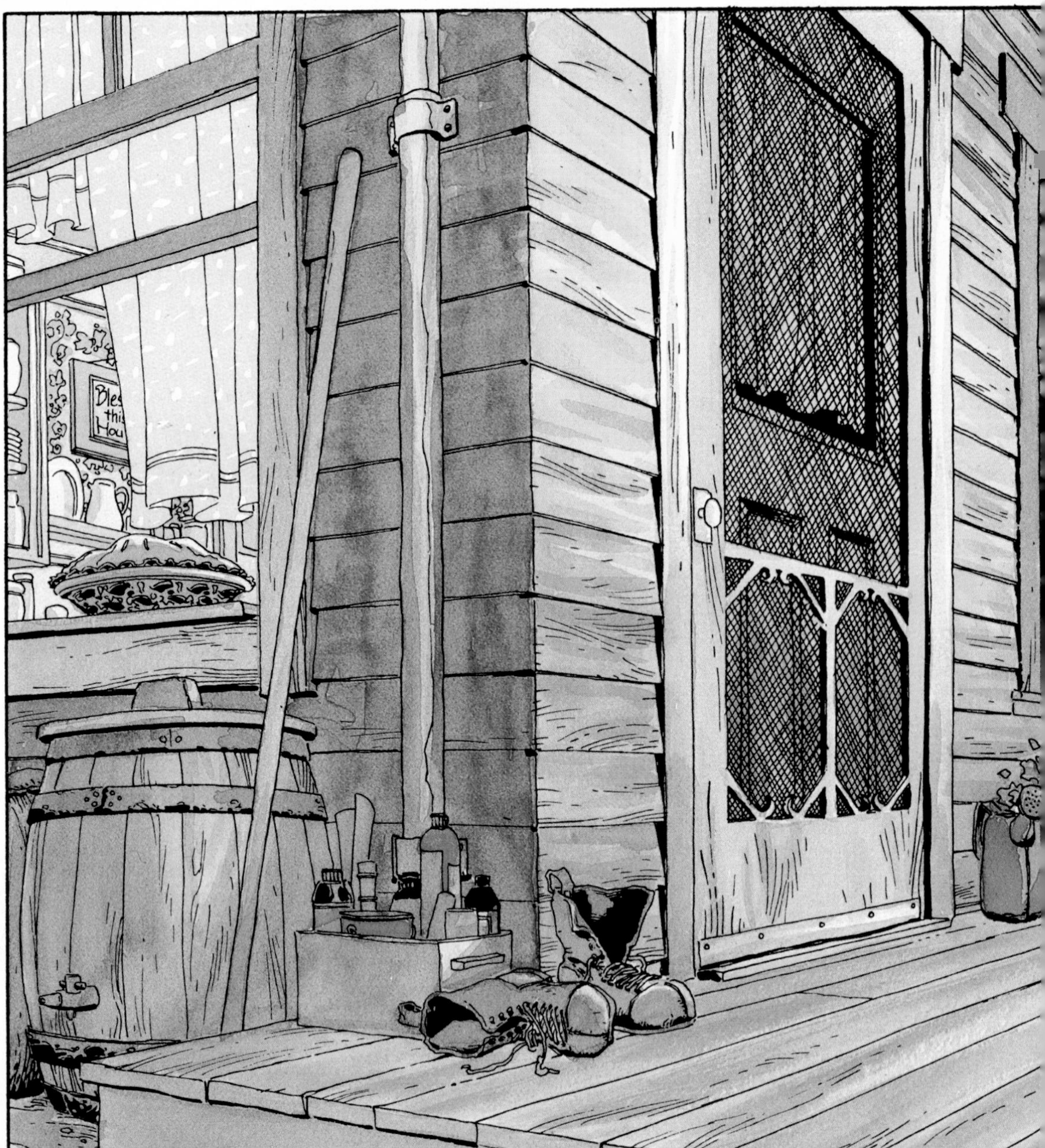

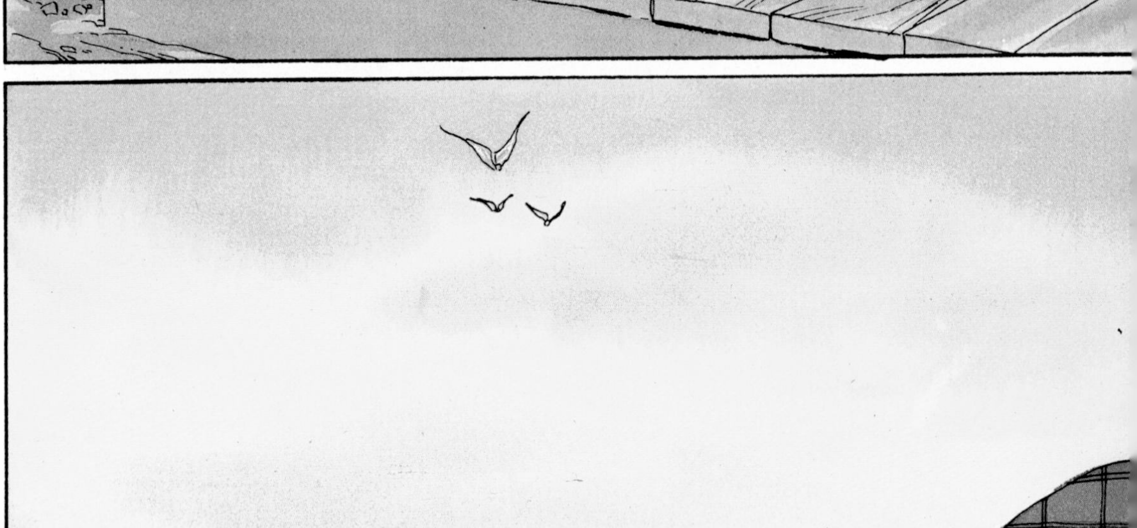

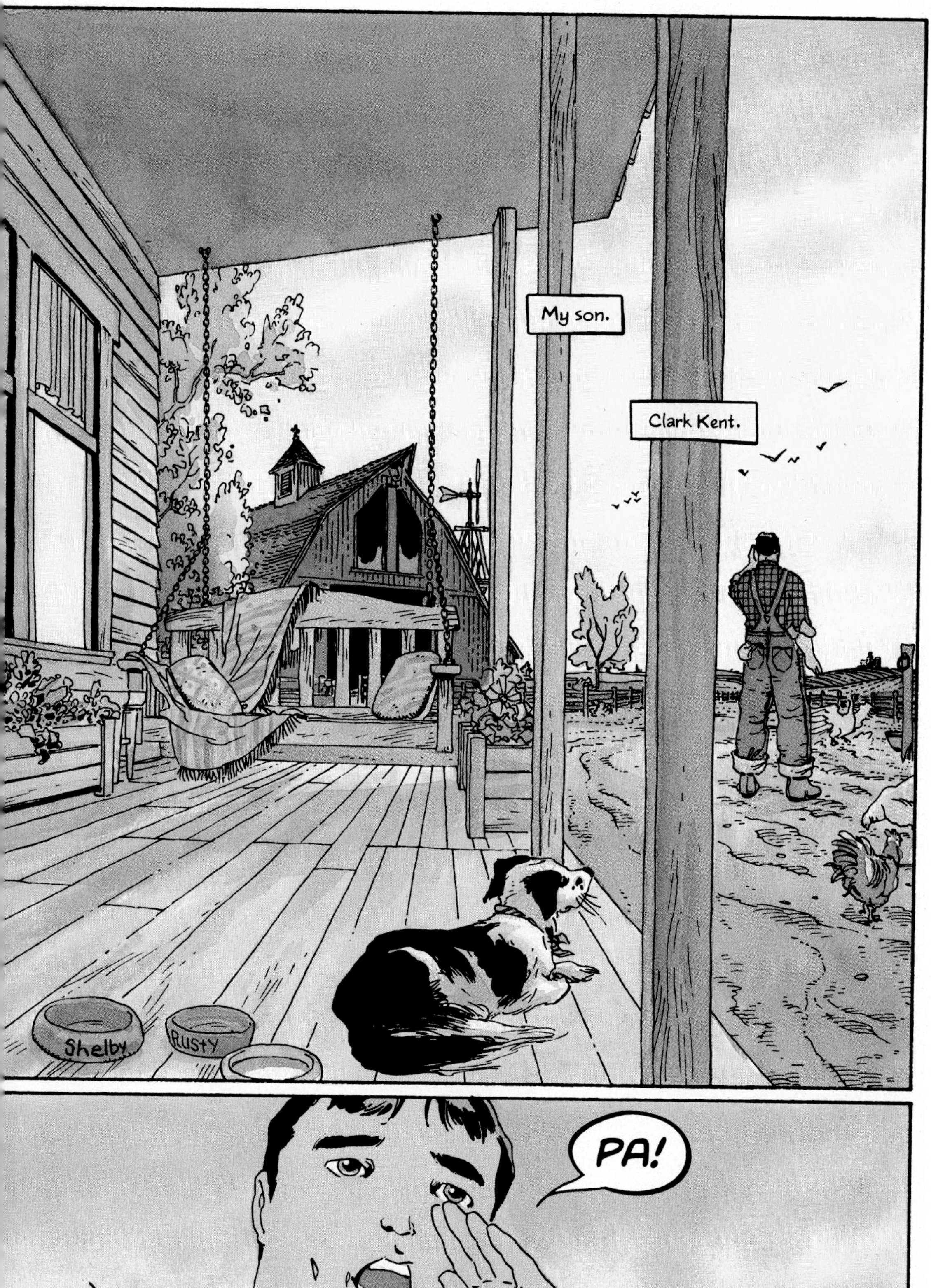
My son.
Clark Kent.
Shelby
Rusty

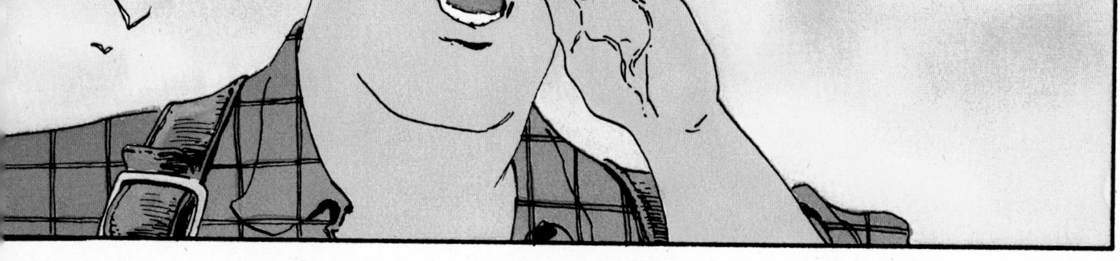
PA!

One night, years ago, a terrible whistling -- loudest thing you ever heard -- came out of the sky.

We drove over to the north field and found some kind of... rocket ship. To this day, I can't think of any other way to describe it.

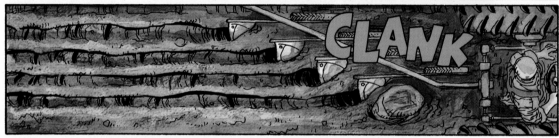

CLANK

Inside it, there was a baby.

A baby.

MA SAYS IT'S GETTING TO BE TIME FOR SUPPER.

And not a scratch on him.

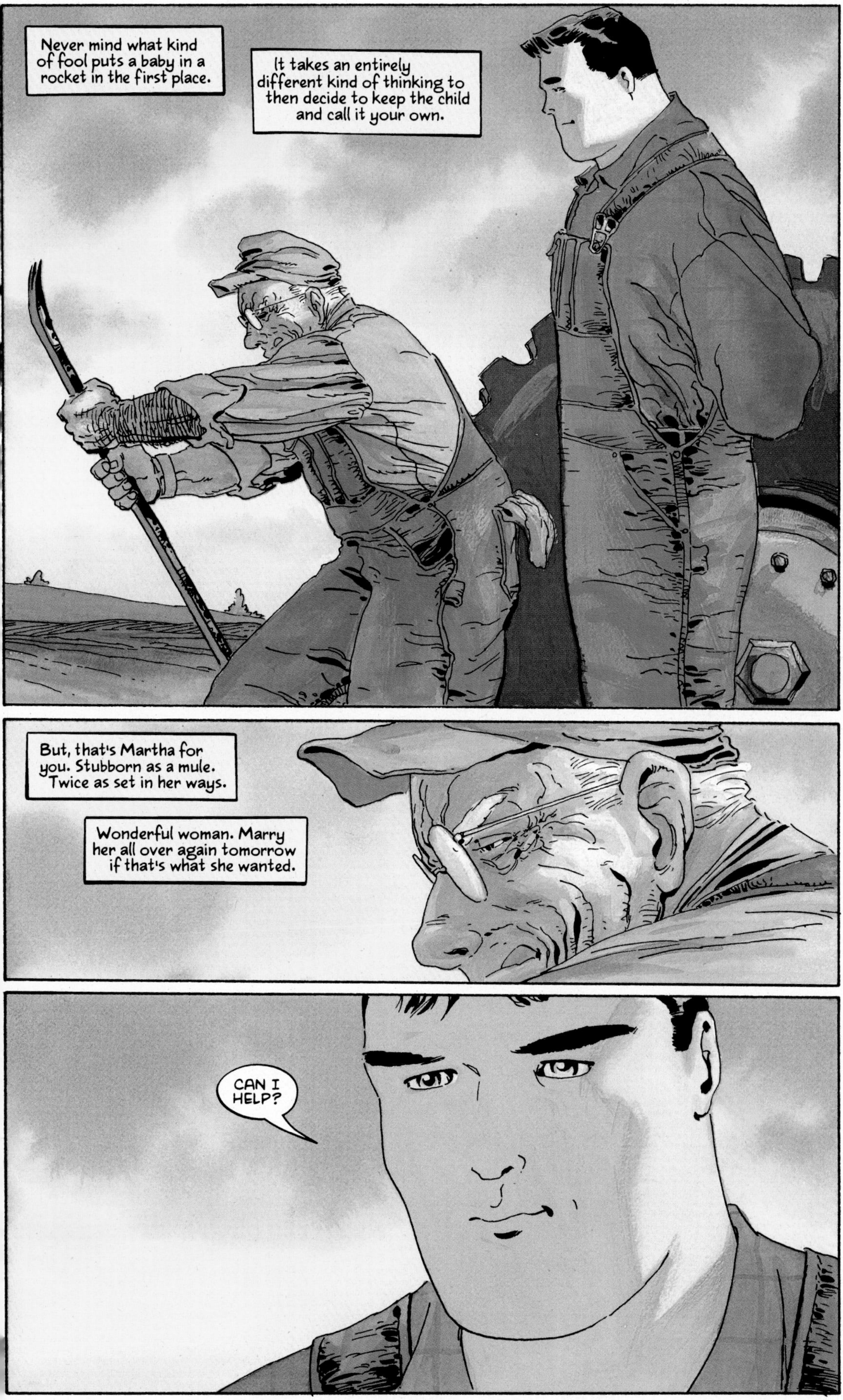

Never mind what kind of fool puts a baby in a rocket in the first place.
It takes an entirely different kind of thinking to then decide to keep the child and call it your own.
But, that's Martha for you. Stubborn as a mule. Twice as set in her ways.
Wonderful woman. Marry her all over again tomorrow if that's what she wanted.
CAN I HELP?

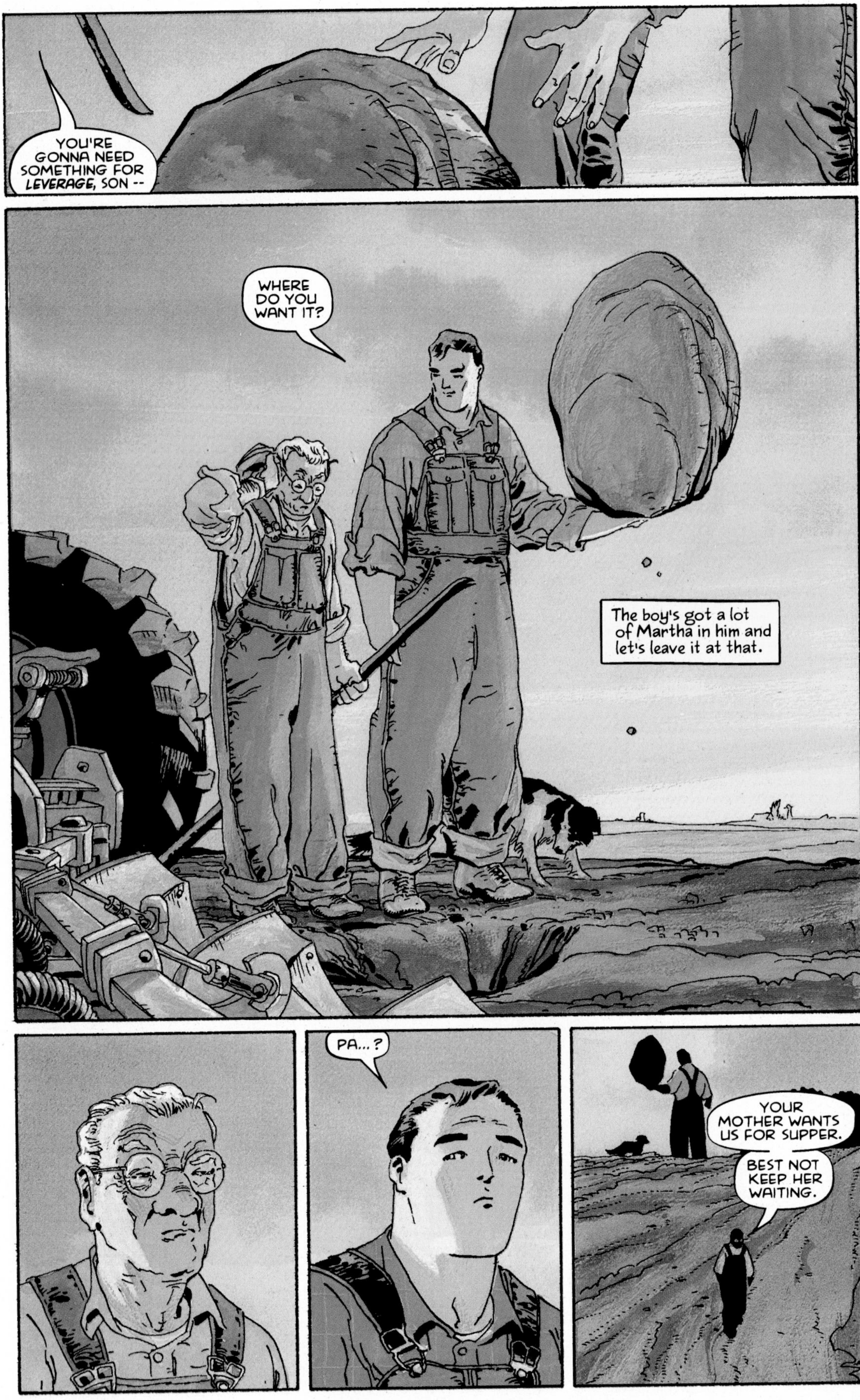

YOU'RE GONNA NEED SOMETHING FOR *LEVERAGE*, SON --
WHERE DO YOU WANT IT?
The boy's got a lot of Martha in him and let's leave it at that.
PA...?
YOUR MOTHER WANTS US FOR SUPPER.
BEST NOT KEEP HER WAITING.

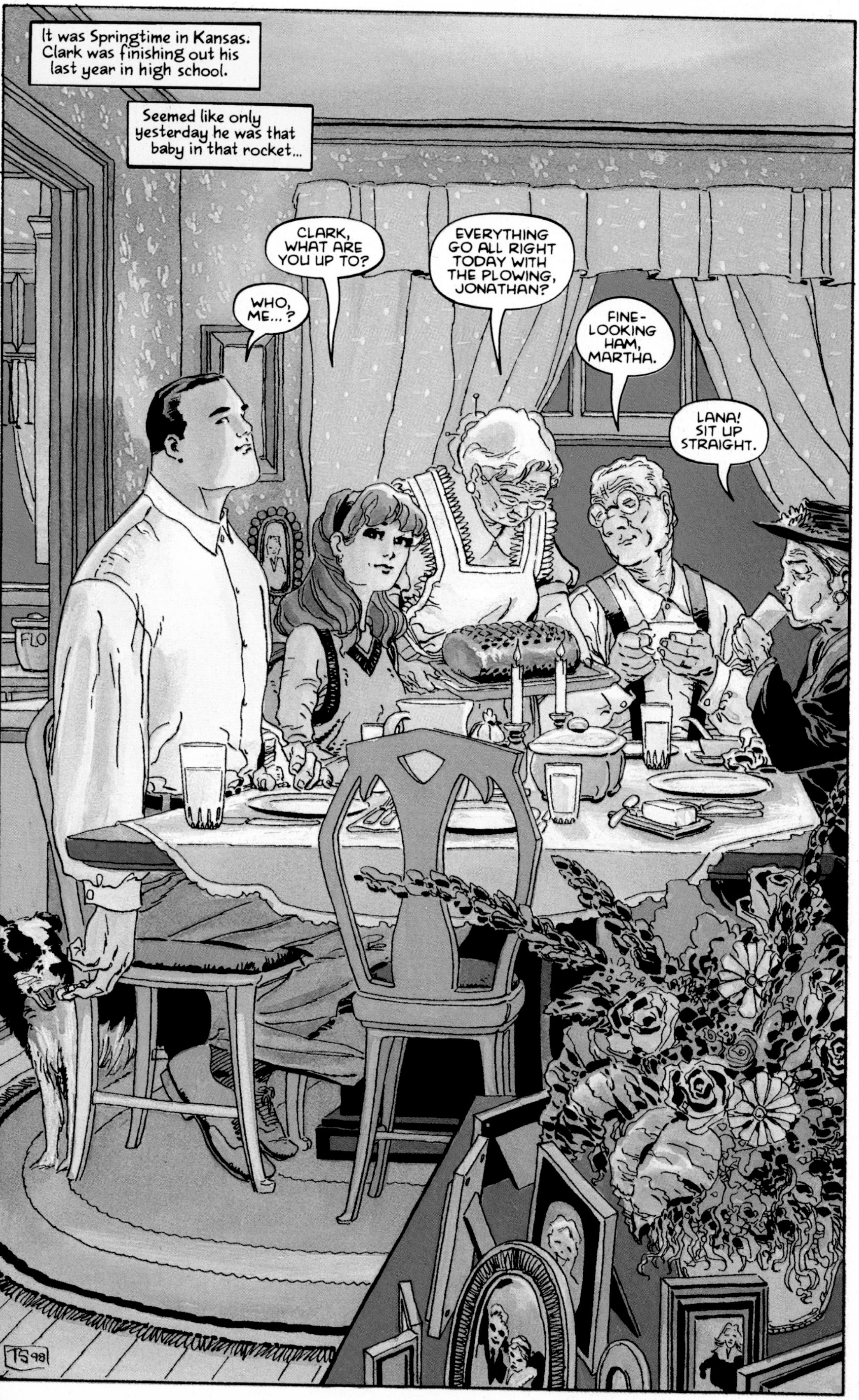
It was Springtime in Kansas. Clark was finishing out his last year in high school.
Seemed like only yesterday he was that baby in that rocket...
WHO, ME...?
CLARK, WHAT ARE YOU UP TO?
EVERYTHING GO ALL RIGHT TODAY WITH THE PLOWING, JONATHAN?
FINE-LOOKING HAM, MARTHA.
LANA! SIT UP STRAIGHT.
TS 98

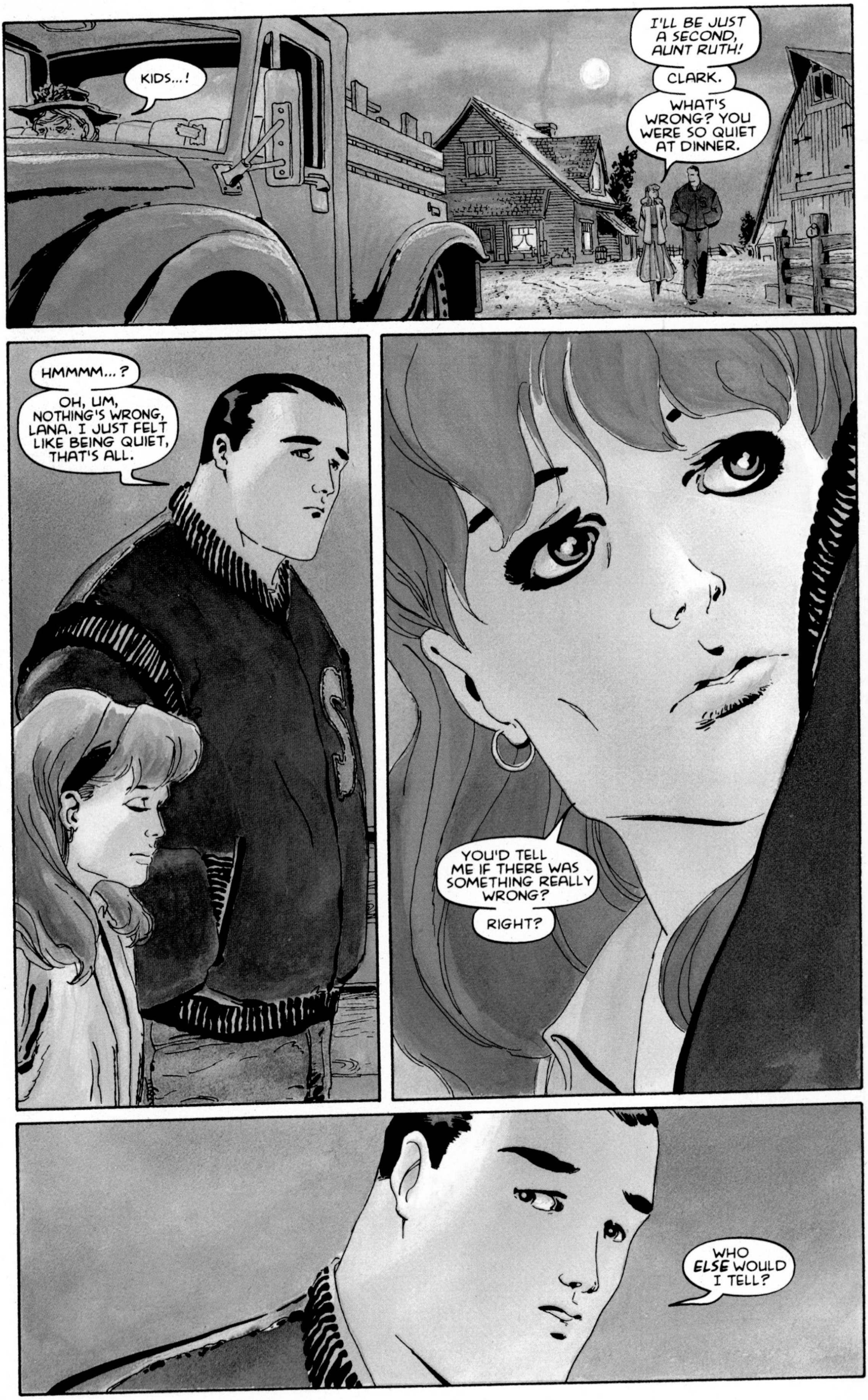

KIDS...!
I'LL BE JUST A SECOND, AUNT RUTH!
CLARK.
WHAT'S WRONG? YOU WERE SO QUIET AT DINNER.
HMMMM...?
OH, UM, NOTHING'S WRONG, LANA. I JUST FELT LIKE BEING QUIET, THAT'S ALL.
YOU'D TELL ME IF THERE WAS SOMETHING REALLY WRONG?
RIGHT?
WHO ELSE WOULD I TELL?

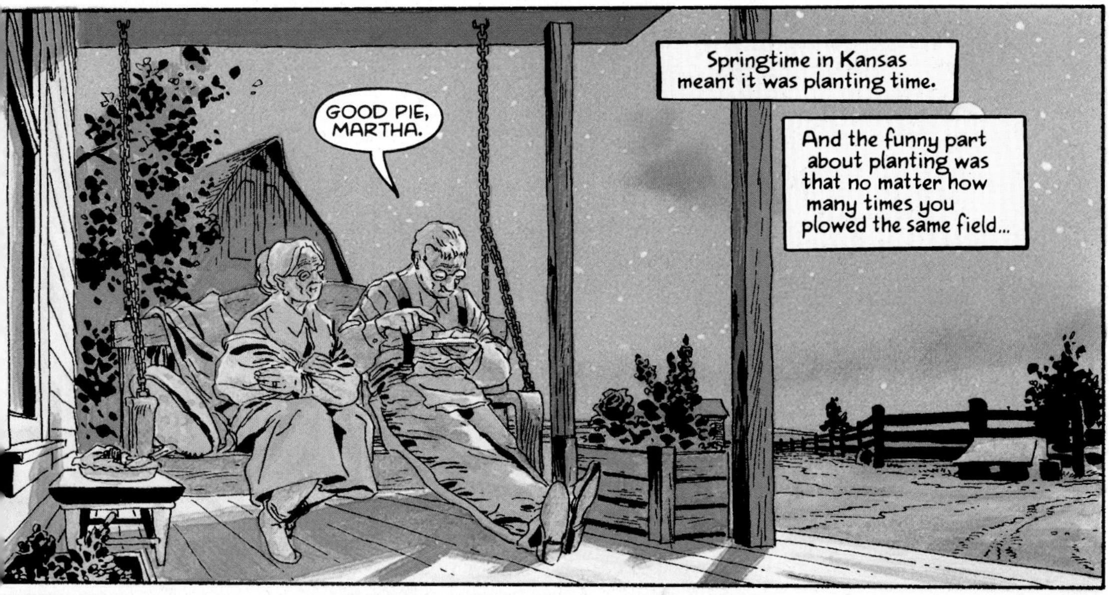
Springtime in Kansas meant it was planting time.
GOOD PIE, MARTHA.
And the funny part about planting was that no matter how many times you plowed the same field...

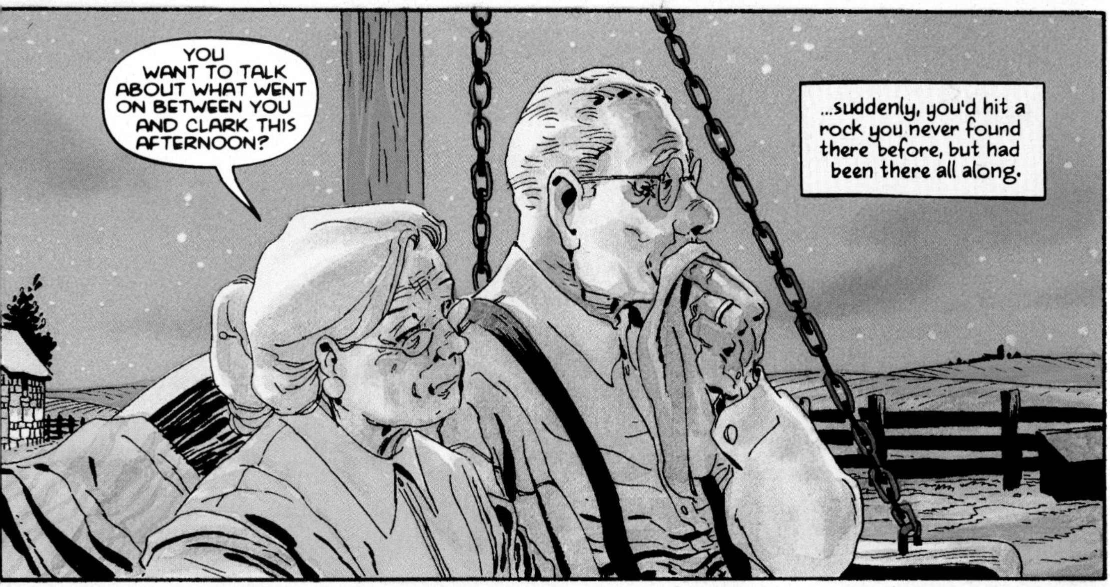
YOU WANT TO TALK ABOUT WHAT WENT ON BETWEEN YOU AND CLARK THIS AFTERNOON?
...suddenly, you'd hit a rock you never found there before, but had been there all along.

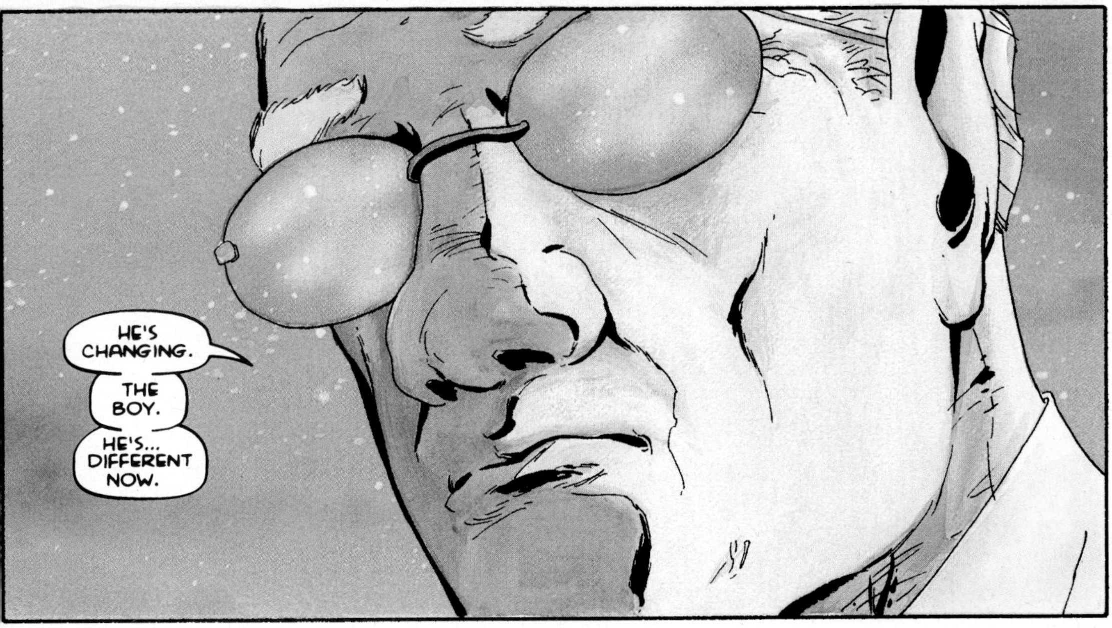
HE'S CHANGING.
THE BOY.
HE'S... DIFFERENT NOW.

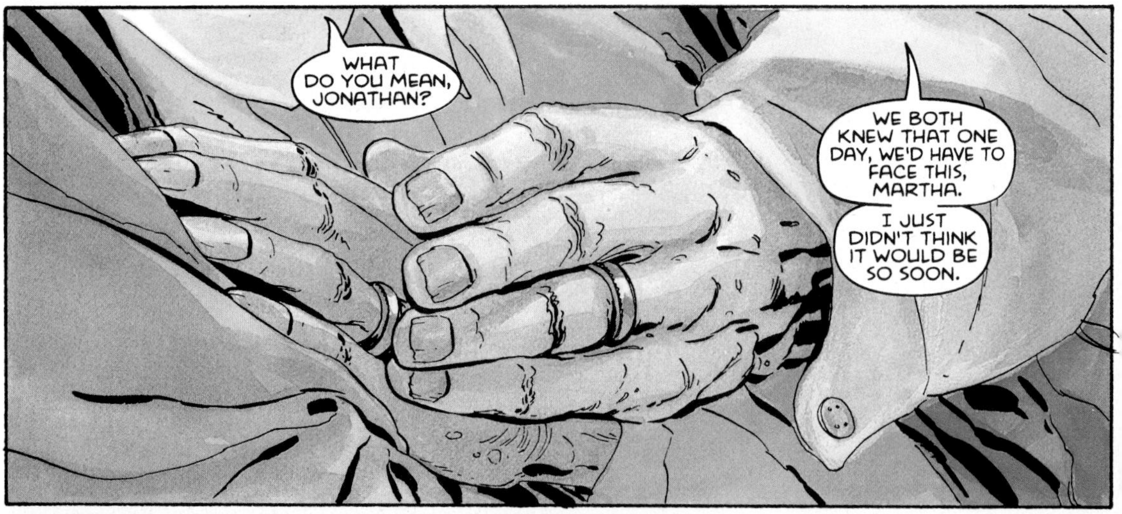
WHAT DO YOU MEAN, JONATHAN?
WE BOTH KNEW THAT ONE DAY, WE'D HAVE TO FACE THIS, MARTHA.
I JUST DIDN'T THINK IT WOULD BE SO SOON.

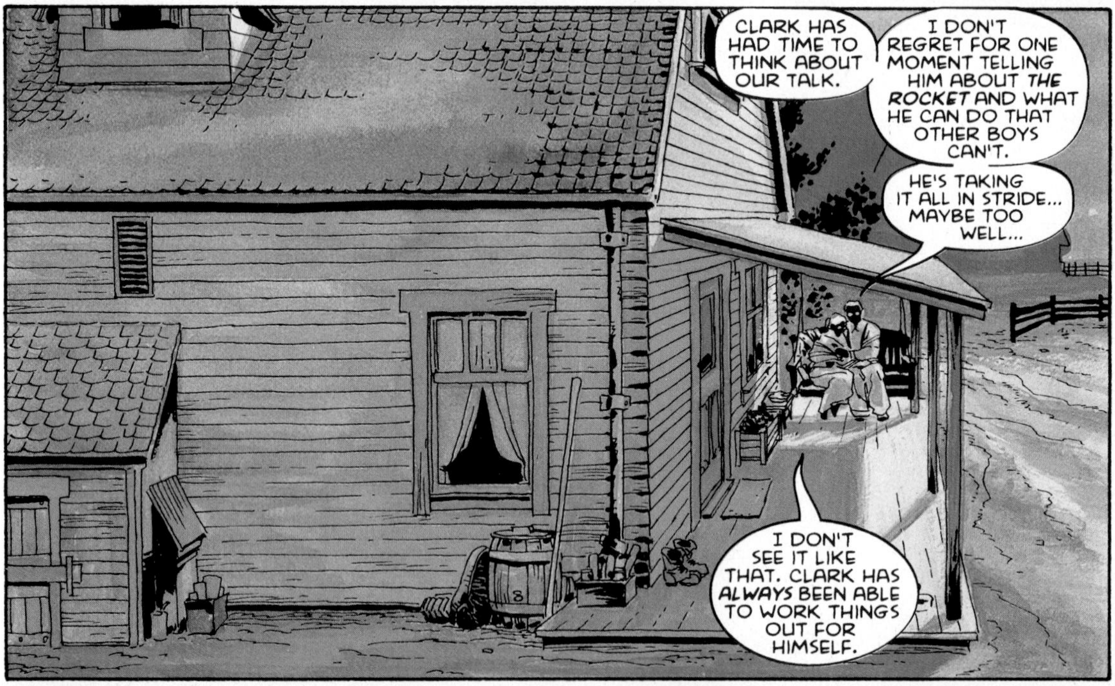
CLARK HAS HAD TIME TO THINK ABOUT OUR TALK.
I DON'T REGRET FOR ONE MOMENT TELLING HIM ABOUT *THE ROCKET* AND WHAT HE CAN DO THAT OTHER BOYS CAN'T.
HE'S TAKING IT ALL IN STRIDE... MAYBE TOO WELL...
I DON'T SEE IT LIKE THAT. CLARK HAS *ALWAYS* BEEN ABLE TO WORK THINGS OUT FOR HIMSELF.

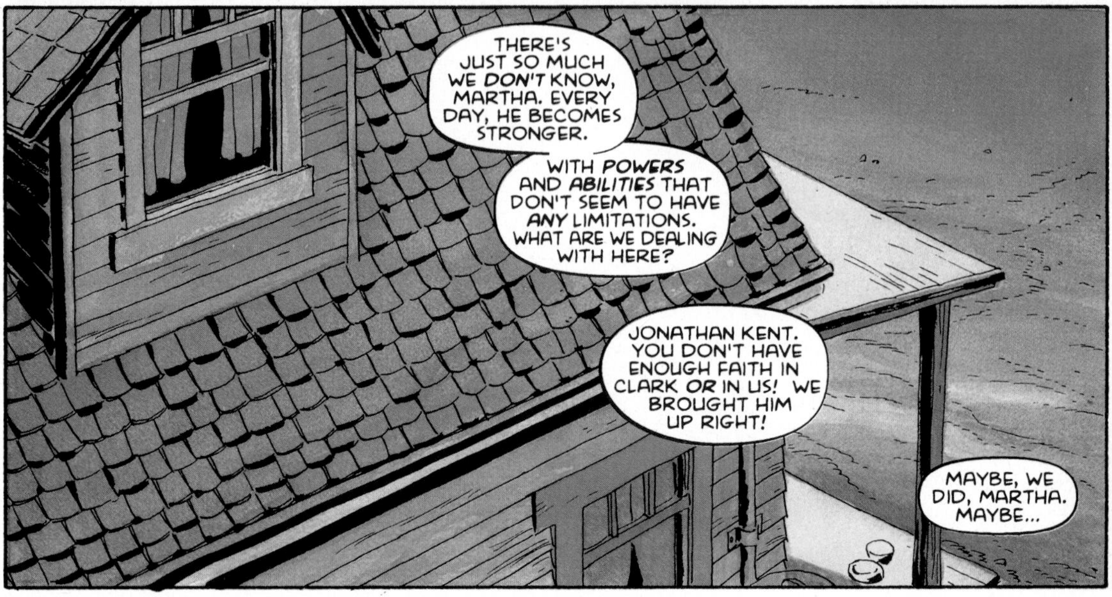
THERE'S JUST SO MUCH WE *DON'T* KNOW, MARTHA. EVERY DAY, HE BECOMES STRONGER.
WITH *POWERS* AND *ABILITIES* THAT DON'T SEEM TO HAVE *ANY* LIMITATIONS. WHAT ARE WE DEALING WITH HERE?
JONATHAN KENT. YOU DON'T HAVE ENOUGH FAITH IN CLARK *OR* IN US! WE BROUGHT HIM UP RIGHT!
MAYBE, WE DID, MARTHA. MAYBE...

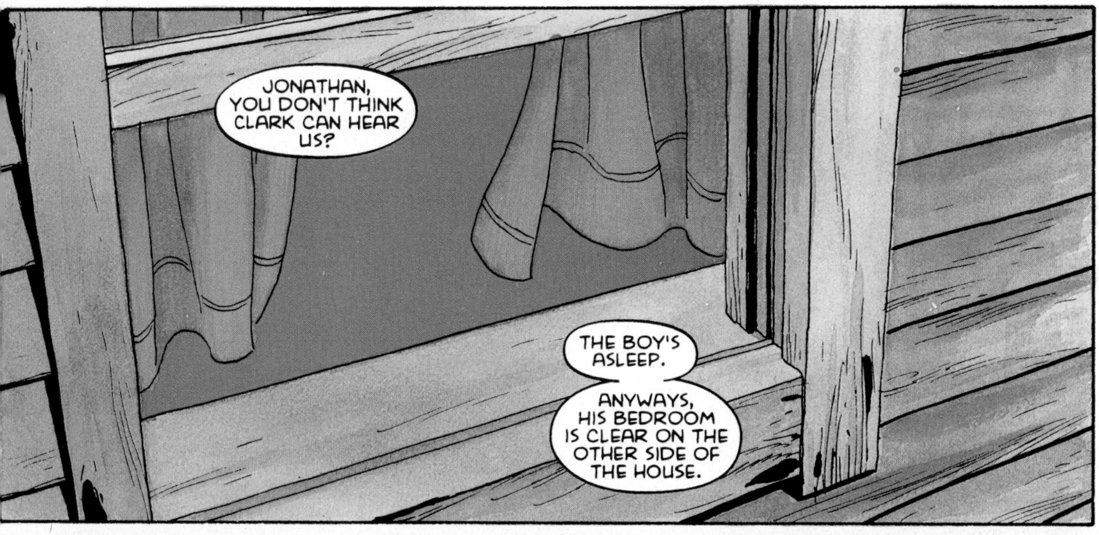
JONATHAN, YOU DON'T THINK CLARK CAN HEAR US?
THE BOY'S ASLEEP.
ANYWAYS, HIS BEDROOM IS CLEAR ON THE OTHER SIDE OF THE HOUSE.

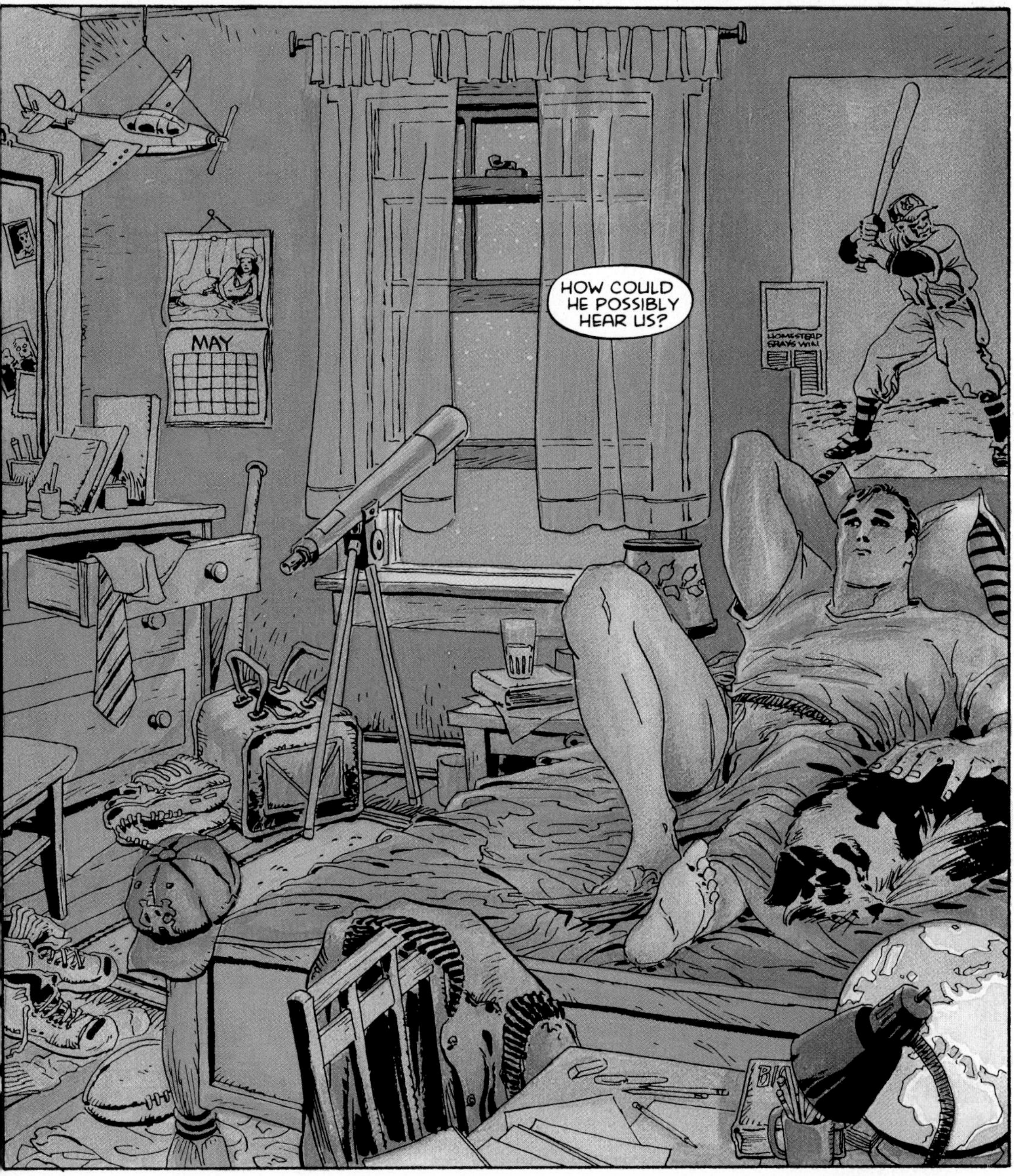
MAY
HOMESTEAD GRAYS WIN
HOW COULD HE POSSIBLY HEAR US?

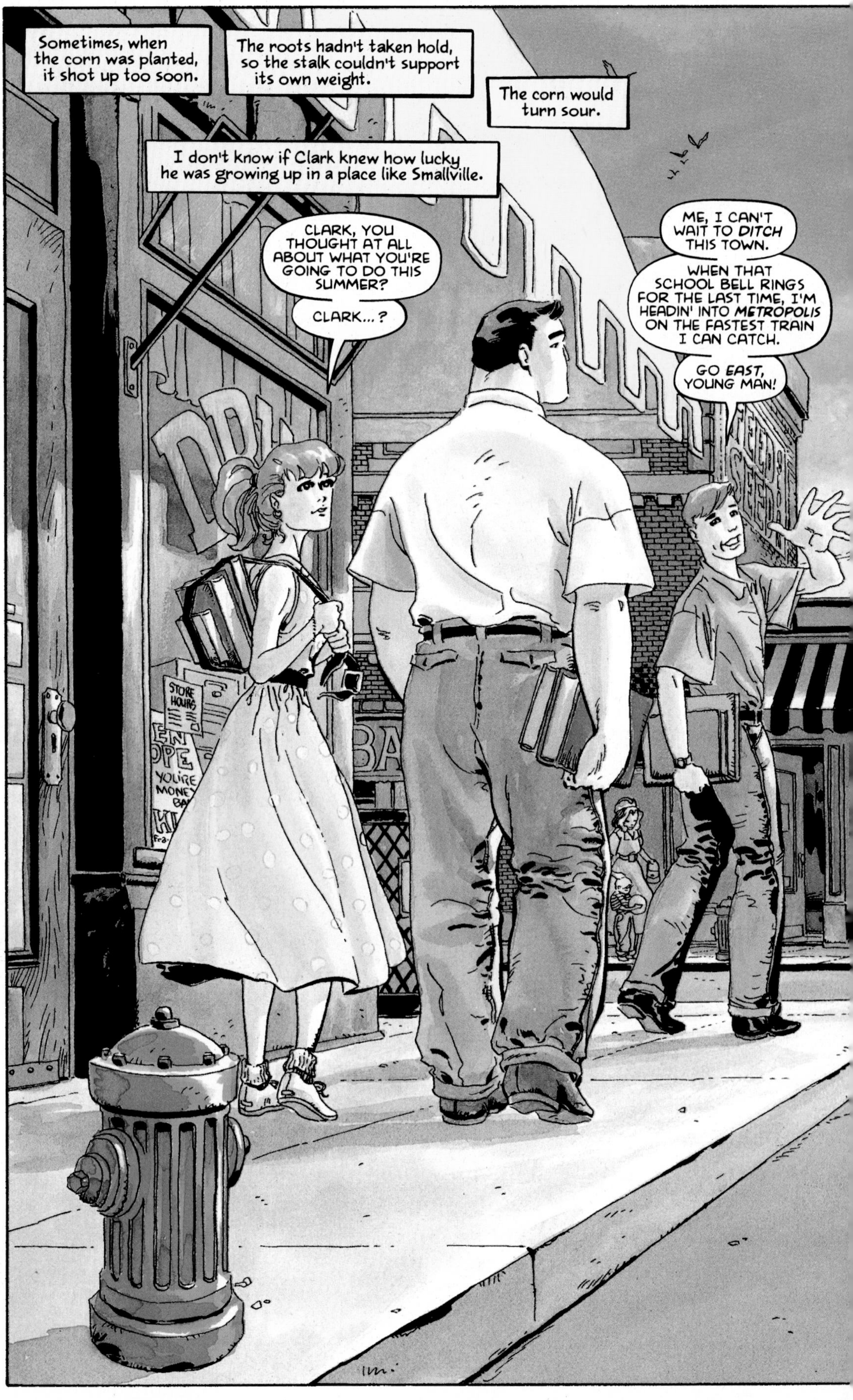
Sometimes, when the corn was planted, it shot up too soon.
The roots hadn't taken hold, so the stalk couldn't support its own weight.
The corn would turn sour.
I don't know if Clark knew how lucky he was growing up in a place like Smallville.
CLARK, YOU THOUGHT AT ALL ABOUT WHAT YOU'RE GOING TO DO THIS SUMMER?
CLARK...?
ME, I CAN'T WAIT TO DITCH THIS TOWN.
WHEN THAT SCHOOL BELL RINGS FOR THE LAST TIME, I'M HEADIN' INTO METROPOLIS ON THE FASTEST TRAIN I CAN CATCH.
GO EAST, YOUNG MAN!
STORE HOURS

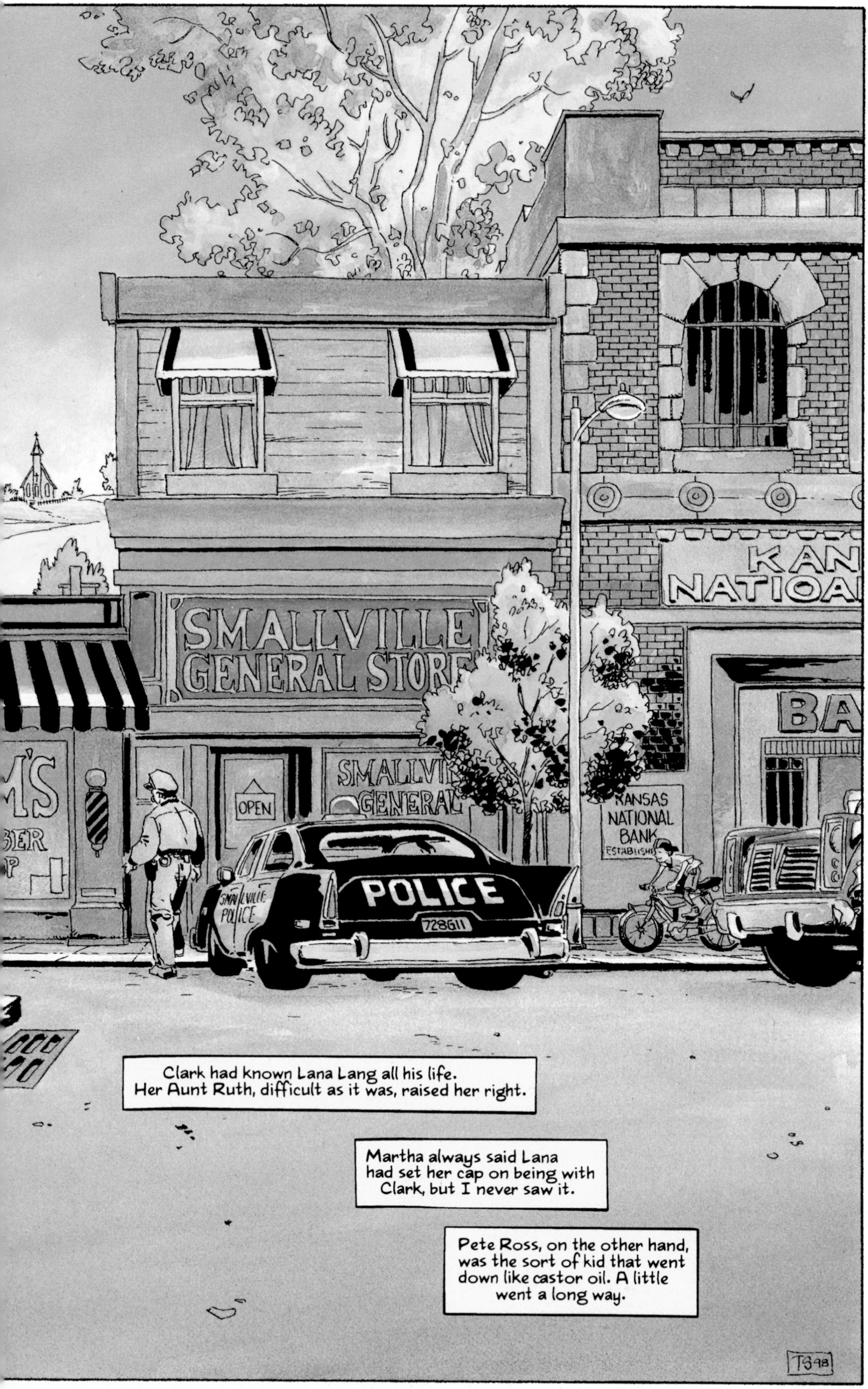
SMALLVILLE GENERAL STORE
OPEN
POLICE
SMALLVILLE POLICE
728G11
KANSAS NATIONAL BANK
Clark had known Lana Lang all his life. Her Aunt Ruth, difficult as it was, raised her right.
Martha always said Lana had set her cap on being with Clark, but I never saw it.
Pete Ross, on the other hand, was the sort of kid that went down like castor oil. A little went a long way.
TS 98

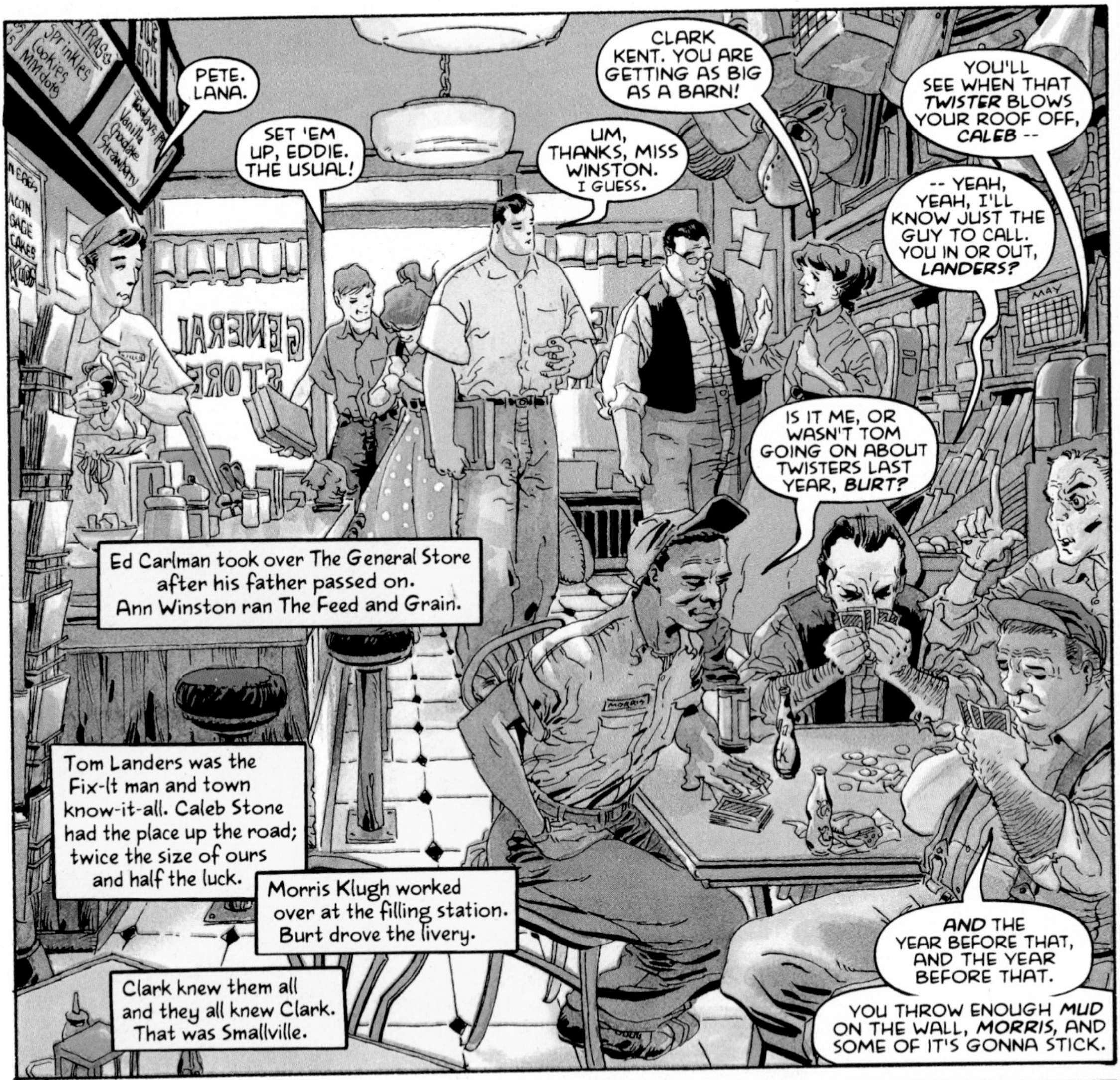
PETE. LANA.
SET 'EM UP, EDDIE. THE USUAL!
CLARK KENT. YOU ARE GETTING AS BIG AS A BARN!
UM, THANKS, MISS WINSTON. I GUESS.
YOU'LL SEE WHEN THAT *TWISTER* BLOWS YOUR ROOF OFF, *CALEB* --
-- YEAH, YEAH, I'LL KNOW JUST THE GUY TO CALL. YOU IN OR OUT, *LANDERS?*
Ed Carlman took over The General Store after his father passed on. Ann Winston ran The Feed and Grain.
IS IT ME, OR WASN'T TOM GOING ON ABOUT TWISTERS LAST YEAR, *BURT?*
Tom Landers was the Fix-It man and town know-it-all. Caleb Stone had the place up the road; twice the size of ours and half the luck.
Morris Klugh worked over at the filling station. Burt drove the livery.
AND THE YEAR BEFORE THAT, AND THE YEAR BEFORE THAT.
YOU THROW ENOUGH *MUD* ON THE WALL, *MORRIS*, AND SOME OF IT'S GONNA STICK.
Clark knew them all and they all knew Clark. That was Smallville.

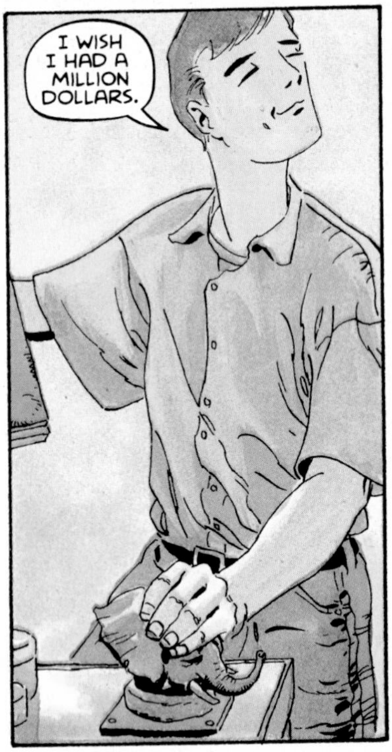
I WISH I HAD A MILLION DOLLARS.

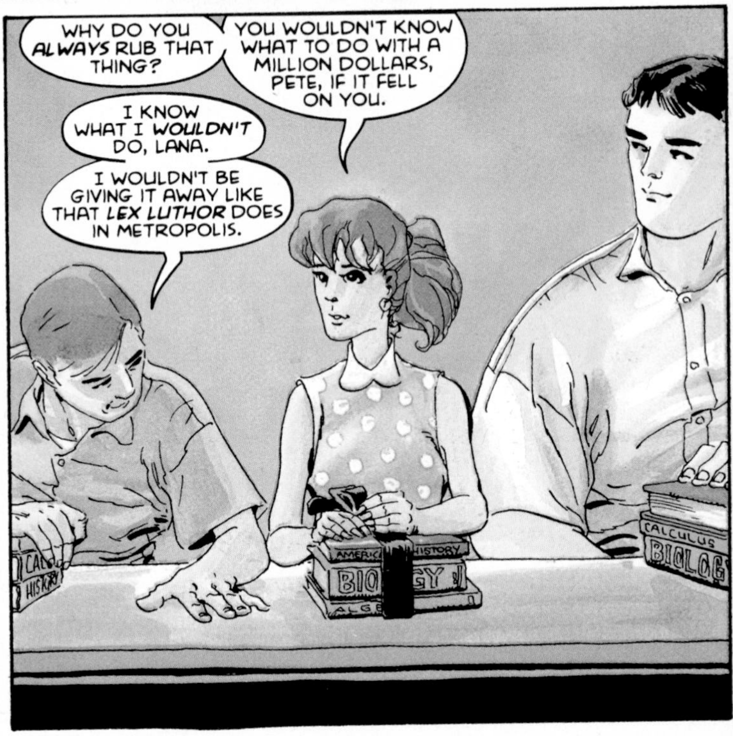
WHY DO YOU *ALWAYS* RUB THAT THING?
YOU WOULDN'T KNOW WHAT TO DO WITH A MILLION DOLLARS, PETE, IF IT FELL ON YOU.
I KNOW WHAT I *WOULDN'T* DO, LANA.
I WOULDN'T BE GIVING IT AWAY LIKE THAT *LEX LUTHOR* DOES IN METROPOLIS.

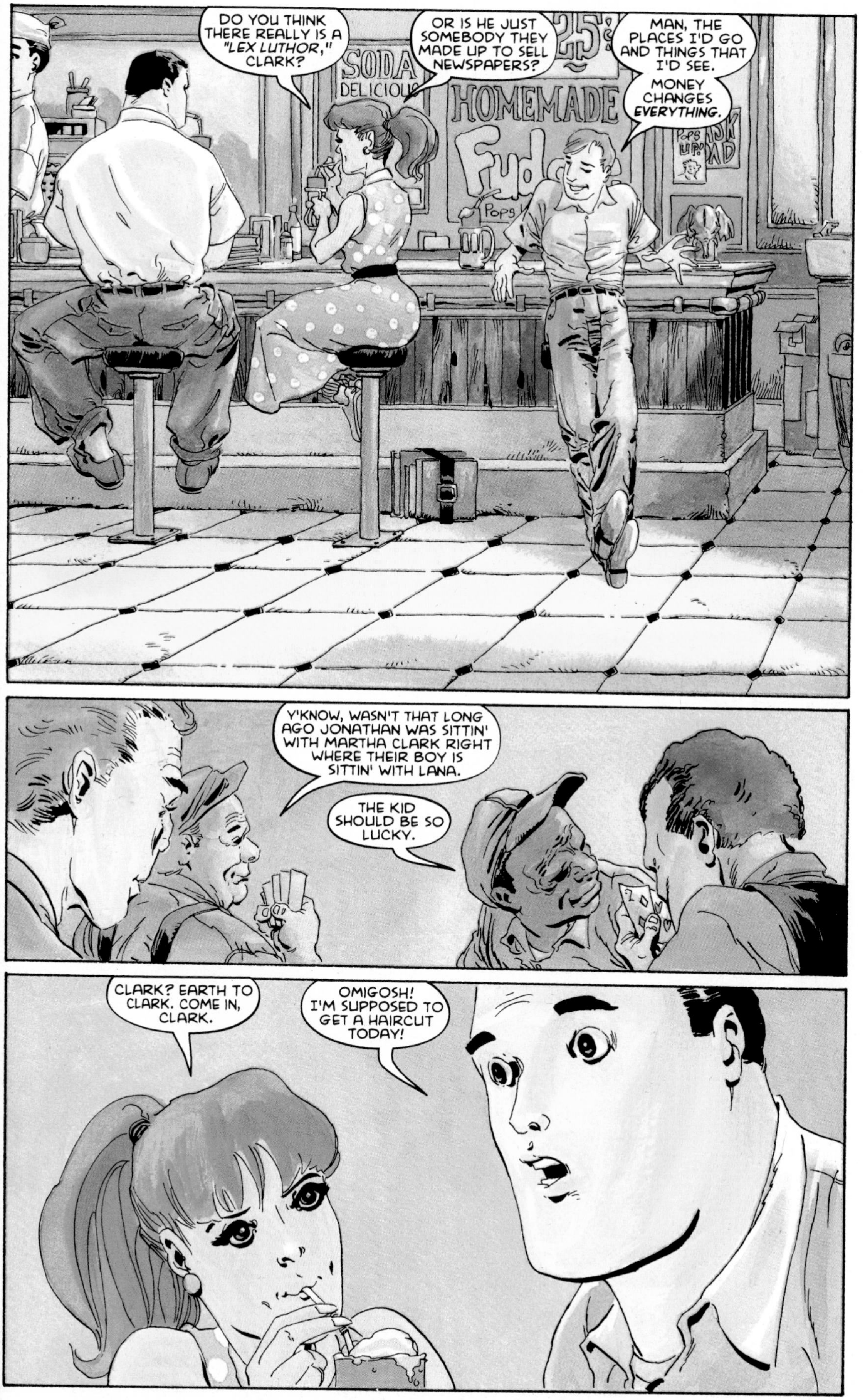
SODA DELICIOUS
25¢
HOMEMADE
DO YOU THINK THERE REALLY IS A "LEX LUTHOR," CLARK?
OR IS HE JUST SOMEBODY THEY MADE UP TO SELL NEWSPAPERS?
MAN, THE PLACES I'D GO AND THINGS THAT I'D SEE.
MONEY CHANGES EVERYTHING.
Y'KNOW, WASN'T THAT LONG AGO JONATHAN WAS SITTIN' WITH MARTHA CLARK RIGHT WHERE THEIR BOY IS SITTIN' WITH LANA.
THE KID SHOULD BE SO LUCKY.
CLARK? EARTH TO CLARK. COME IN, CLARK.
OMIGOSH! I'M SUPPOSED TO GET A HAIRCUT TODAY!

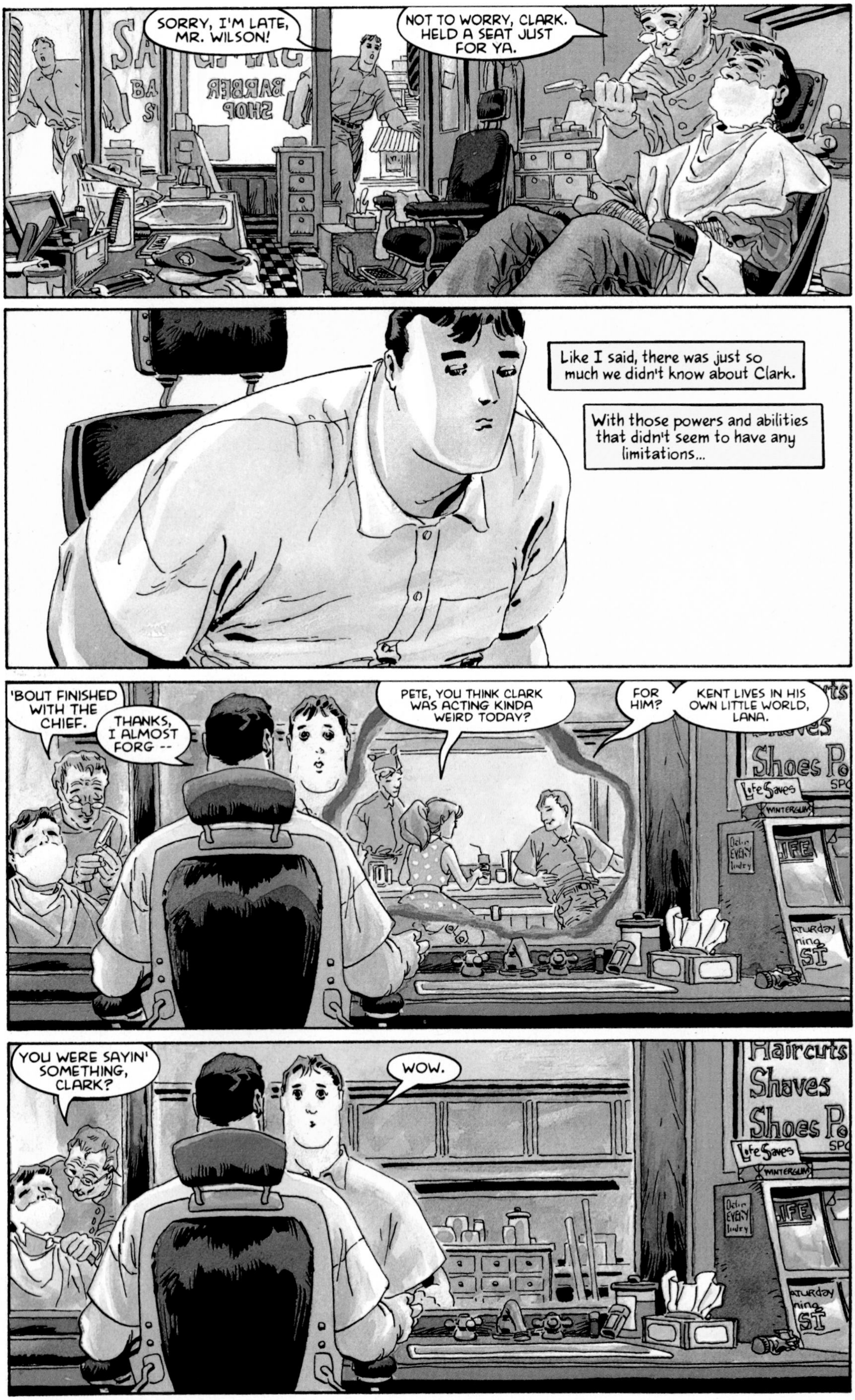
SORRY, I'M LATE, MR. WILSON!
NOT TO WORRY, CLARK. HELD A SEAT JUST FOR YA.
BARBER SHOP
Like I said, there was just so much we didn't know about Clark.
With those powers and abilities that didn't seem to have any limitations...
'BOUT FINISHED WITH THE CHIEF.
THANKS, I ALMOST FORG --
PETE, YOU THINK CLARK WAS ACTING KINDA WEIRD TODAY?
FOR HIM?
KENT LIVES IN HIS OWN LITTLE WORLD, LANA.
Shoes
Life Saves
WINTERGUM
YOU WERE SAYIN' SOMETHING, CLARK?
WOW.
Haircuts
Shaves
Shoes
Life Saves
WINTERGUM

SAME AS USUAL, CLARK? LITTLE OFF THE TOP?

YEAH. UM. SURE.

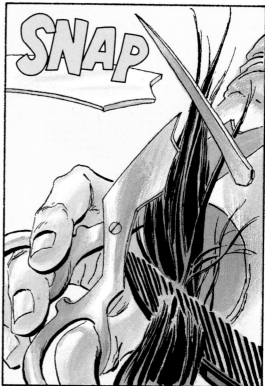

SNAP

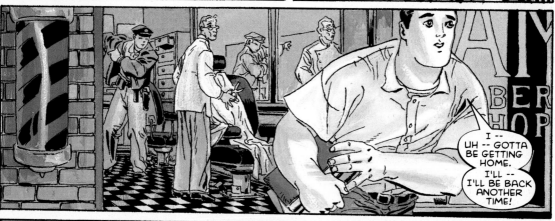

I -- UH -- GOTTA BE GETTING HOME. I'LL -- I'LL BE BACK ANOTHER TIME!

DAMNEDEST THING I EVER SAW. THEY CAN'T MAKE A PAIR OF SCISSORS WORTH A NICKEL ANYMORE...

Sam Wilson was the sort of man who made everybody's business his own, even when he didn't have the right to.

Chief Parker, on the other hand, had the right to, but believed in letting folks go about their business...

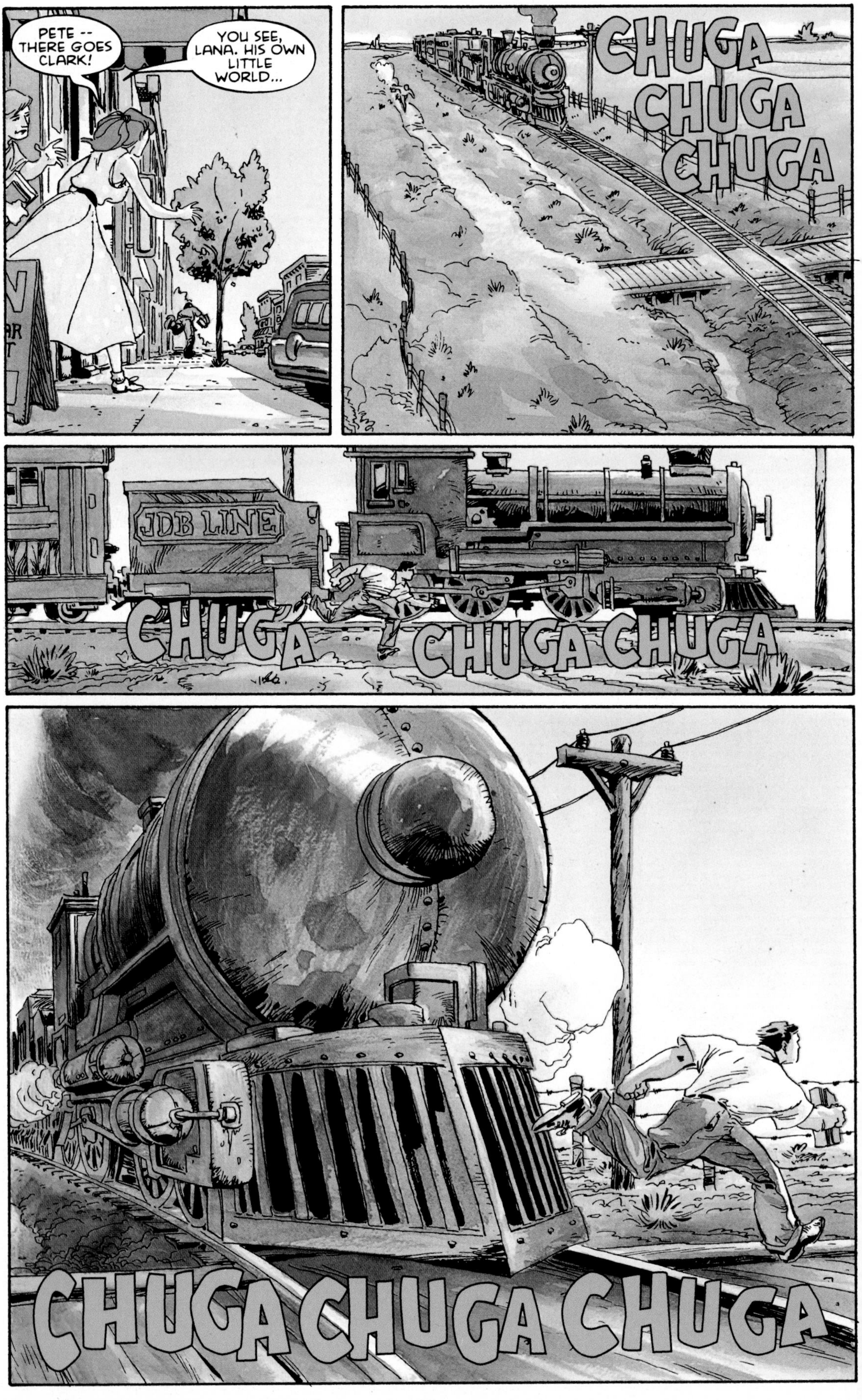
PETE -- THERE GOES CLARK!
YOU SEE, LANA. HIS OWN LITTLE WORLD...
CHUGA
CHUGA
CHUGA
JDB LINE
CHUGA
CHUGA CHUGA
CHUGA CHUGA CHUGA

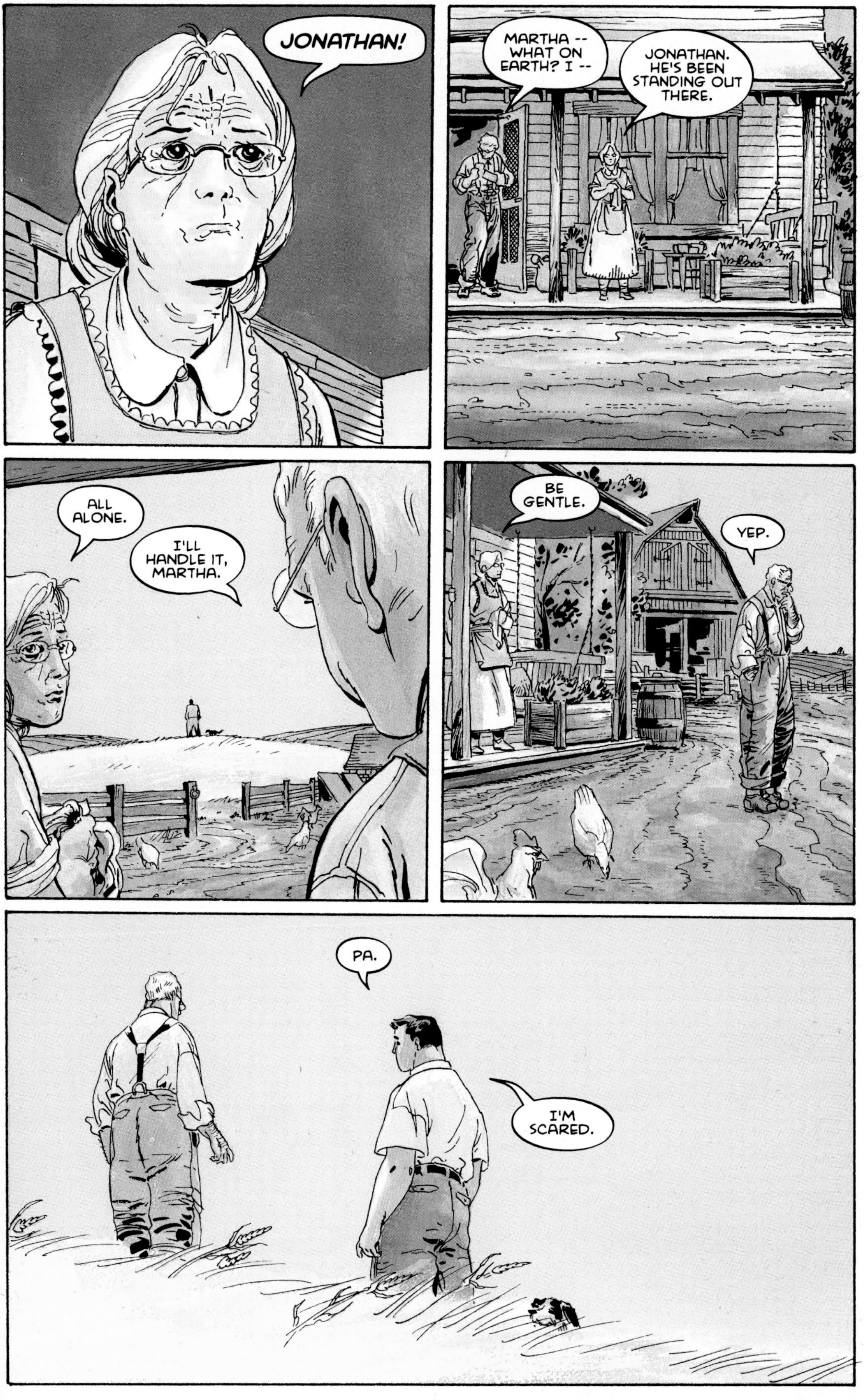
JONATHAN!
MARTHA -- WHAT ON EARTH? I --
JONATHAN. HE'S BEEN STANDING OUT THERE.
ALL ALONE.
I'LL HANDLE IT, MARTHA.
BE GENTLE.
YEP.
PA.
I'M SCARED.

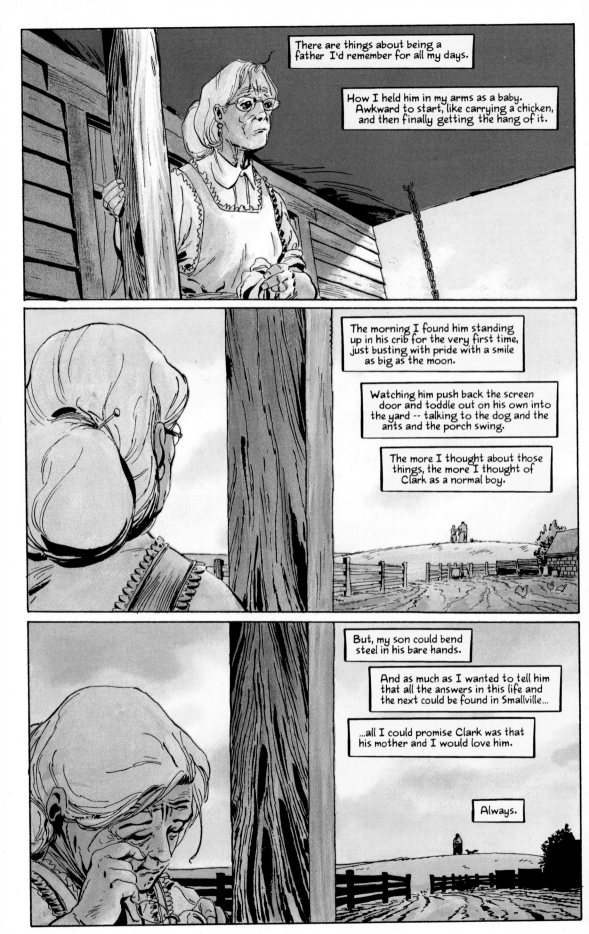

There are things about being a father I'd remember for all my days.

How I held him in my arms as a baby. Awkward to start, like carrying a chicken, and then finally getting the hang of it.

The morning I found him standing up in his crib for the very first time, just busting with pride with a smile as big as the moon.

Watching him push back the screen door and toddle out on his own into the yard -- talking to the dog and the ants and the porch swing.

The more I thought about those things, the more I thought of Clark as a normal boy.

But, my son could bend steel in his bare hands.

And as much as I wanted to tell him that all the answers in this life and the next could be found in Smallville...

...all I could promise Clark was that his mother and I would love him.

Always.

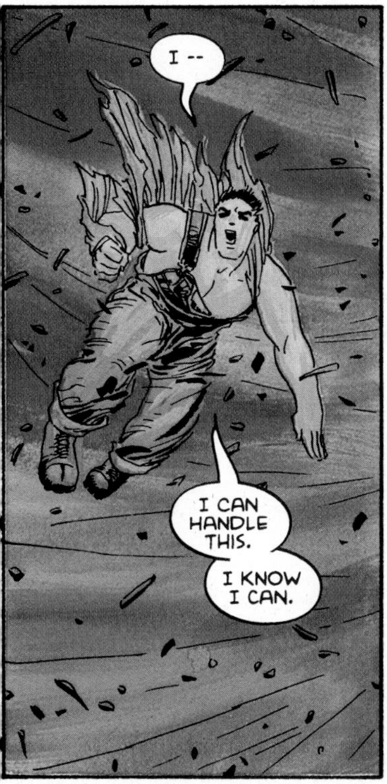
I --
I CAN HANDLE THIS.
I KNOW I CAN.

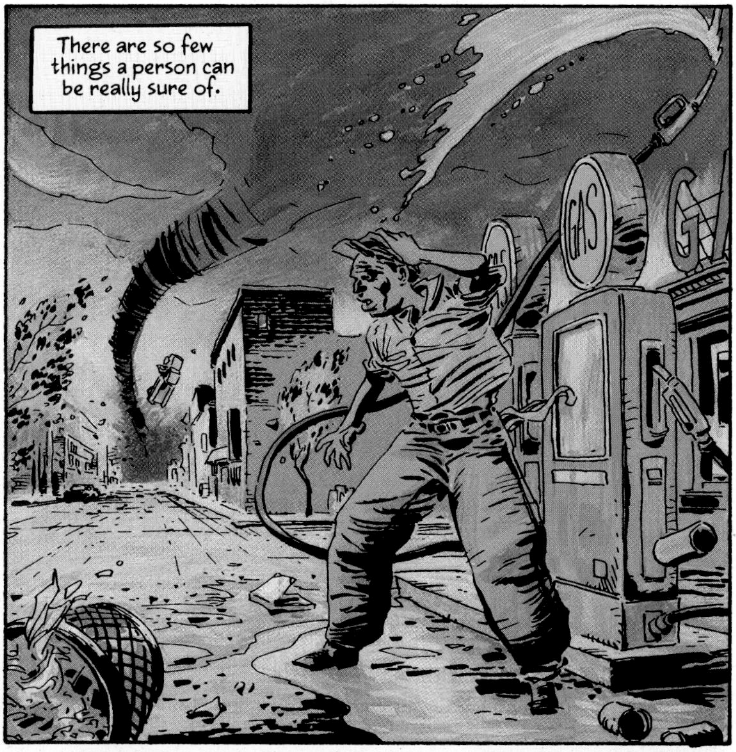
There are so few things a person can be really sure of.
GAS

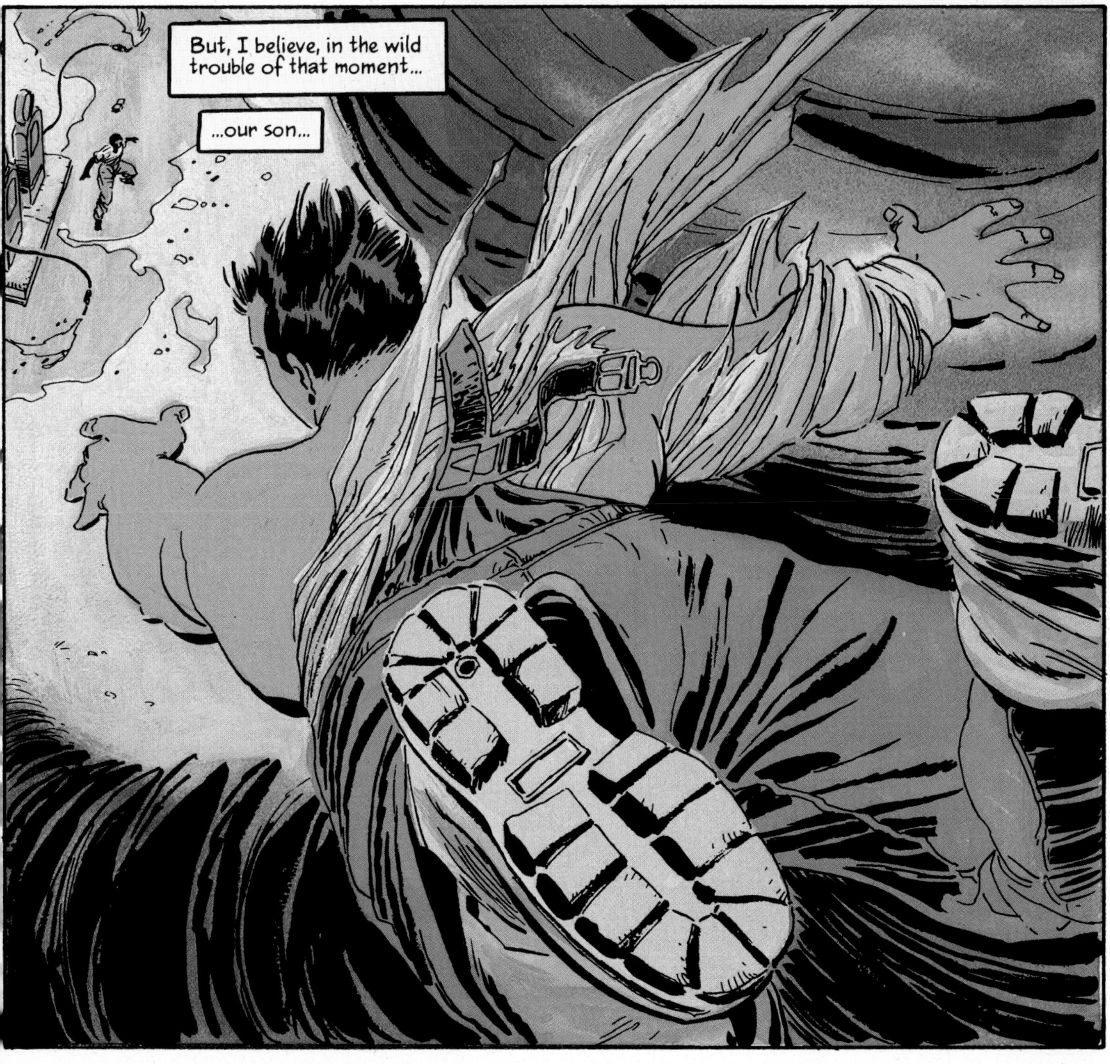
But, I believe, in the wild trouble of that moment...
...our son...

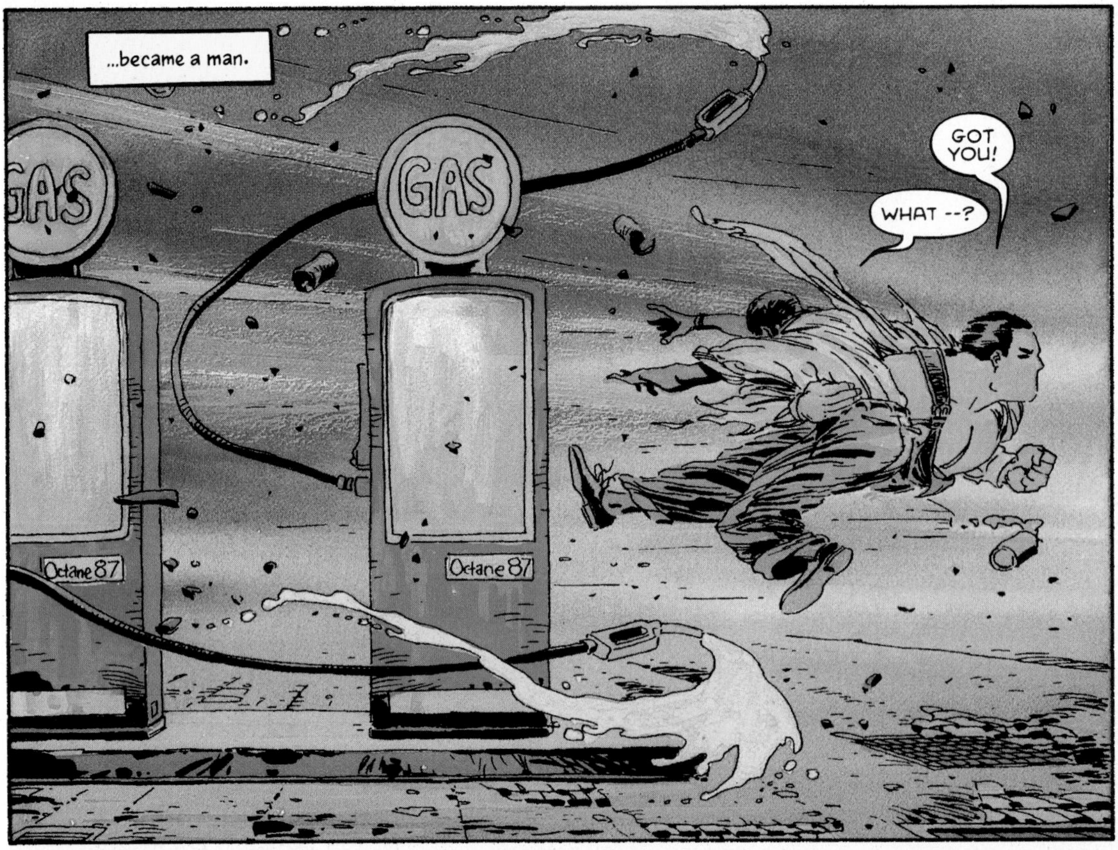
...became a man.
GAS
GAS
GOT YOU!
WHAT --?
Octane 87
Octane 87

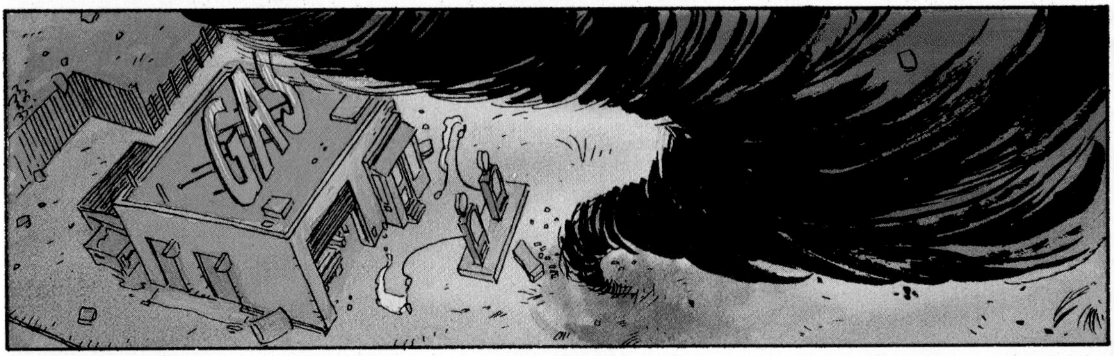
GAS

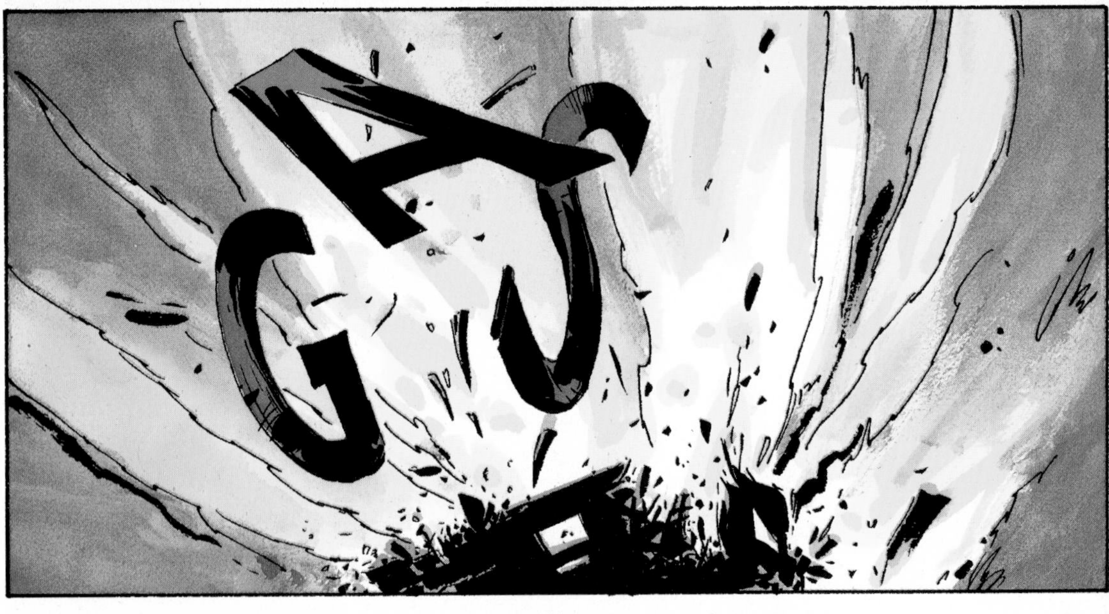

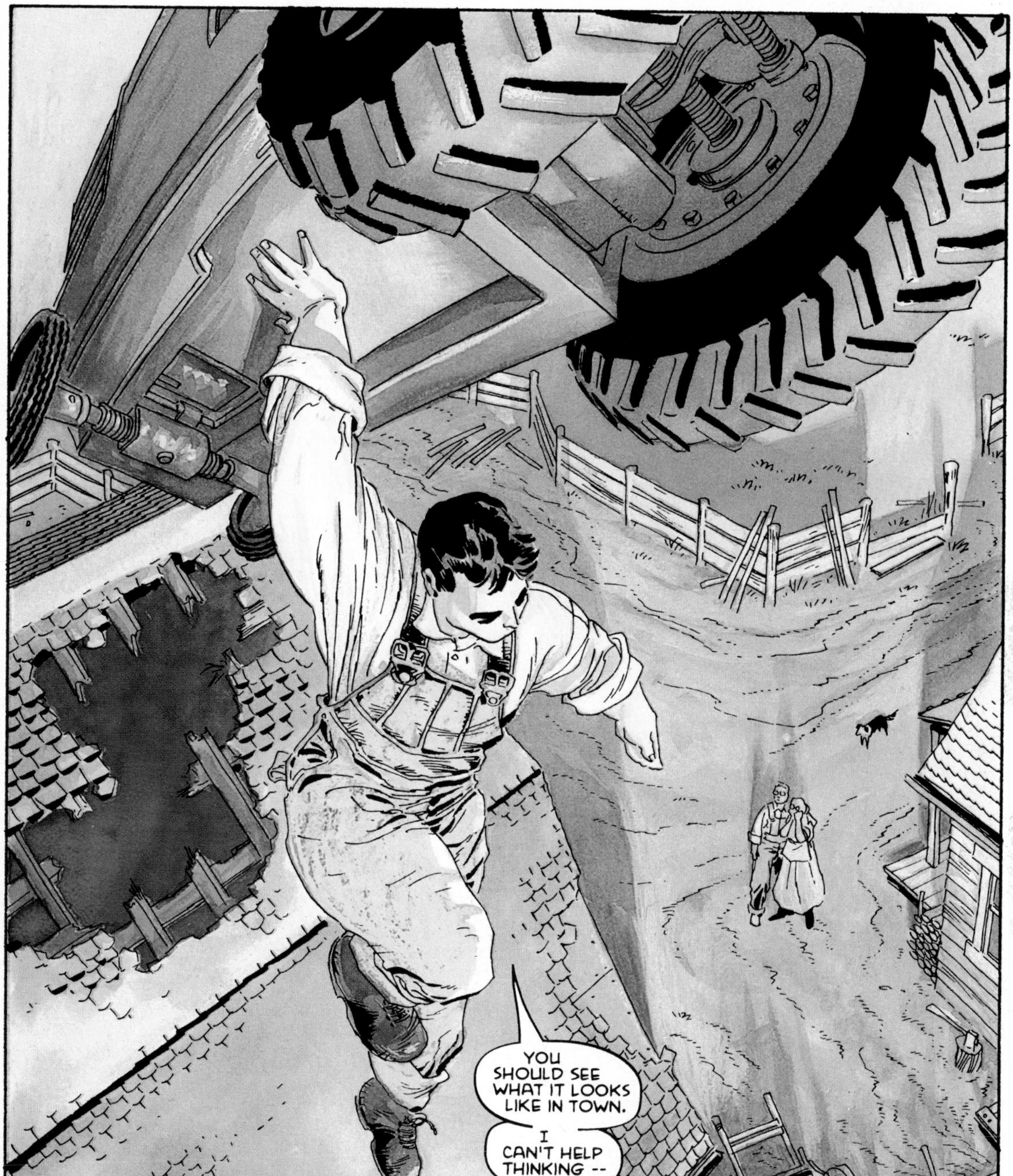
YOU SHOULD SEE WHAT IT LOOKS LIKE IN TOWN.
I CAN'T HELP THINKING --

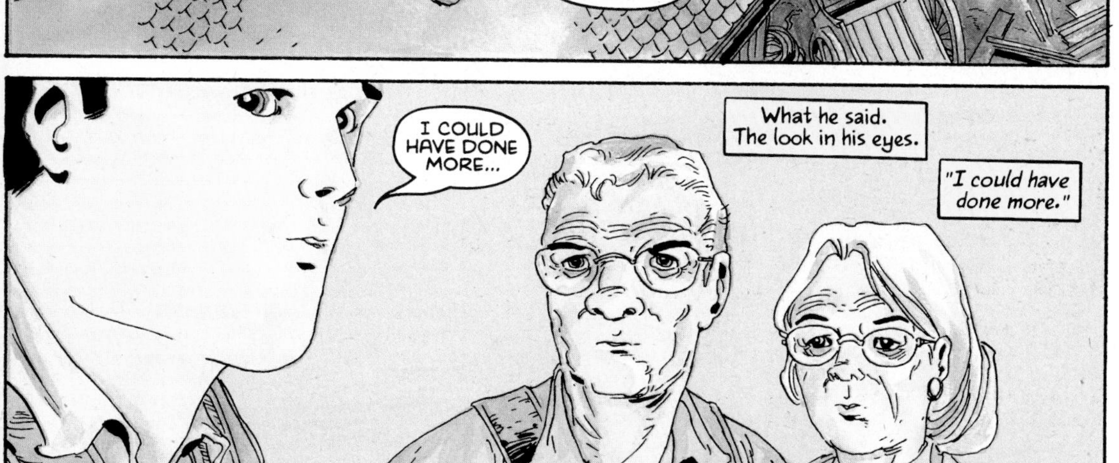
I COULD HAVE DONE MORE...
What he said. The look in his eyes.
"I could have done more."

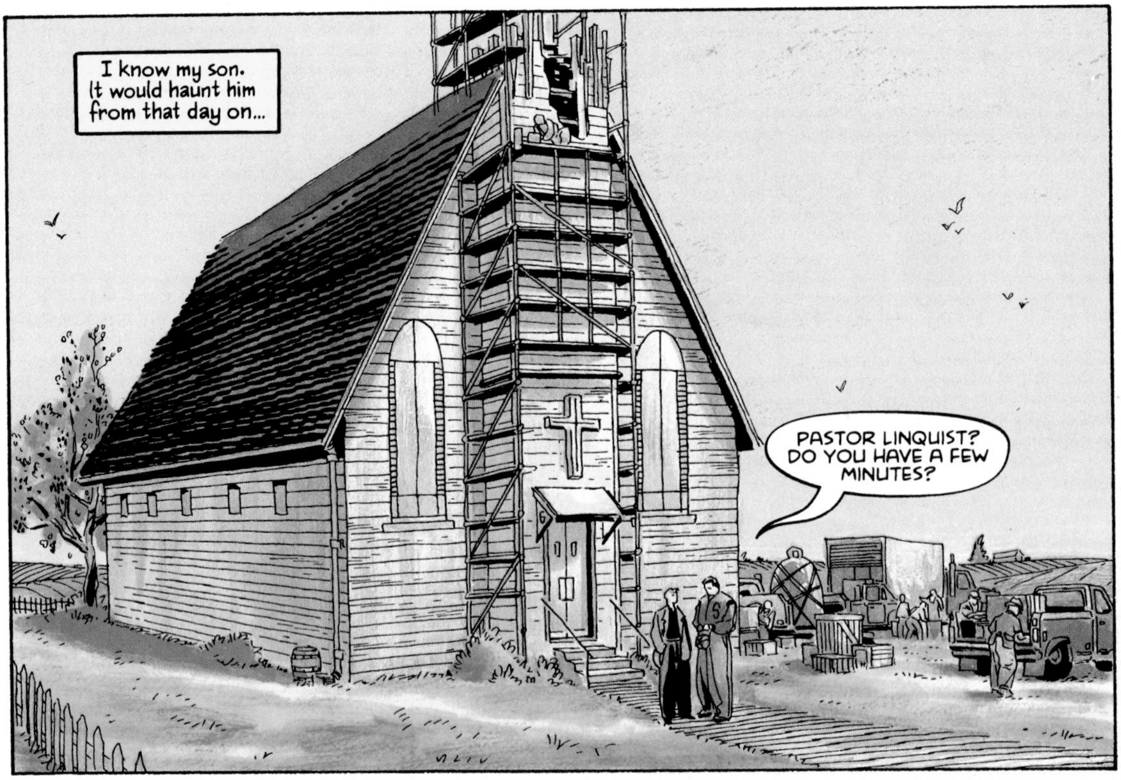
I know my son.
It would haunt him
from that day on...
PASTOR LINQUIST? DO YOU HAVE A FEW MINUTES?

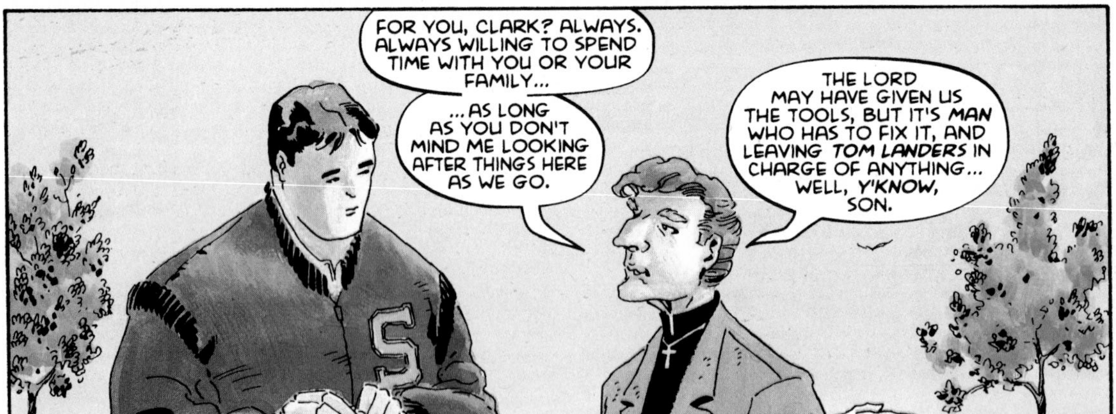
FOR YOU, CLARK? ALWAYS. ALWAYS WILLING TO SPEND TIME WITH YOU OR YOUR FAMILY...
...AS LONG AS YOU DON'T MIND ME LOOKING AFTER THINGS HERE AS WE GO.
THE LORD MAY HAVE GIVEN US THE TOOLS, BUT IT'S MAN WHO HAS TO FIX IT, AND LEAVING TOM LANDERS IN CHARGE OF ANYTHING... WELL, Y'KNOW, SON.

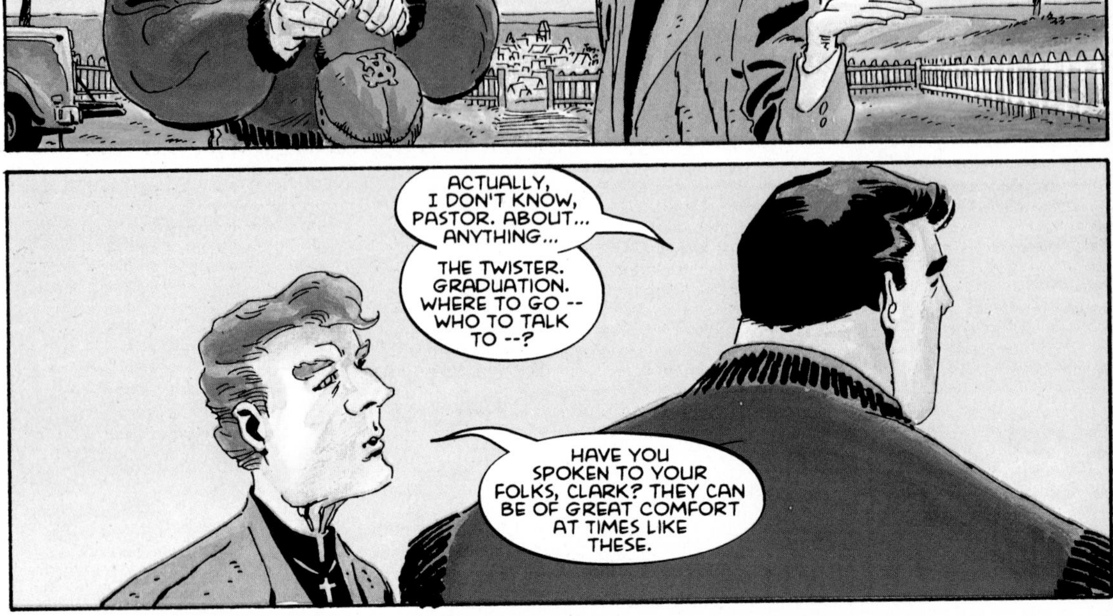
ACTUALLY, I DON'T KNOW, PASTOR. ABOUT... ANYTHING...
THE TWISTER. GRADUATION. WHERE TO GO -- WHO TO TALK TO --?
HAVE YOU SPOKEN TO YOUR FOLKS, CLARK? THEY CAN BE OF GREAT COMFORT AT TIMES LIKE THESE.

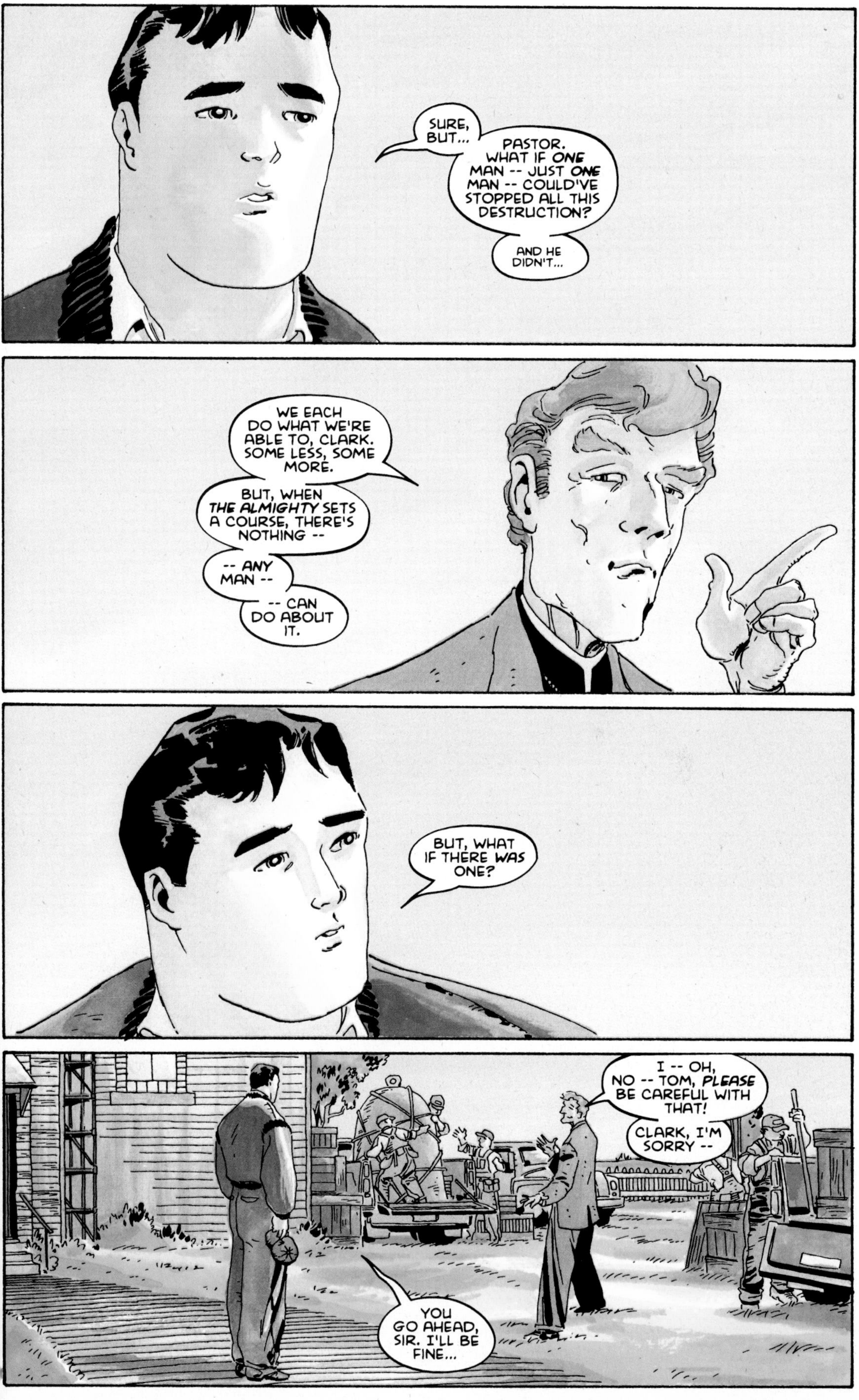
SURE, BUT...
PASTOR. WHAT IF ONE MAN -- JUST ONE MAN -- COULD'VE STOPPED ALL THIS DESTRUCTION?
AND HE DIDN'T...
WE EACH DO WHAT WE'RE ABLE TO, CLARK. SOME LESS, SOME MORE.
BUT, WHEN THE ALMIGHTY SETS A COURSE, THERE'S NOTHING --
-- ANY MAN --
-- CAN DO ABOUT IT.
BUT, WHAT IF THERE WAS ONE?
I -- OH, NO -- TOM, PLEASE BE CAREFUL WITH THAT!
CLARK, I'M SORRY --
YOU GO AHEAD, SIR. I'LL BE FINE...

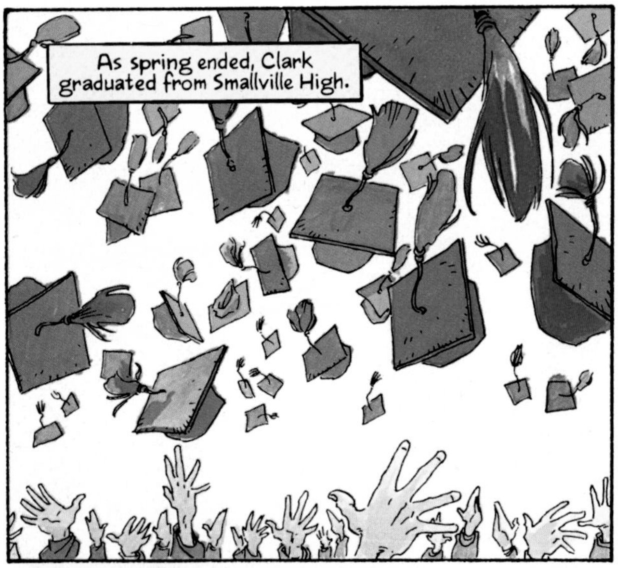
As spring ended, Clark graduated from Smallville High.

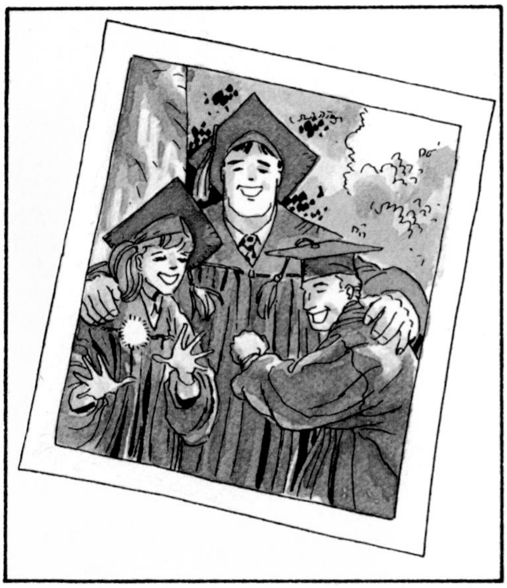

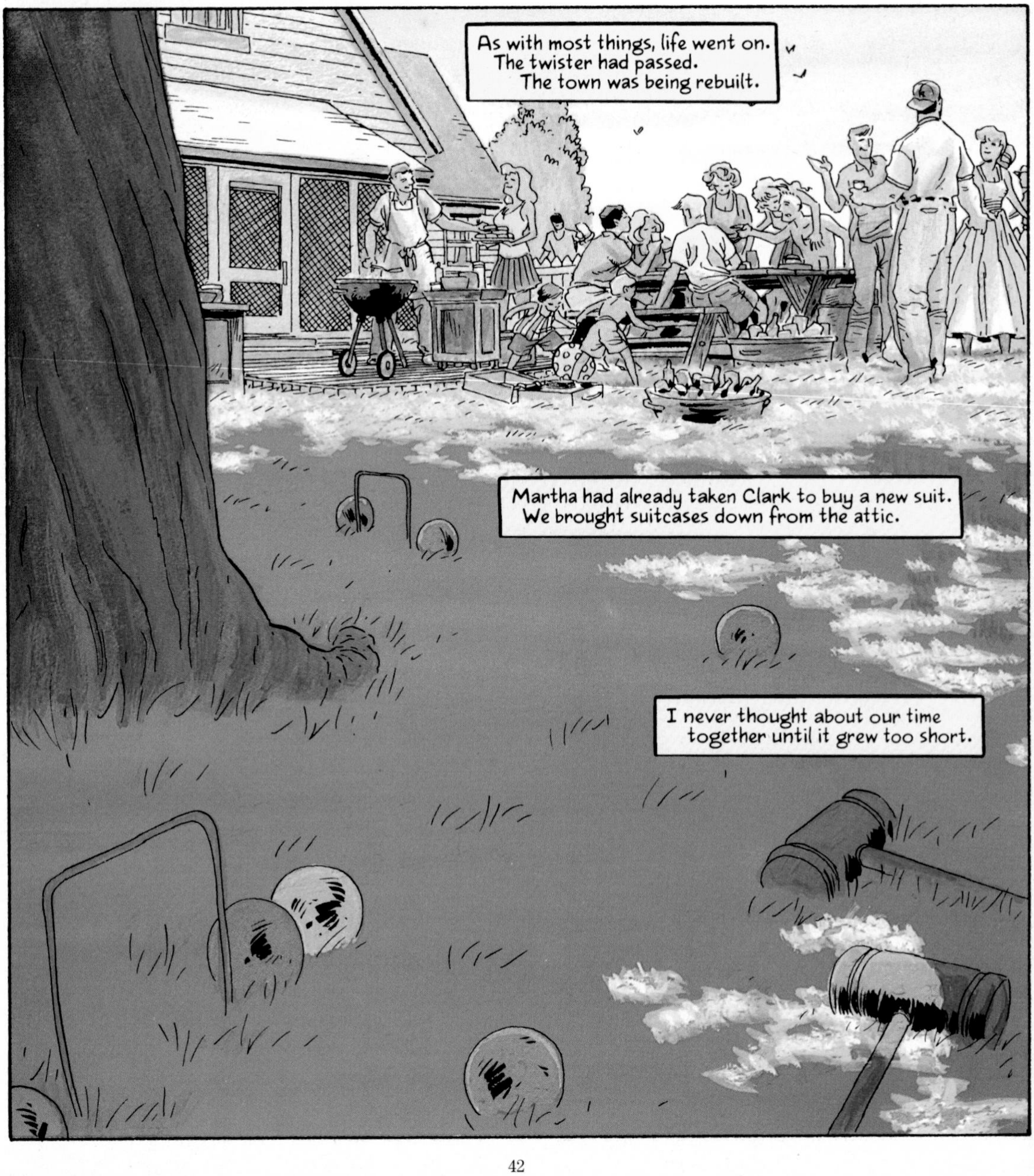
As with most things, life went on. The twister had passed. The town was being rebuilt.
Martha had already taken Clark to buy a new suit. We brought suitcases down from the attic.
I never thought about our time together until it grew too short.

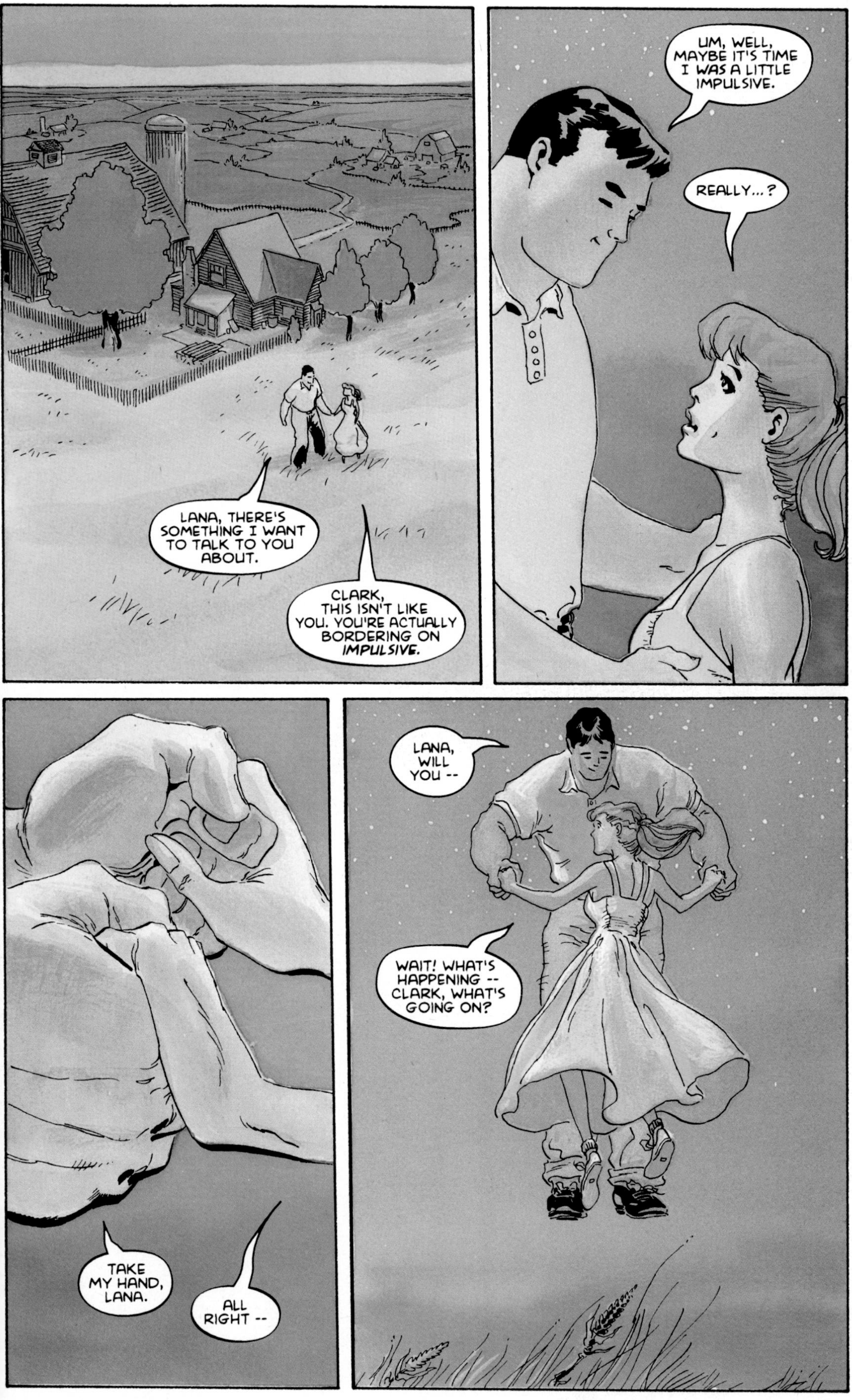

LANA, THERE'S SOMETHING I WANT TO TALK TO YOU ABOUT.
CLARK, THIS ISN'T LIKE YOU. YOU'RE ACTUALLY BORDERING ON *IMPULSIVE*.
UM, WELL, MAYBE IT'S TIME I WAS A LITTLE IMPULSIVE.
REALLY...?
TAKE MY HAND, LANA.
ALL RIGHT --
LANA, WILL YOU --
WAIT! WHAT'S HAPPENING -- CLARK, WHAT'S GOING ON?

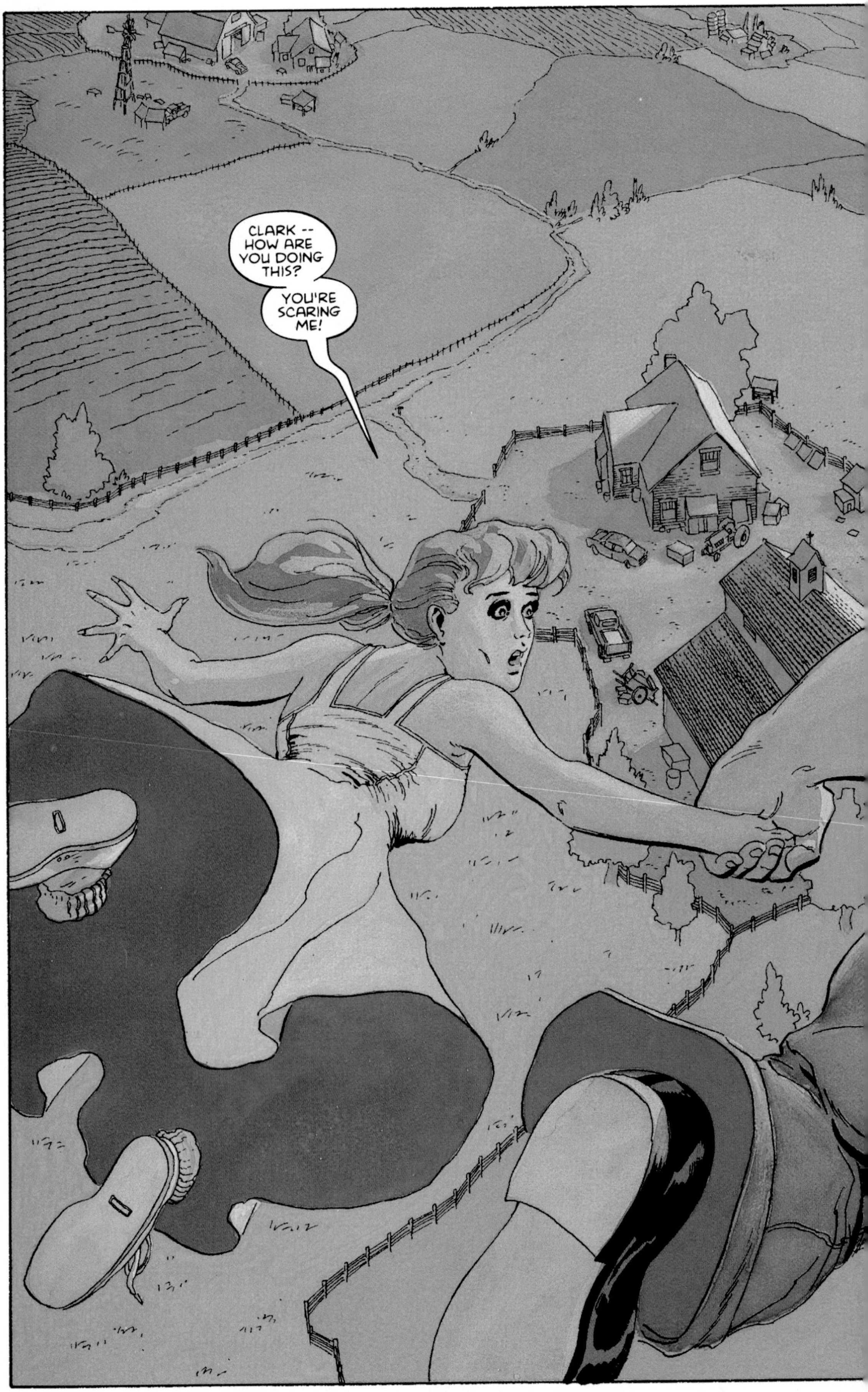
CLARK -- HOW ARE YOU DOING THIS?
YOU'RE SCARING ME!

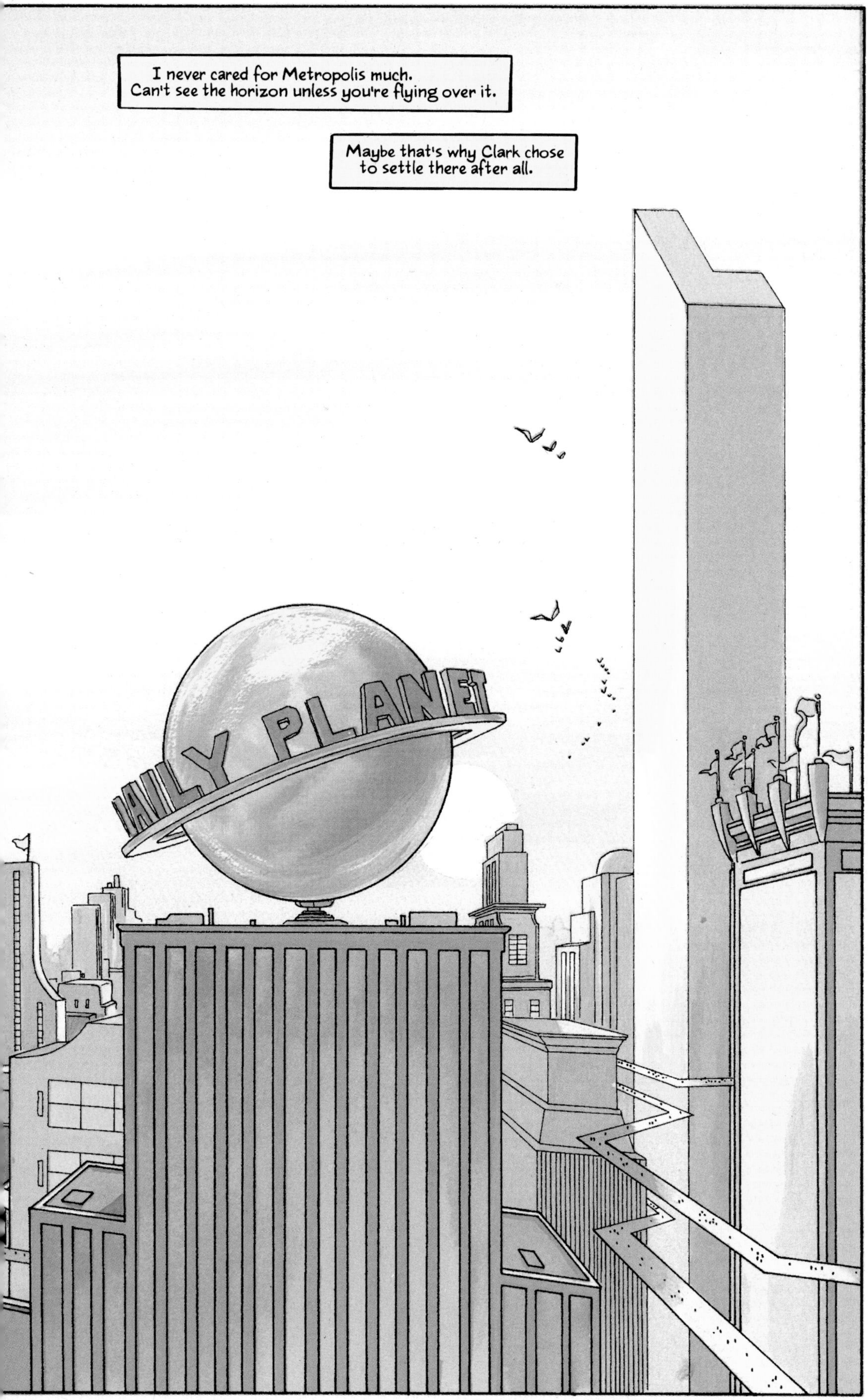
I never cared for Metropolis much.
Can't see the horizon unless you're flying over it.
Maybe that's why Clark chose to settle there after all.
DAILY PLANET

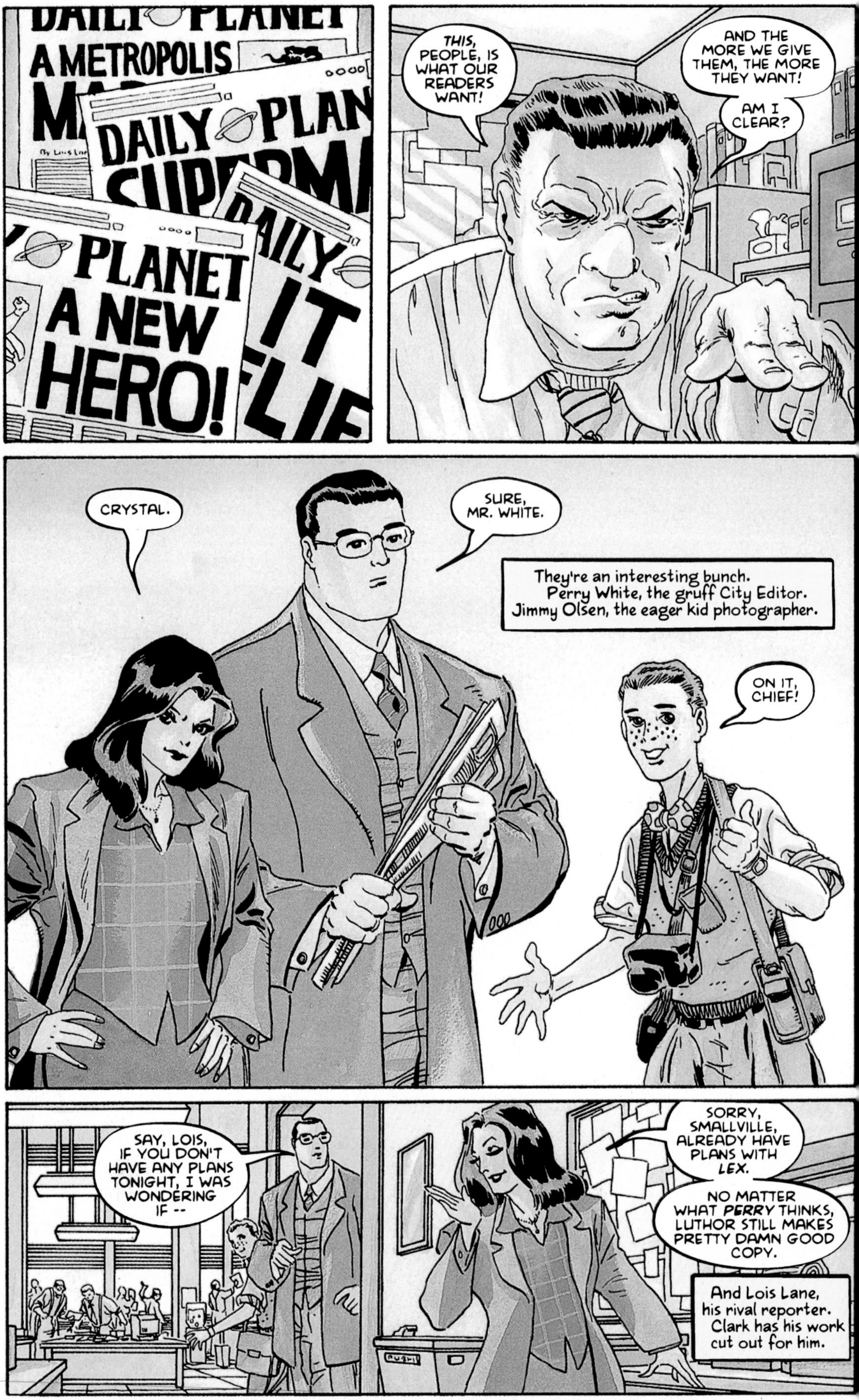
DAILY PLANET
A METROPOLIS
DAILY PLANET
SUPERM
DAILY
PLANET
A NEW
HERO!
IT
THIS, PEOPLE, IS WHAT OUR READERS WANT!
AND THE MORE WE GIVE THEM, THE MORE THEY WANT!
AM I CLEAR?
CRYSTAL.
SURE, MR. WHITE.
They're an interesting bunch. Perry White, the gruff City Editor. Jimmy Olsen, the eager kid photographer.
ON IT, CHIEF!
SAY, LOIS, IF YOU DON'T HAVE ANY PLANS TONIGHT, I WAS WONDERING IF --
SORRY, SMALLVILLE, ALREADY HAVE PLANS WITH *LEX.*
NO MATTER WHAT *PERRY* THINKS, LUTHOR STILL MAKES PRETTY DAMN GOOD COPY.
And Lois Lane, his rival reporter. Clark has his work cut out for him.

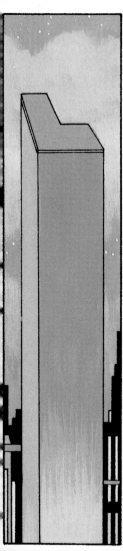

JOIN ME FOR A NIGHTCAP?

I HAD A LOVELY EVENING, LEX --

I SENSE A "BUT" COMING --

WHOOSH

-- BUT I'VE GOT AN EARLY DEADLINE --

-- AND YOU'VE GOT A HAT TO CATCH...

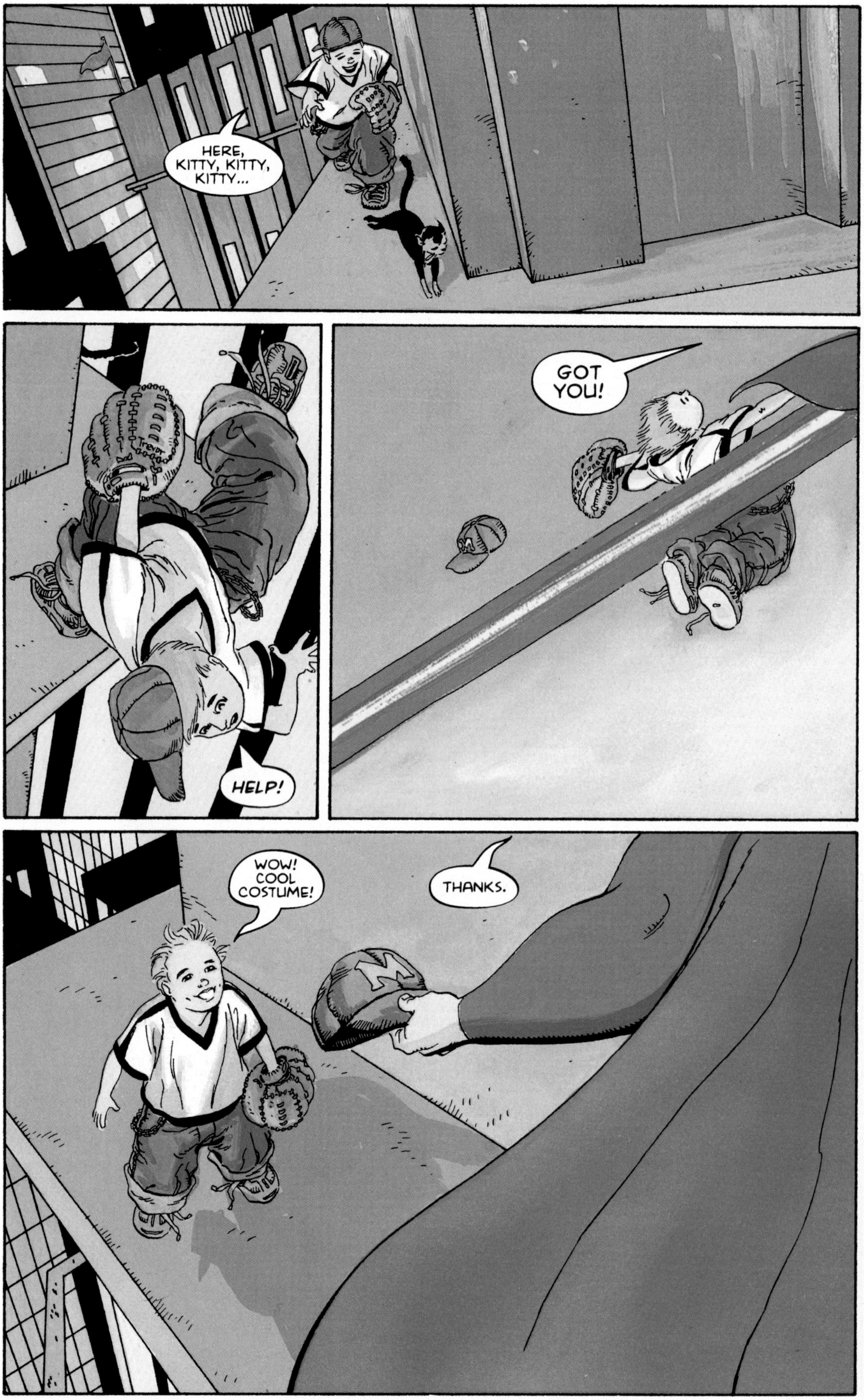
HERE, KITTY, KITTY, KITTY...
HELP!
GOT YOU!
WOW! COOL COSTUME!
THANKS.

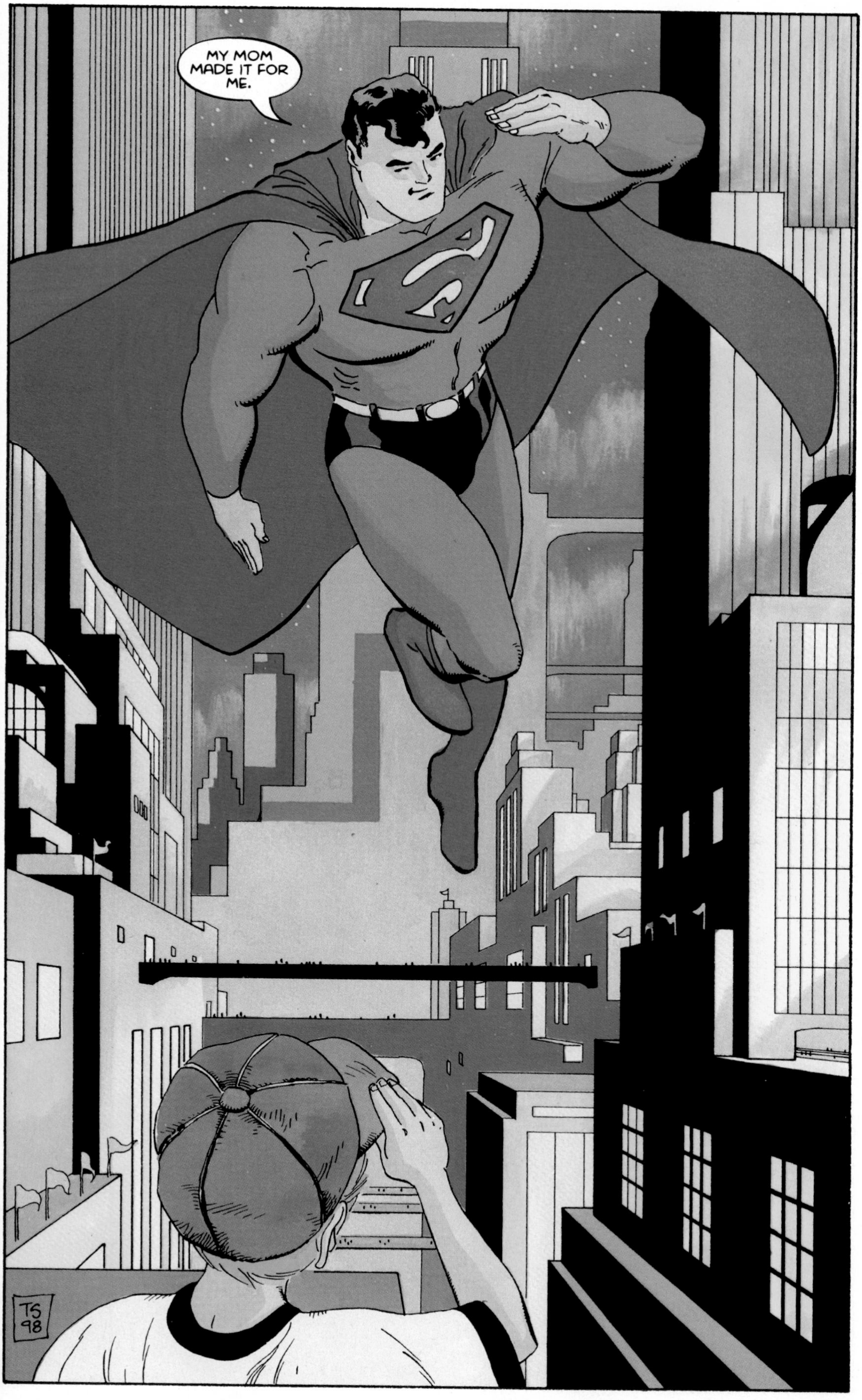
MY MOM MADE IT FOR ME.
TS 98

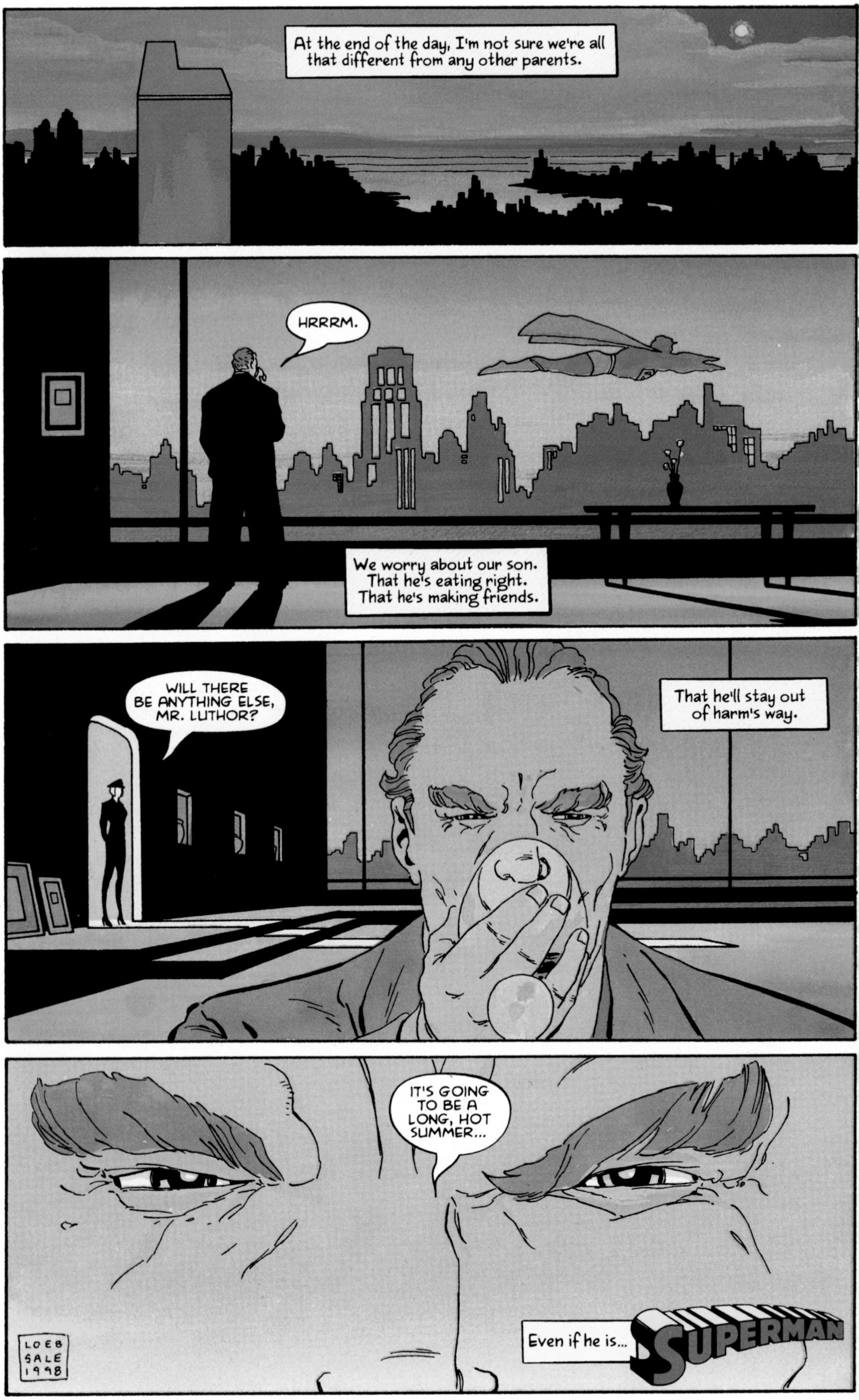

At the end of the day, I'm not sure we're all that different from any other parents.
HRRRM.
We worry about our son. That he's eating right. That he's making friends.
WILL THERE BE ANYTHING ELSE, MR. LUTHOR?
That he'll stay out of harm's way.
IT'S GOING TO BE A LONG, HOT SUMMER...
LOEB SALE 1998
Even if he is...
SUPERMAN

Summer

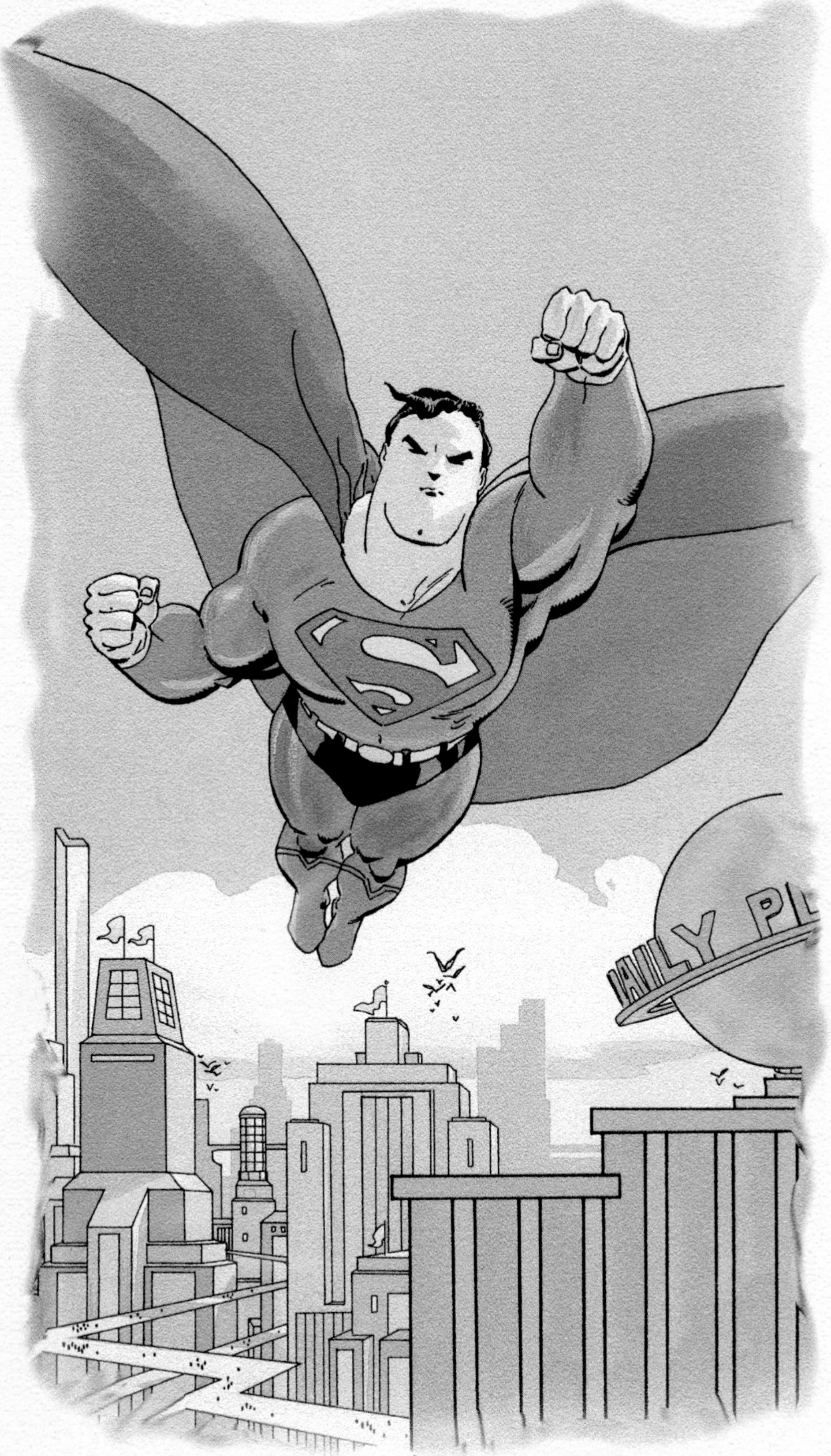

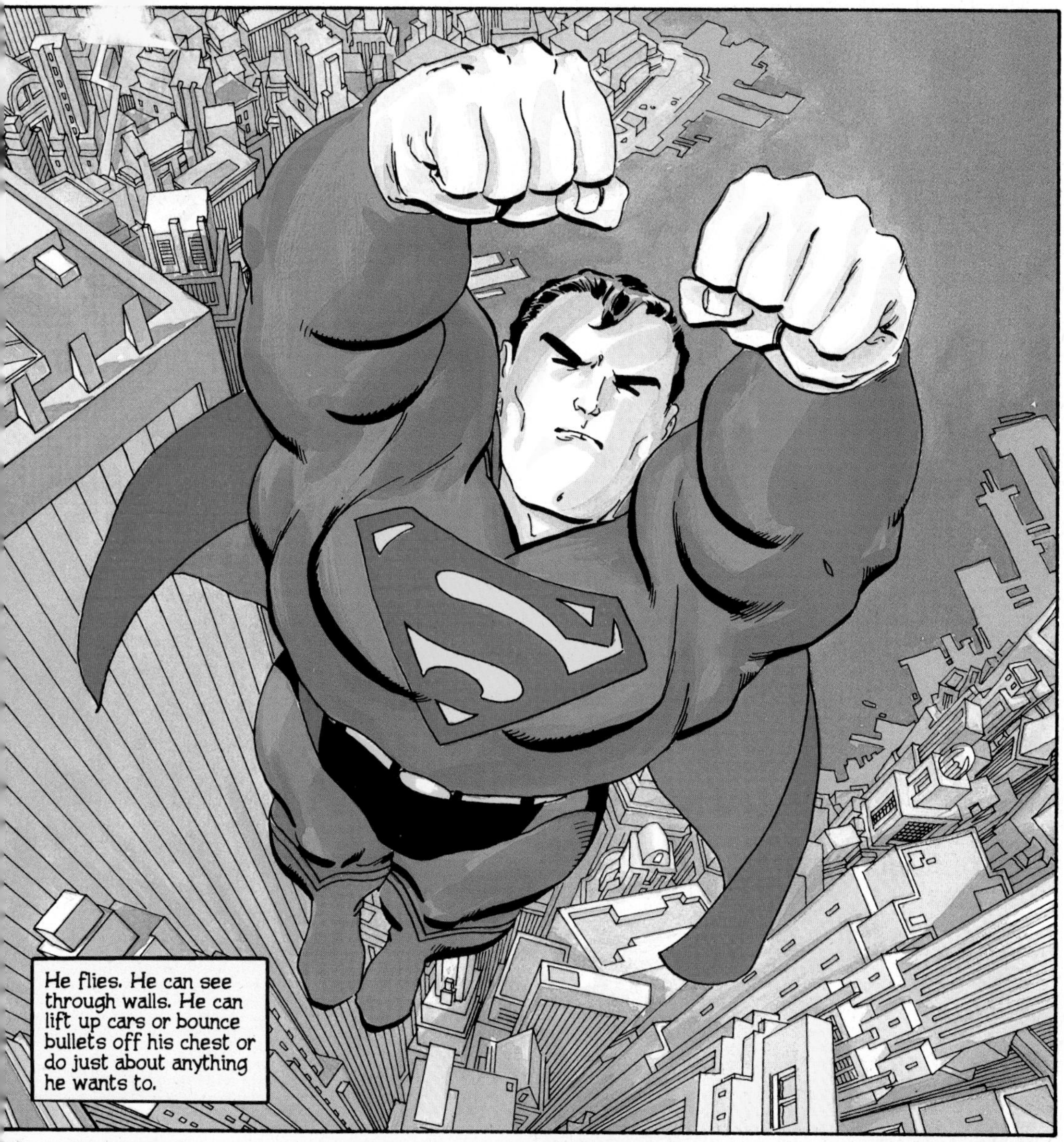
He flies. He can see through walls. He can lift up cars or bounce bullets off his chest or do just about anything he wants to.

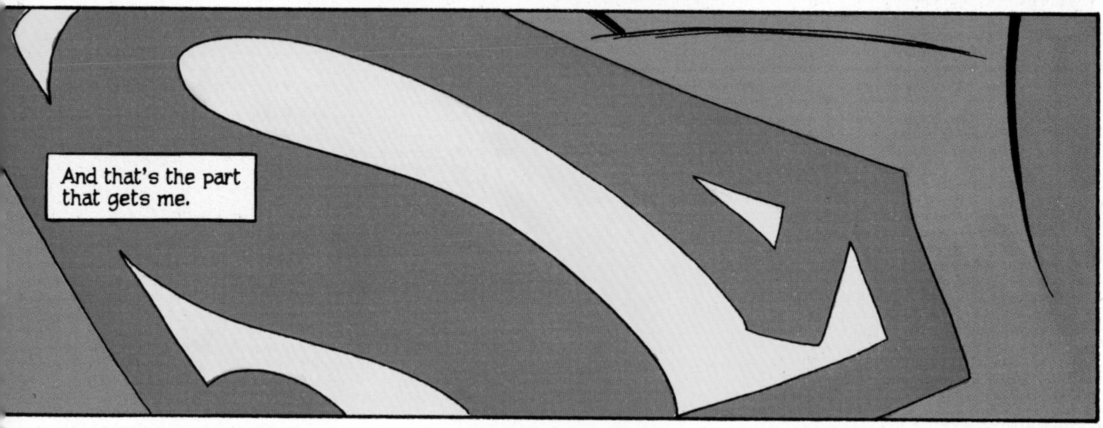
And that's the part that gets me.

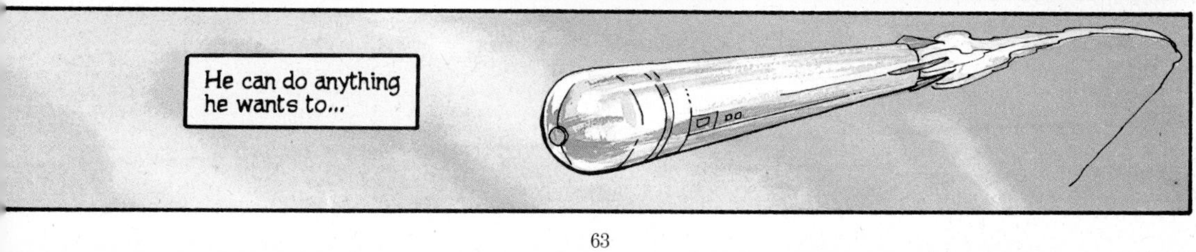
He can do anything he wants to...

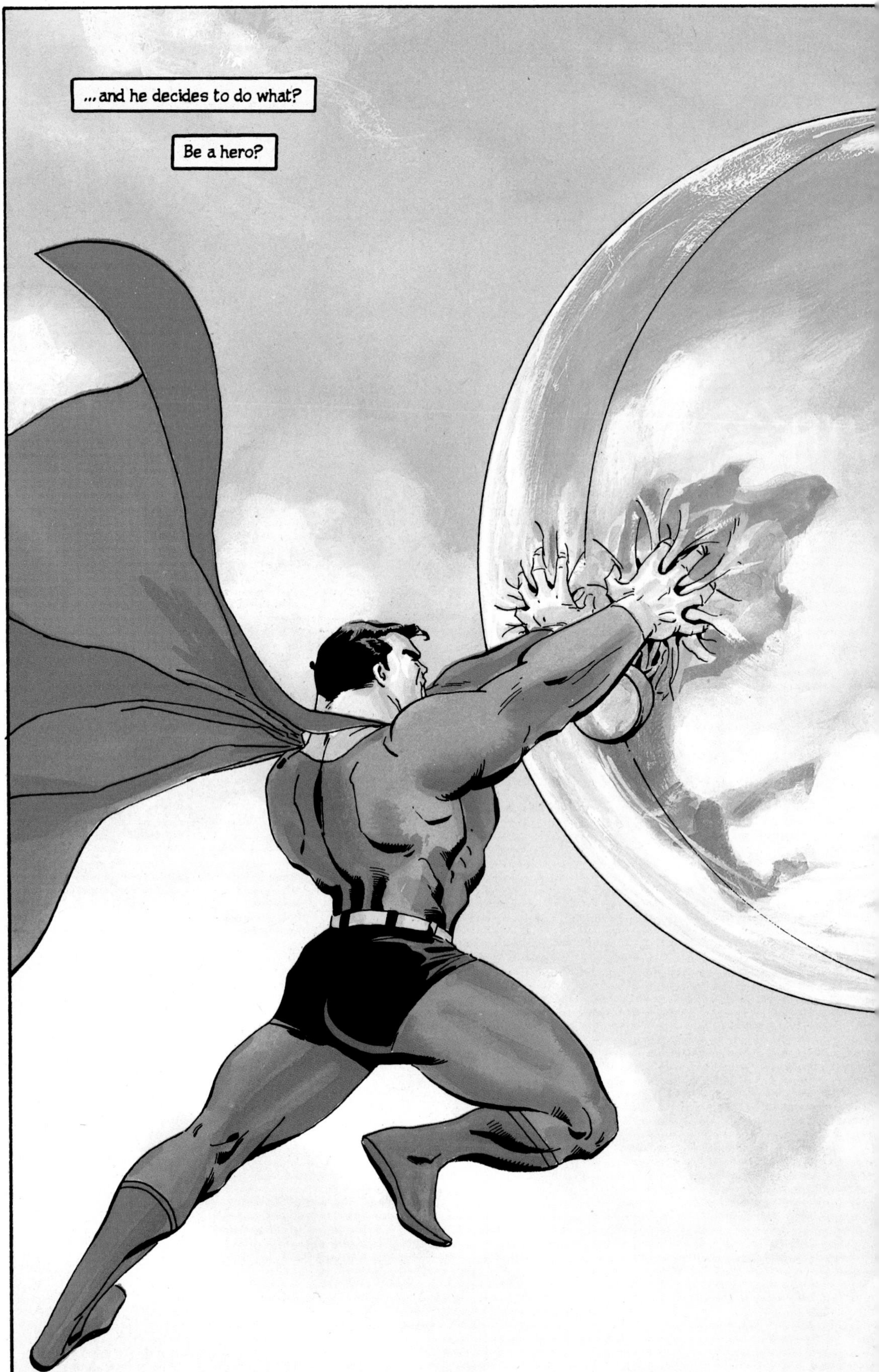
...and he decides to do what?
Be a hero?

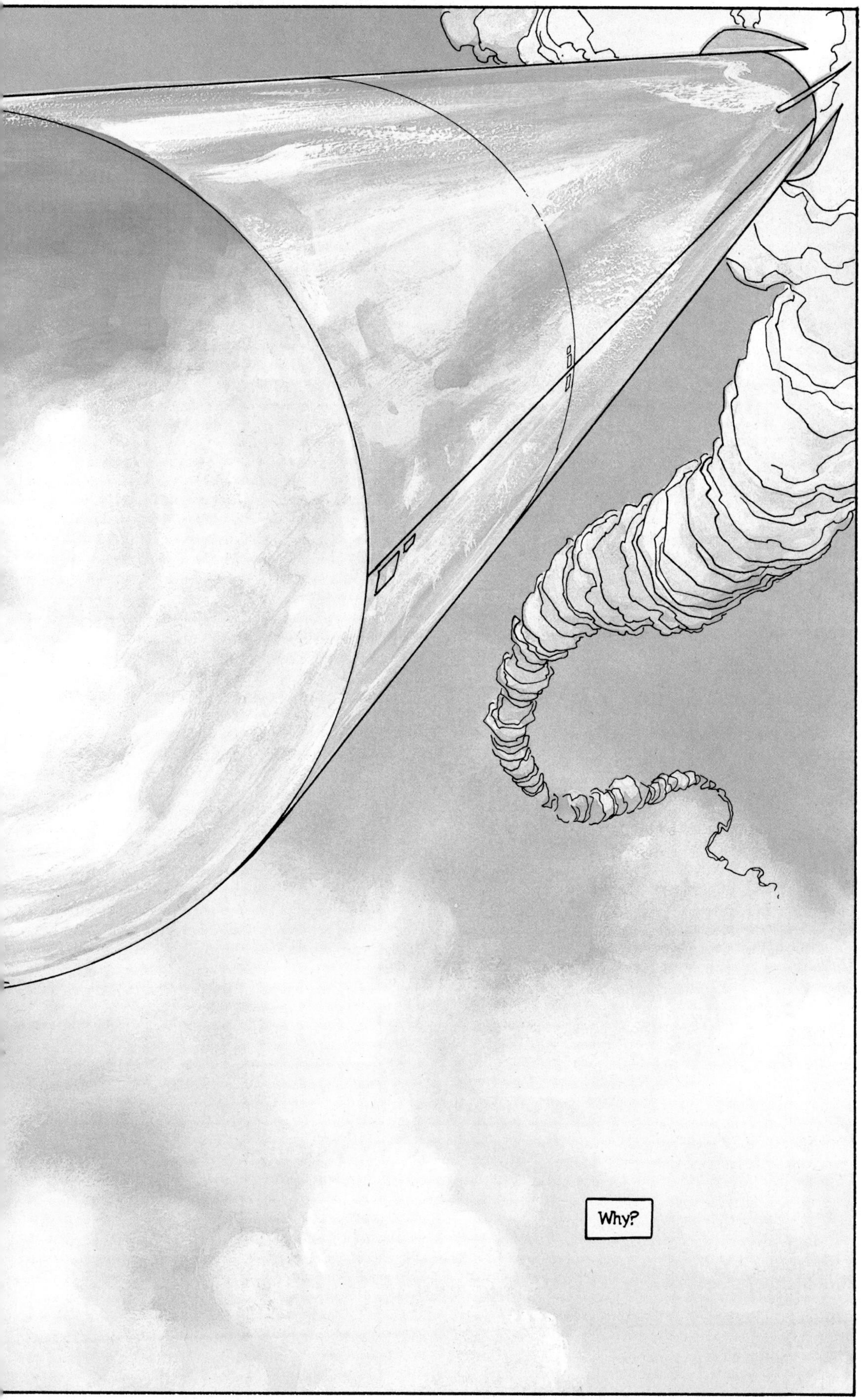
Why?

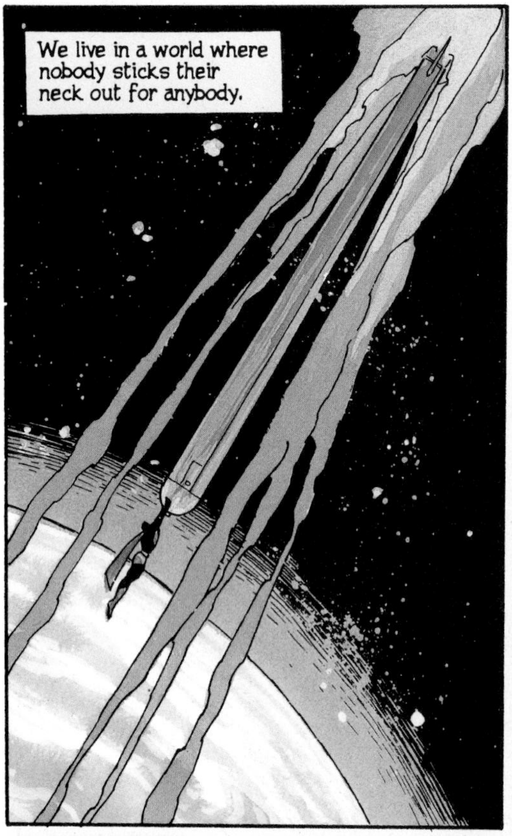
We live in a world where nobody sticks their neck out for anybody.

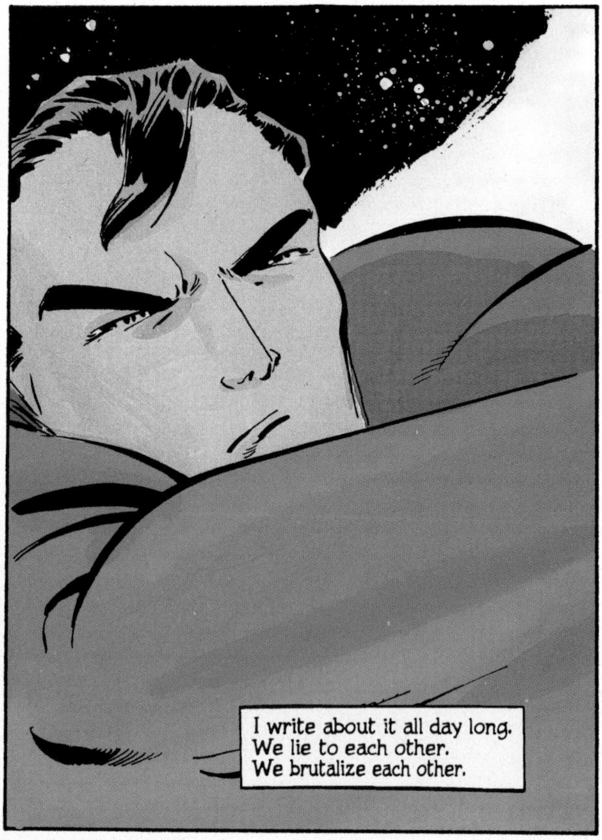
I write about it all day long.
We lie to each other.
We brutalize each other.

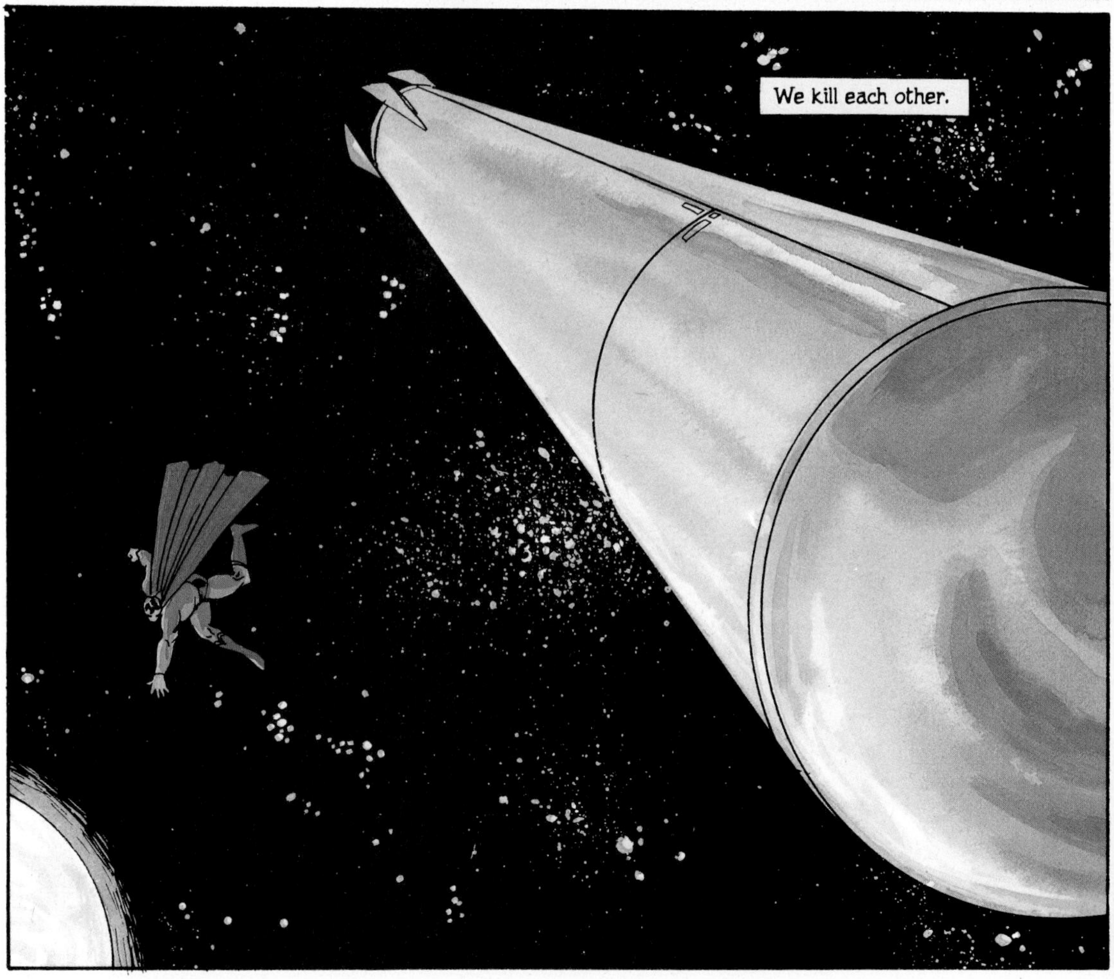
We kill each other.

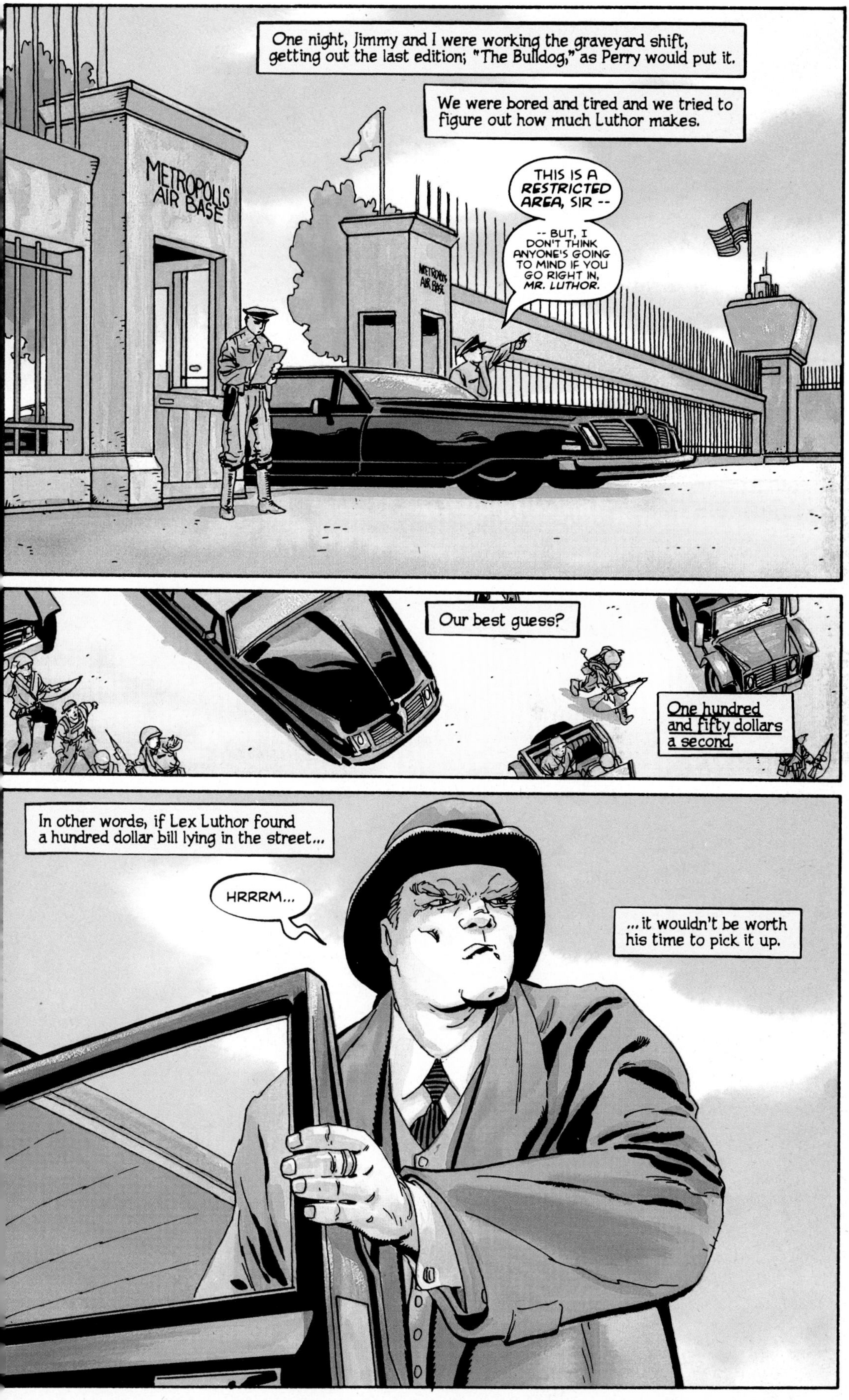
One night, Jimmy and I were working the graveyard shift, getting out the last edition; "The Bulldog," as Perry would put it.
We were bored and tired and we tried to figure out how much Luthor makes.
METROPOLIS AIR BASE
THIS IS A RESTRICTED AREA, SIR --
-- BUT, I DON'T THINK ANYONE'S GOING TO MIND IF YOU GO RIGHT IN, MR. LUTHOR.
Our best guess?
One hundred and fifty dollars a second.
In other words, if Lex Luthor found a hundred dollar bill lying in the street...
HRRRM...
...it wouldn't be worth his time to pick it up.

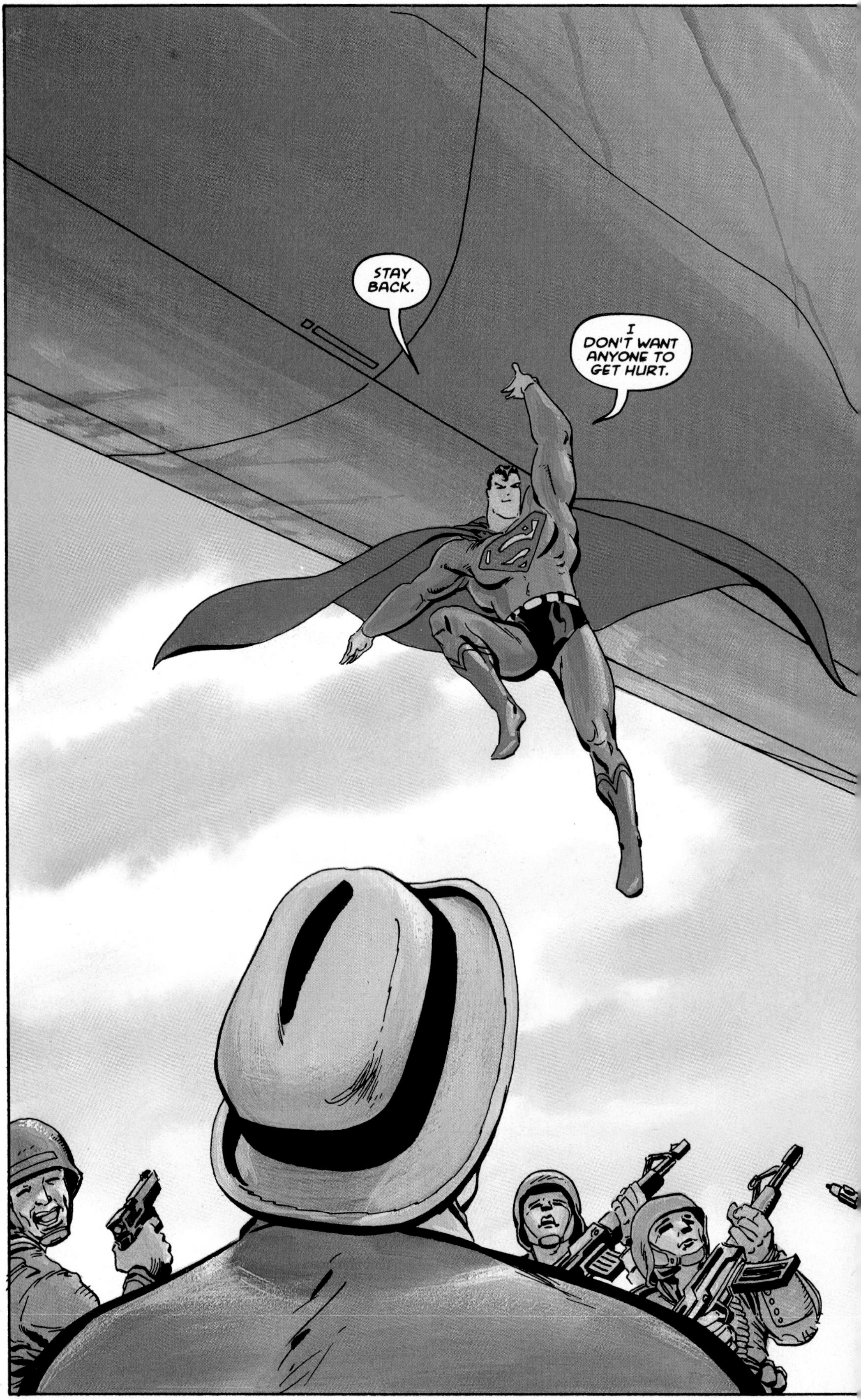

STAY BACK.
I DON'T WANT ANYONE TO GET HURT.

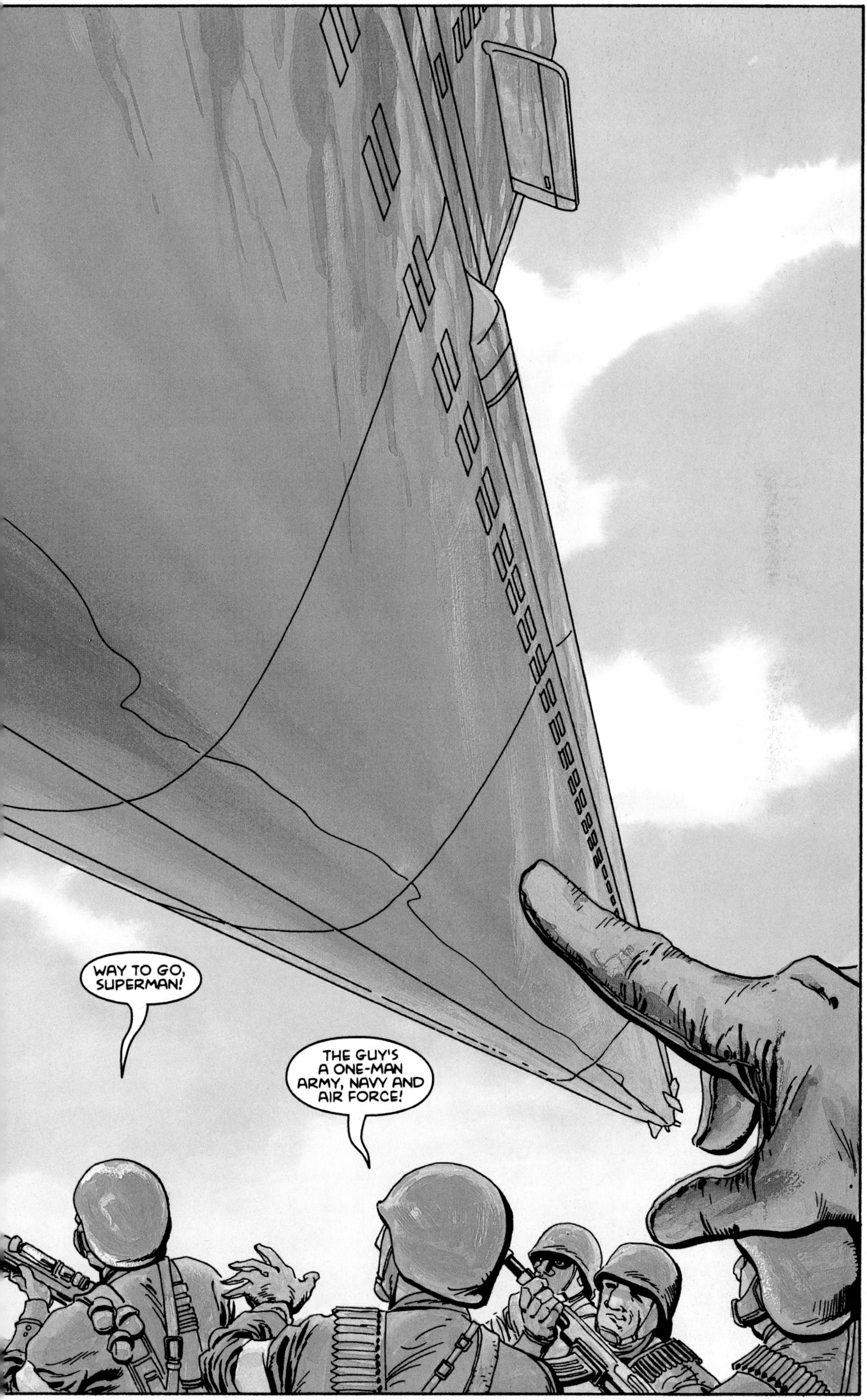
WAY TO GO, SUPERMAN!
THE GUY'S A ONE-MAN ARMY, NAVY AND AIR FORCE!

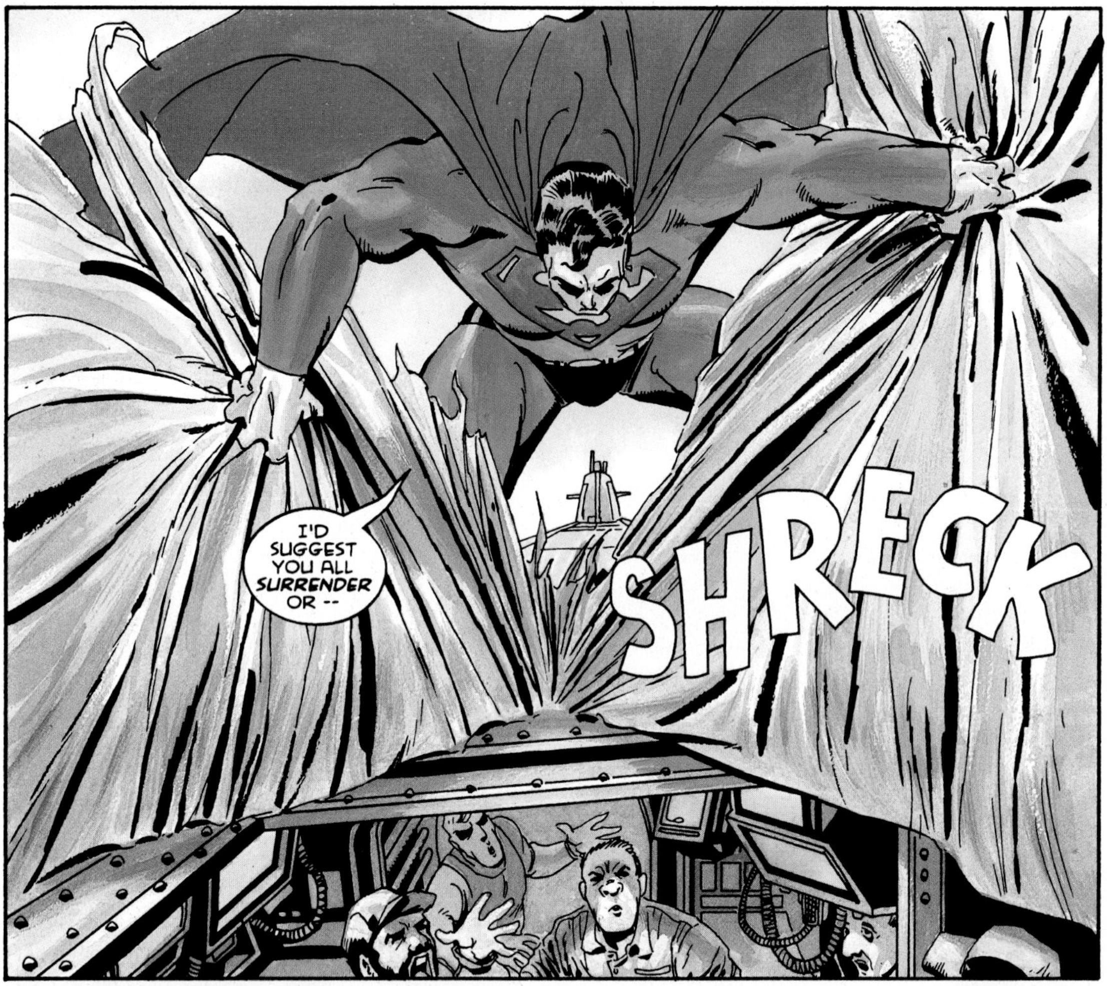
I'D SUGGEST YOU ALL SURRENDER OR --
SHRECK

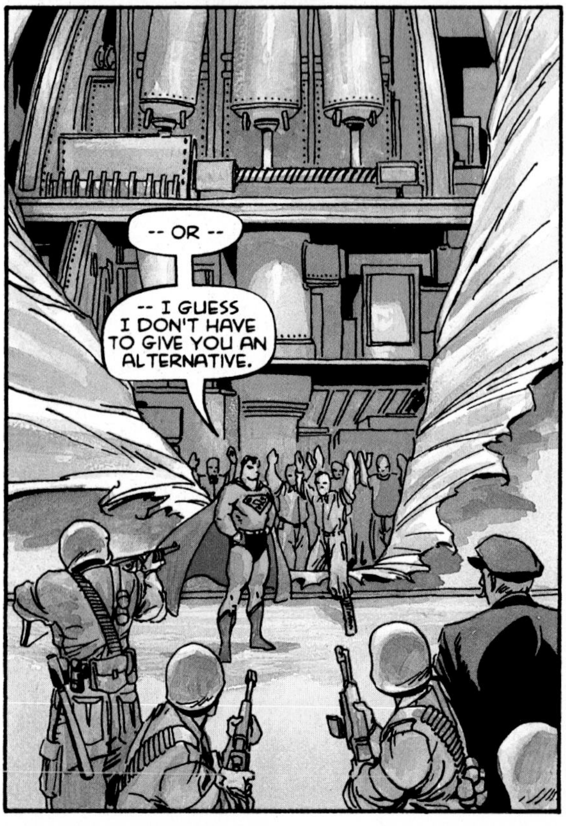
-- OR --
-- I GUESS I DON'T HAVE TO GIVE YOU AN ALTERNATIVE.

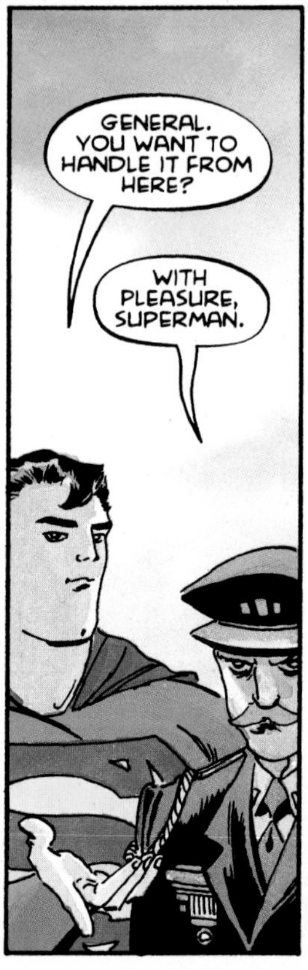
GENERAL. YOU WANT TO HANDLE IT FROM HERE?
WITH PLEASURE, SUPERMAN.

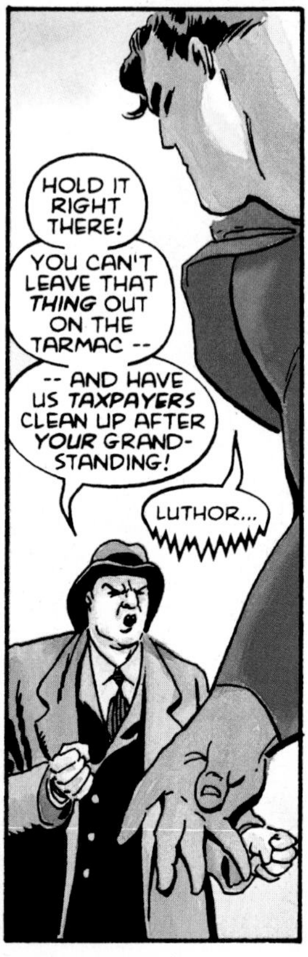
HOLD IT RIGHT THERE!
YOU CAN'T LEAVE THAT THING OUT ON THE TARMAC --
-- AND HAVE US TAXPAYERS CLEAN UP AFTER YOUR GRAND-STANDING!
LUTHOR...

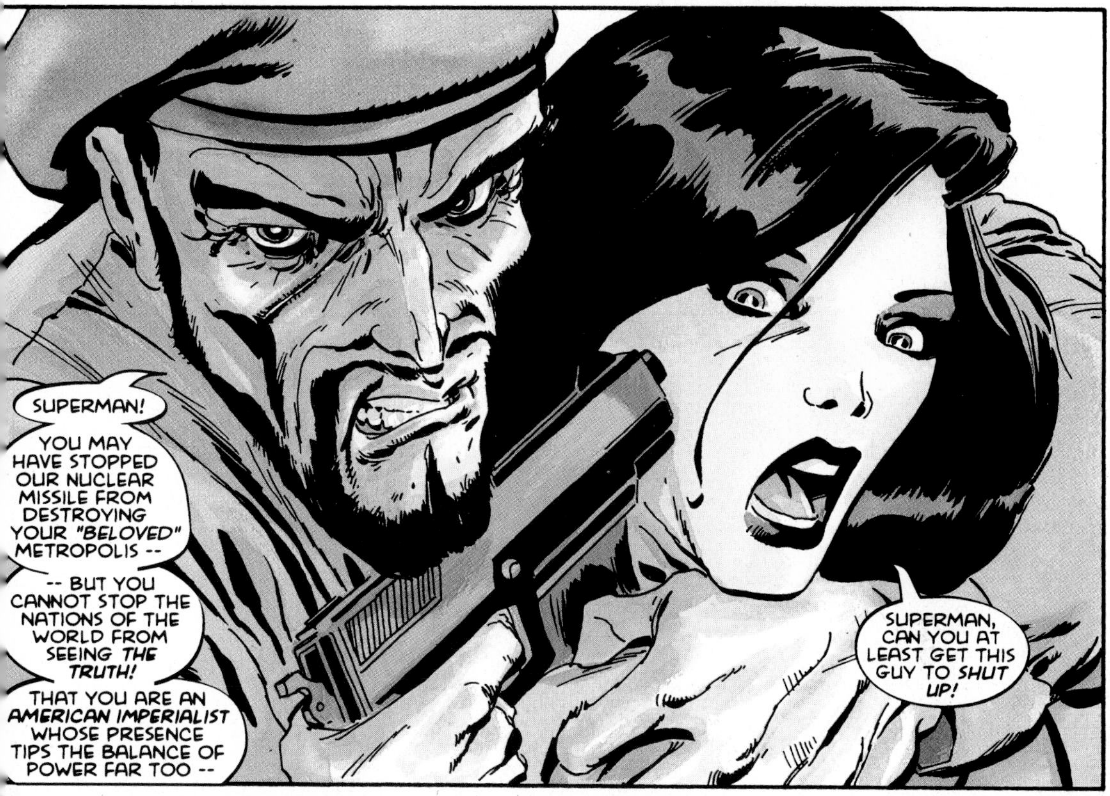
SUPERMAN!
YOU MAY HAVE STOPPED OUR NUCLEAR MISSILE FROM DESTROYING YOUR "BELOVED" METROPOLIS --
-- BUT YOU CANNOT STOP THE NATIONS OF THE WORLD FROM SEEING THE TRUTH!
THAT YOU ARE AN AMERICAN IMPERIALIST WHOSE PRESENCE TIPS THE BALANCE OF POWER FAR TOO --
SUPERMAN, CAN YOU AT LEAST GET THIS GUY TO SHUT UP!

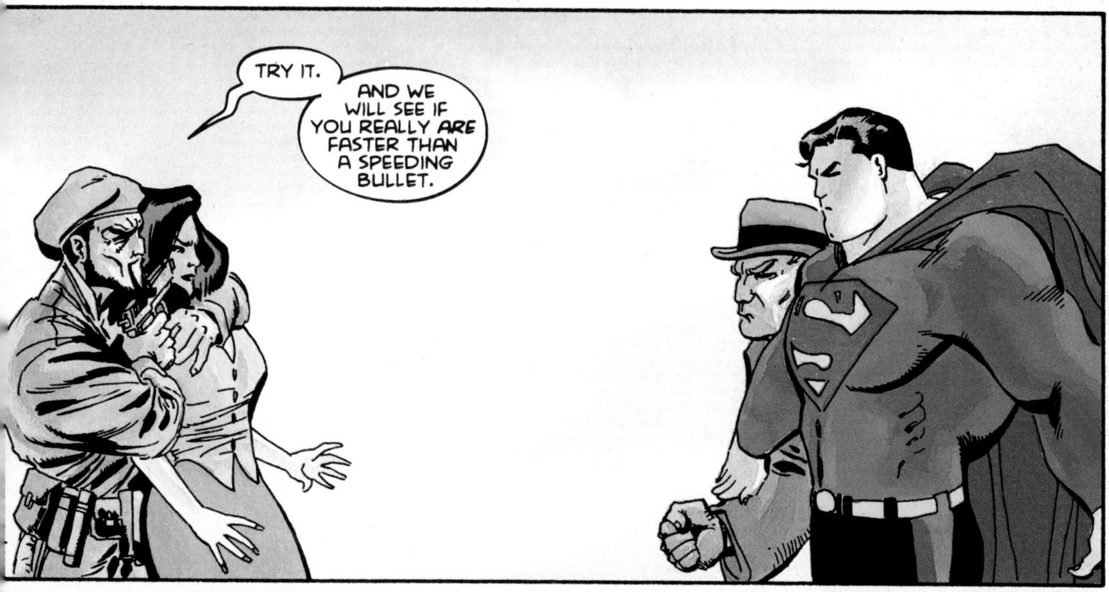
TRY IT.
AND WE WILL SEE IF YOU REALLY ARE FASTER THAN A SPEEDING BULLET.

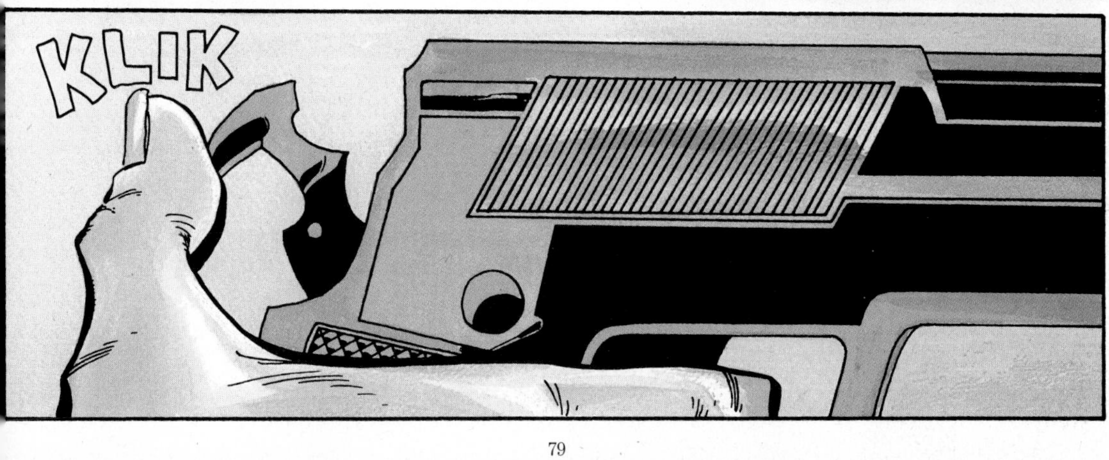
KLIK

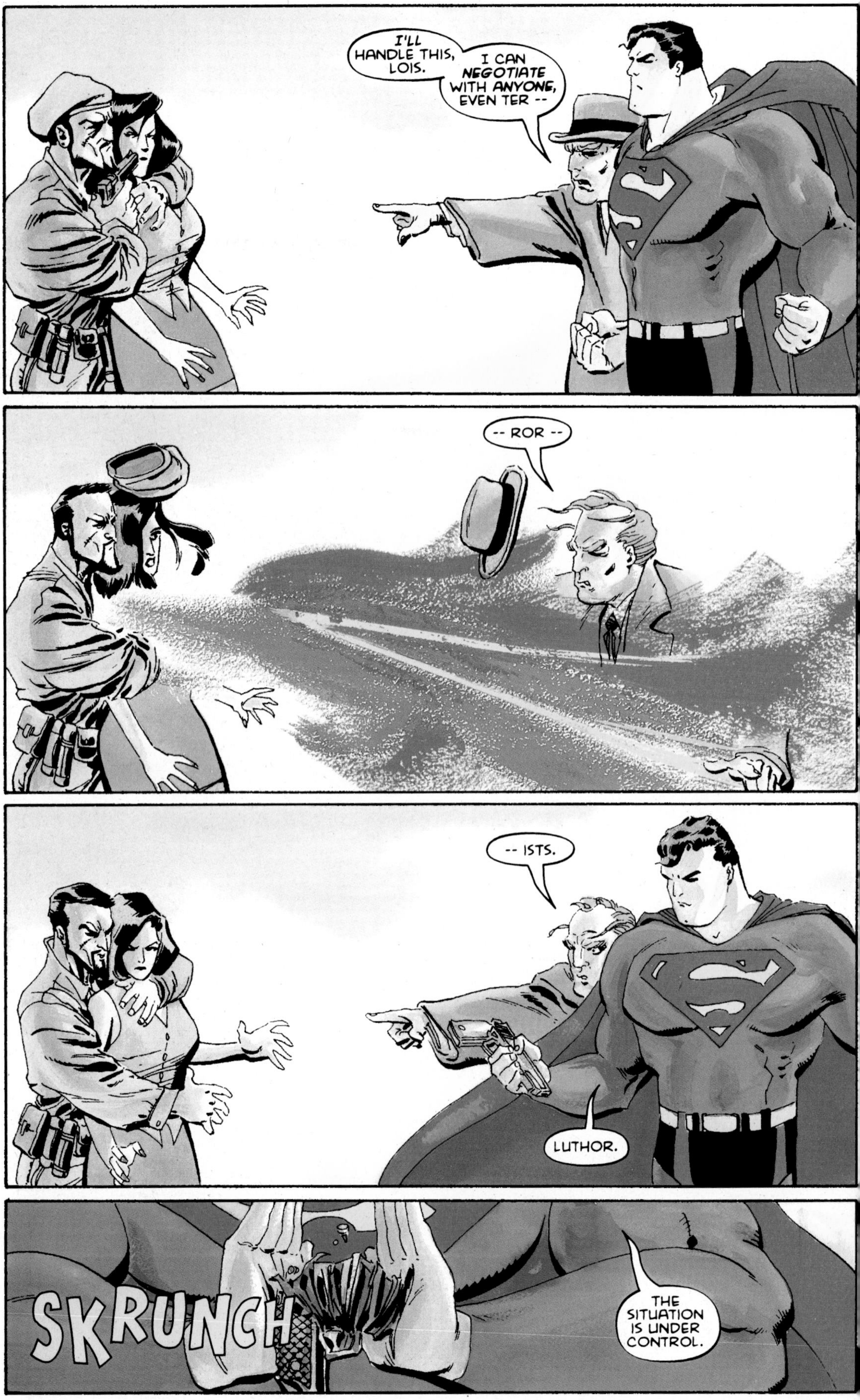
I'LL HANDLE THIS, LOIS.
I CAN NEGOTIATE WITH ANYONE, EVEN TER --
-- ROR --
-- ISTS.
LUTHOR.
SKRUNCH
THE SITUATION IS UNDER CONTROL.

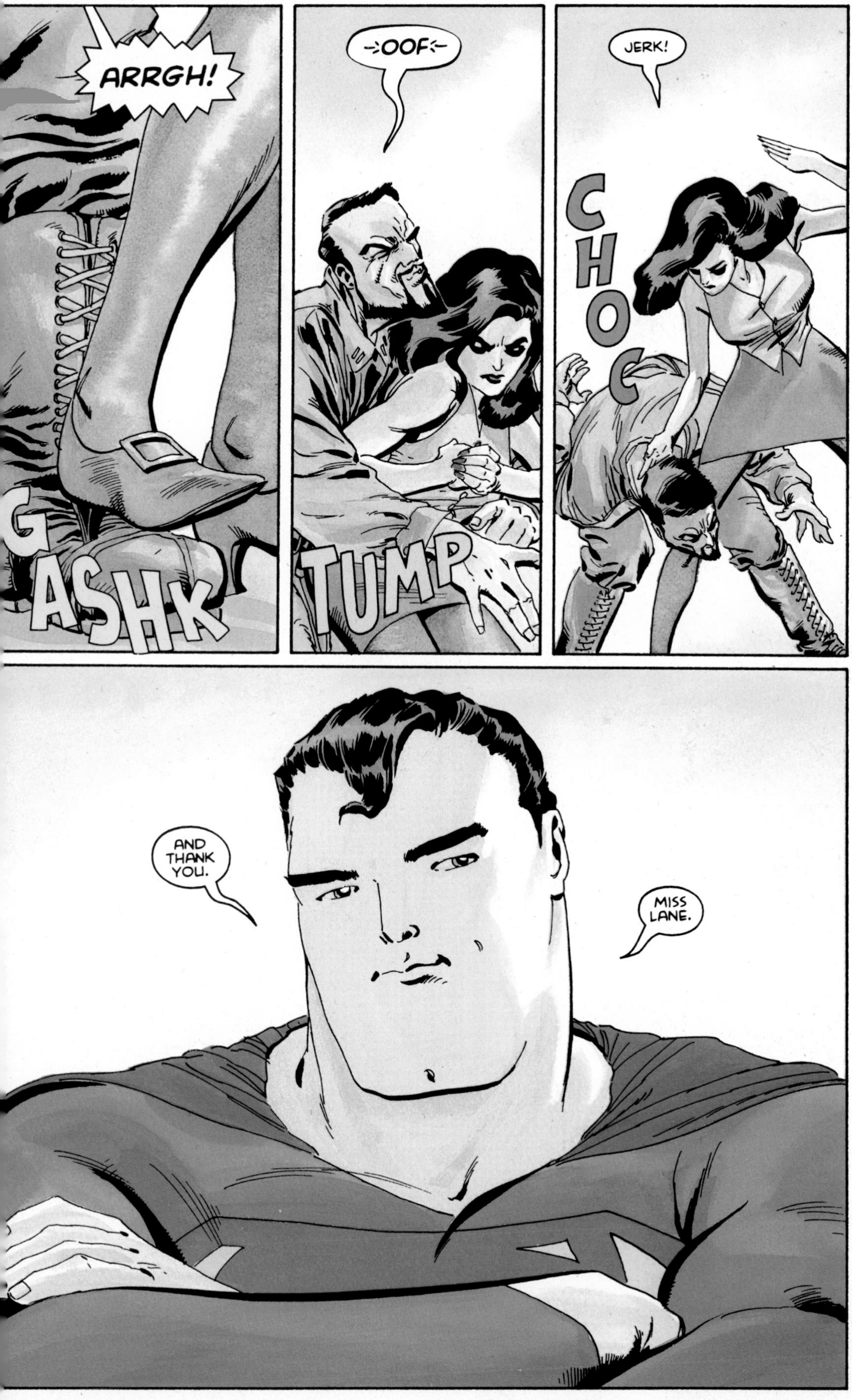
ARRGH!
GASHK
-OOF-
TUMP
JERK!
CHOC
AND THANK YOU.
MISS LANE.

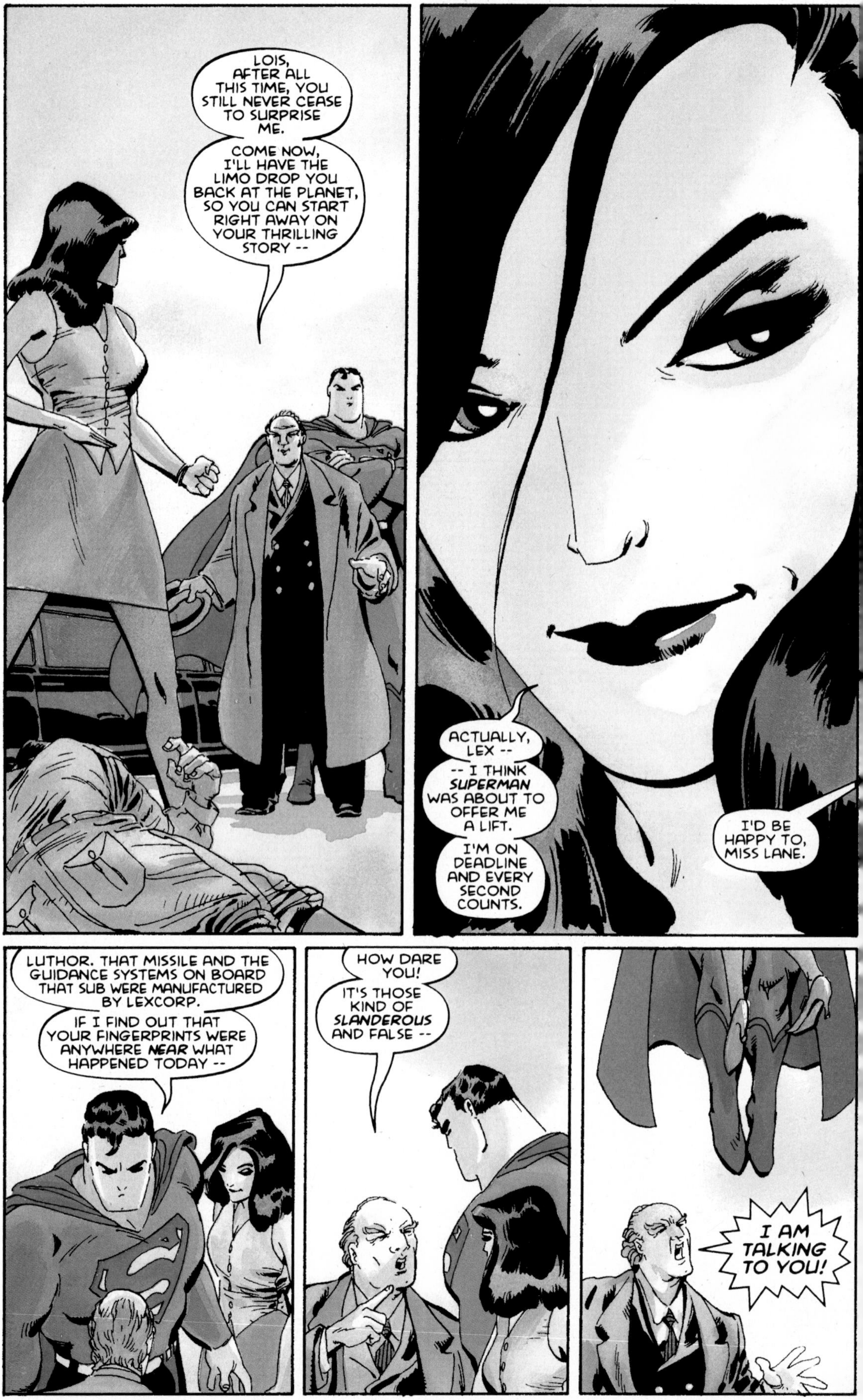
LOIS, AFTER ALL THIS TIME, YOU STILL NEVER CEASE TO SURPRISE ME.
COME NOW, I'LL HAVE THE LIMO DROP YOU BACK AT THE PLANET, SO YOU CAN START RIGHT AWAY ON YOUR THRILLING STORY --
ACTUALLY, LEX --
-- I THINK SUPERMAN WAS ABOUT TO OFFER ME A LIFT.
I'M ON DEADLINE AND EVERY SECOND COUNTS.
I'D BE HAPPY TO, MISS LANE.
LUTHOR. THAT MISSILE AND THE GUIDANCE SYSTEMS ON BOARD THAT SUB WERE MANUFACTURED BY LEXCORP.
IF I FIND OUT THAT YOUR FINGERPRINTS WERE ANYWHERE NEAR WHAT HAPPENED TODAY --
HOW DARE YOU!
IT'S THOSE KIND OF SLANDEROUS AND FALSE --
I AM TALKING TO YOU!

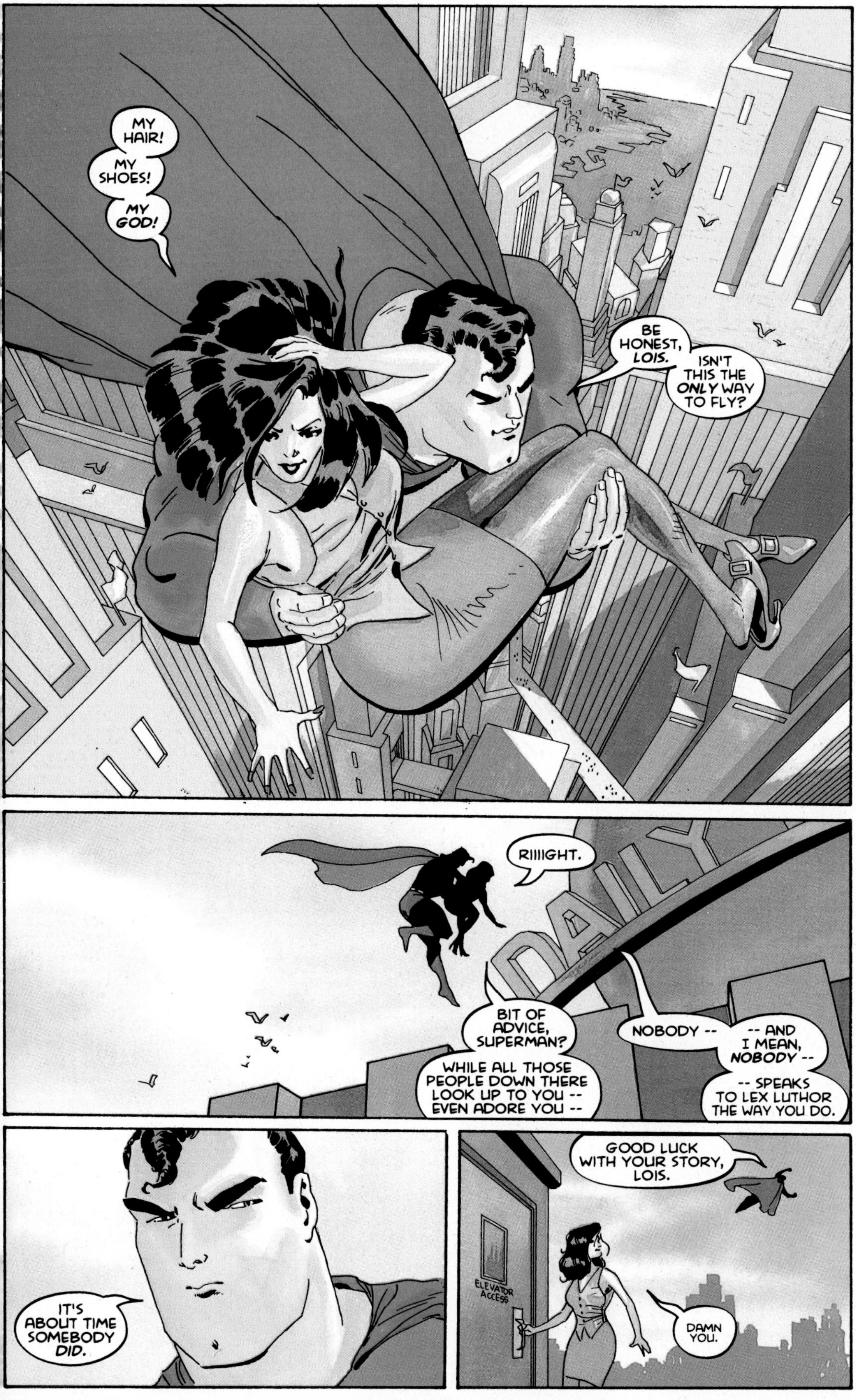
MY HAIR!
MY SHOES!
MY GOD!
BE HONEST, LOIS.
ISN'T THIS THE ONLY WAY TO FLY?
DAILY
RIIIIGHT.
BIT OF ADVICE, SUPERMAN?
WHILE ALL THOSE PEOPLE DOWN THERE LOOK UP TO YOU -- EVEN ADORE YOU --
NOBODY --
-- AND I MEAN, NOBODY --
-- SPEAKS TO LEX LUTHOR THE WAY YOU DO.
IT'S ABOUT TIME SOMEBODY DID.
GOOD LUCK WITH YOUR STORY, LOIS.
ELEVATOR ACCESS
DAMN YOU.

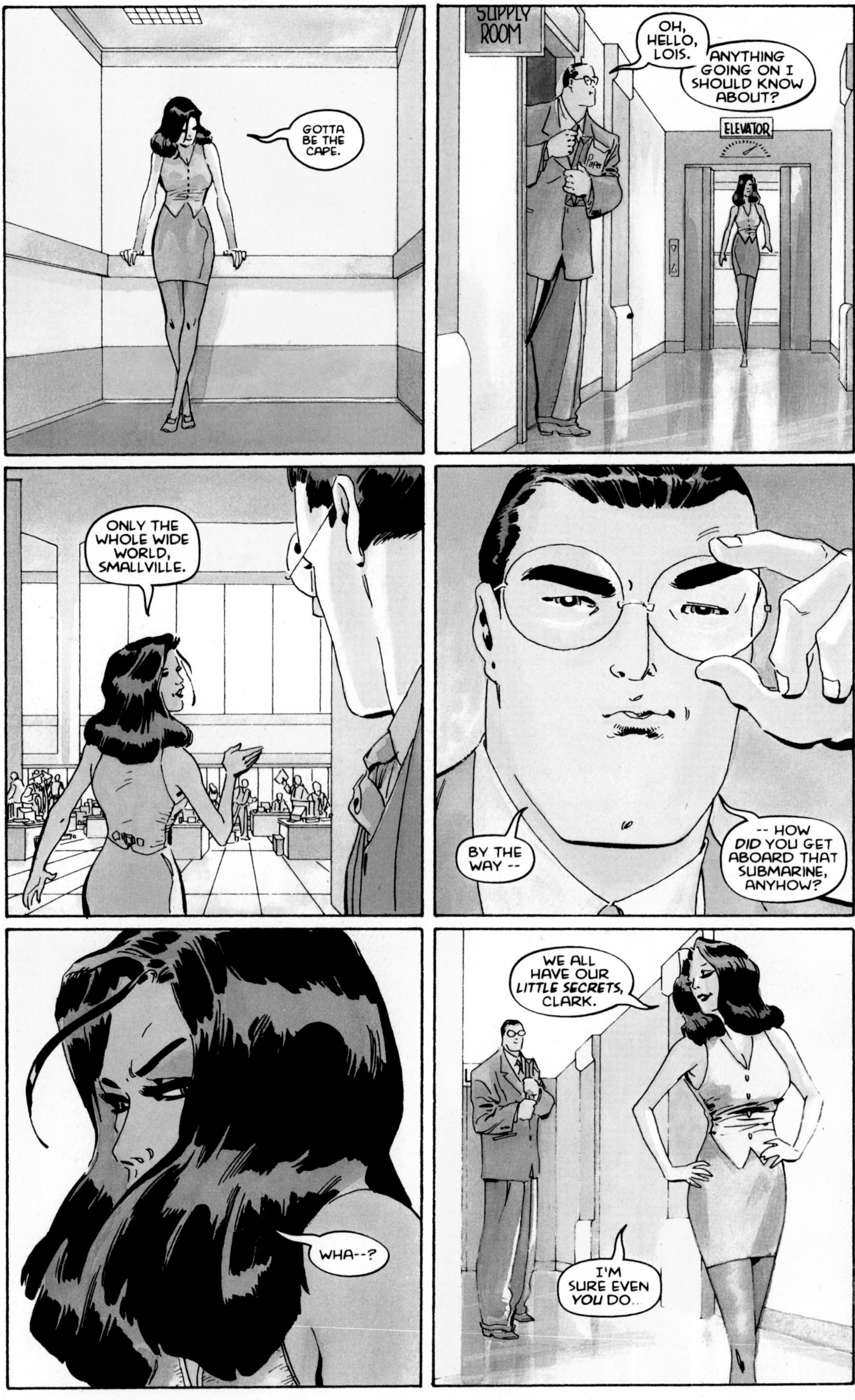
GOTTA BE THE CAPE.
SUPPLY ROOM
OH, HELLO, LOIS.
ANYTHING GOING ON I SHOULD KNOW ABOUT?
ELEVATOR
ONLY THE WHOLE WIDE WORLD, SMALLVILLE.
BY THE WAY --
-- HOW *DID* YOU GET ABOARD THAT SUBMARINE, ANYHOW?
WHA--?
WE ALL HAVE OUR *LITTLE SECRETS*, CLARK.
I'M SURE EVEN *YOU* DO...

The problem, of course, with the whole "Prince Charming" thing is that it's a recipe for disaster.

344 CLINTON

A woman has this ideal man in mind and since no such man exists, no man can live up to that standard.

And then, along comes Superman...

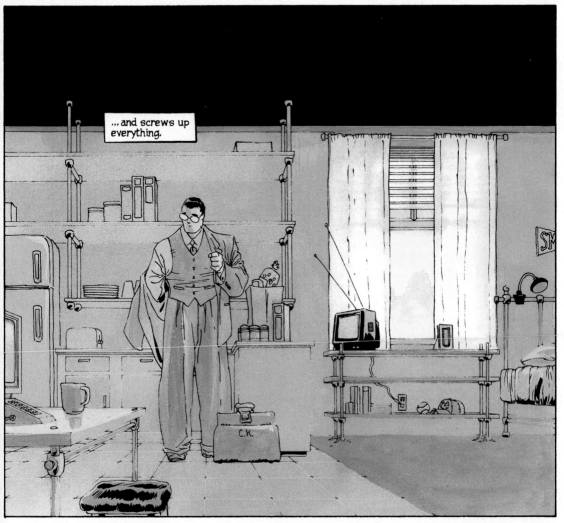

...and screws up everything.

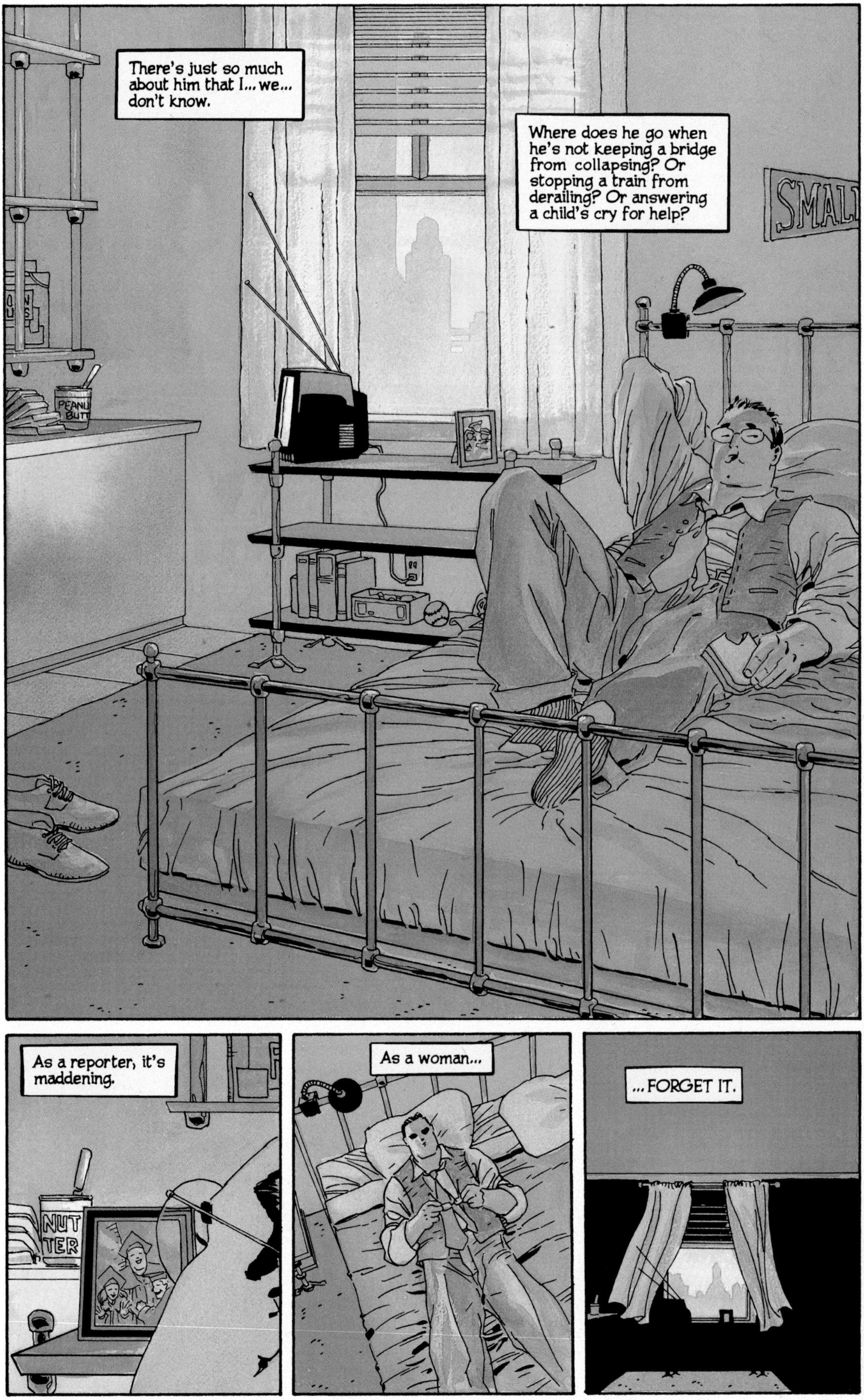
There's just so much about him that I... we... don't know.
Where does he go when he's not keeping a bridge from collapsing? Or stopping a train from derailing? Or answering a child's cry for help?
As a reporter, it's maddening.
As a woman...
...FORGET IT.

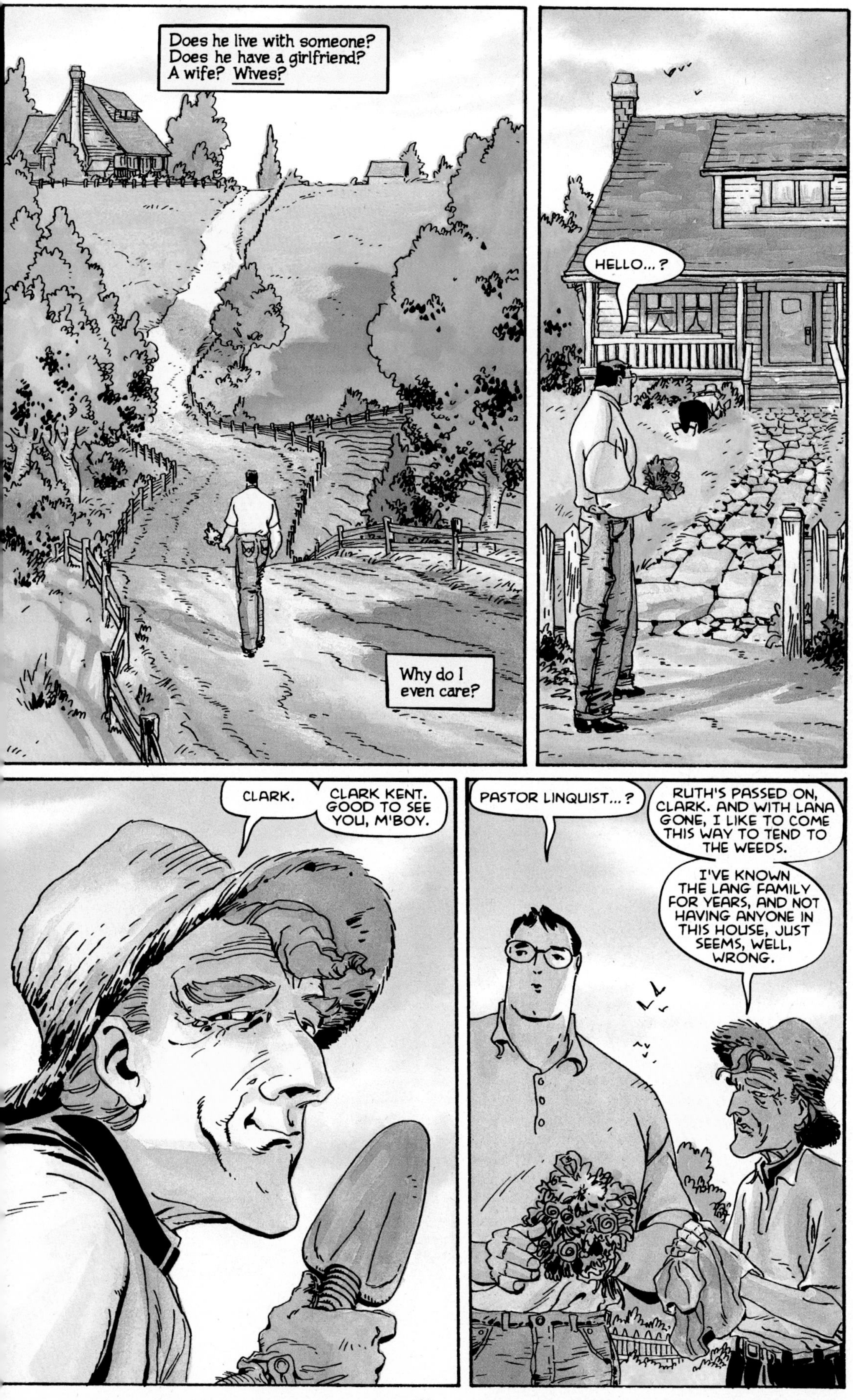

Does he live with someone? Does he have a girlfriend? A wife? Wives?
Why do I even care?
HELLO...?
CLARK.
CLARK KENT. GOOD TO SEE YOU, M'BOY.
PASTOR LINQUIST...?
RUTH'S PASSED ON, CLARK. AND WITH LANA GONE, I LIKE TO COME THIS WAY TO TEND TO THE WEEDS.
I'VE KNOWN THE LANG FAMILY FOR YEARS, AND NOT HAVING ANYONE IN THIS HOUSE, JUST SEEMS, WELL, WRONG.

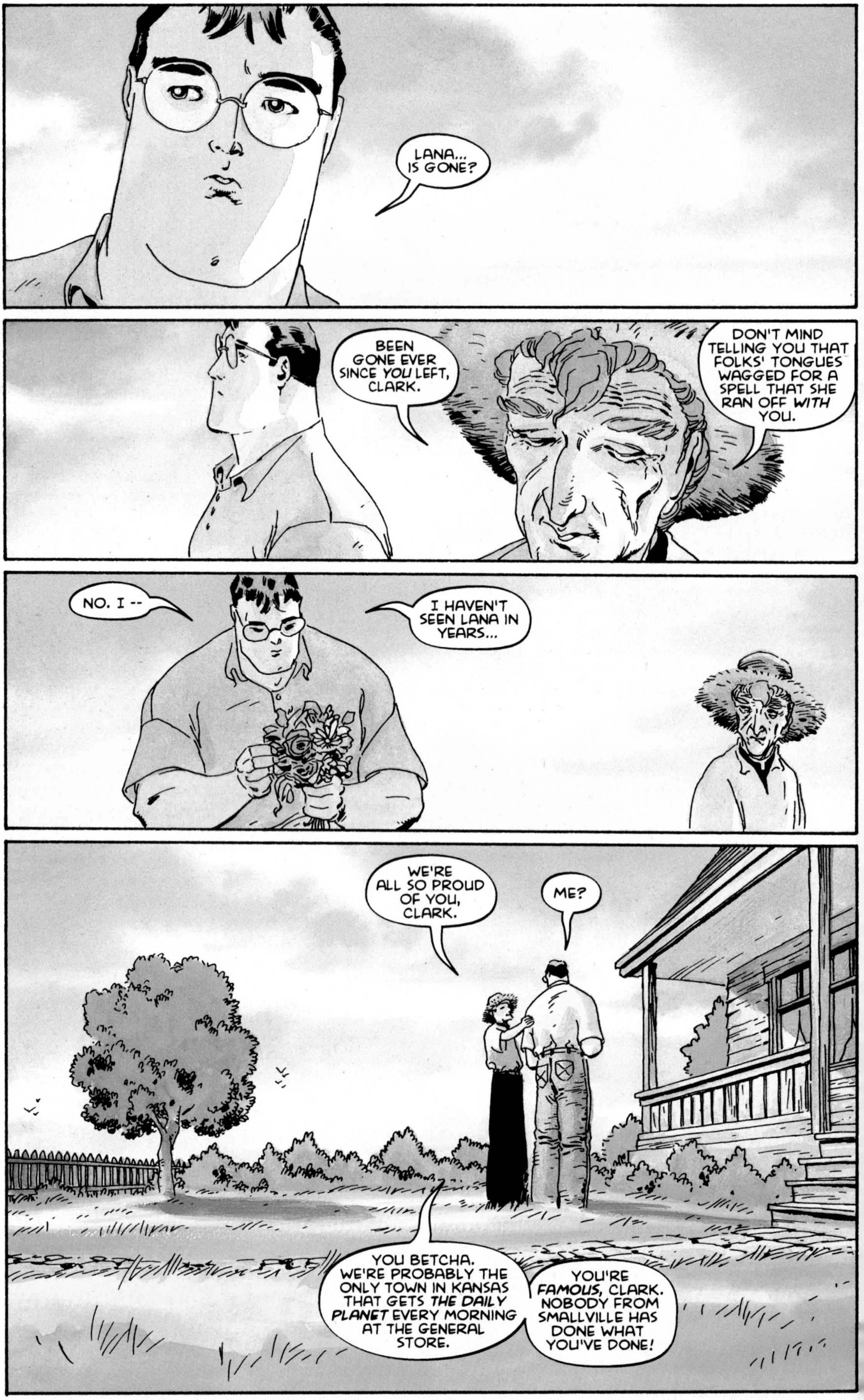
LANA... IS GONE?
BEEN GONE EVER SINCE YOU LEFT, CLARK.
DON'T MIND TELLING YOU THAT FOLKS' TONGUES WAGGED FOR A SPELL THAT SHE RAN OFF WITH YOU.
NO. I --
I HAVEN'T SEEN LANA IN YEARS...
WE'RE ALL SO PROUD OF YOU, CLARK.
ME?
YOU BETCHA. WE'RE PROBABLY THE ONLY TOWN IN KANSAS THAT GETS THE DAILY PLANET EVERY MORNING AT THE GENERAL STORE.
YOU'RE FAMOUS, CLARK. NOBODY FROM SMALLVILLE HAS DONE WHAT YOU'VE DONE!

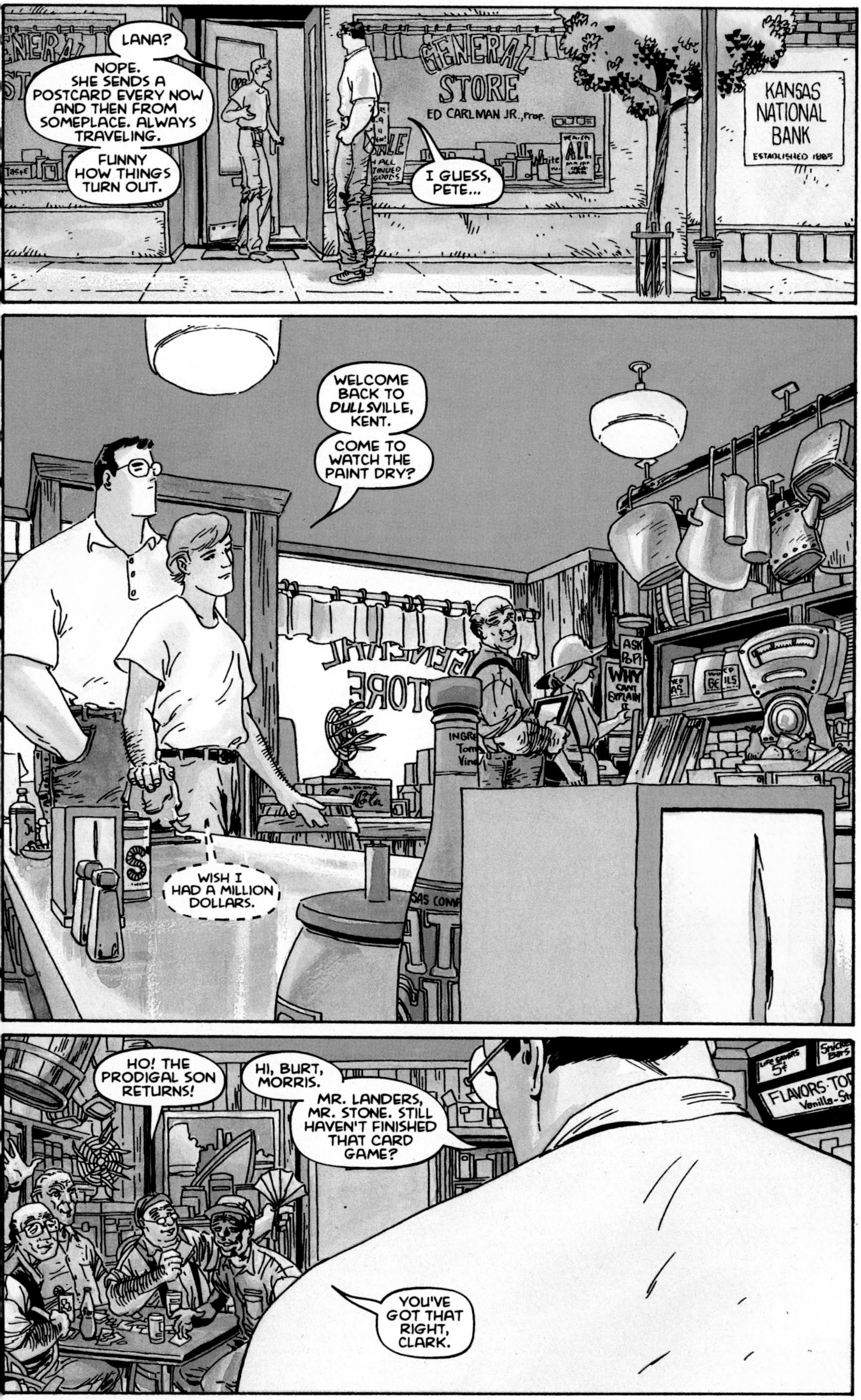
GENERAL STORE
ED CARLMAN JR., Prop.
KANSAS NATIONAL BANK
LANA?
NOPE. SHE SENDS A POSTCARD EVERY NOW AND THEN FROM SOMEPLACE. ALWAYS TRAVELING.
FUNNY HOW THINGS TURN OUT.
I GUESS, PETE...
WELCOME BACK TO *DULLSVILLE*, KENT.
COME TO WATCH THE PAINT DRY?
WISH I HAD A MILLION DOLLARS.
HO! THE PRODIGAL SON RETURNS!
HI, BURT, MORRIS.
MR. LANDERS, MR. STONE. STILL HAVEN'T FINISHED THAT CARD GAME?
YOU'VE GOT THAT RIGHT, CLARK.

SET 'EM UP, EDDIE. THE USUAL.

THESE ARE ON ME, MISTER BIG CITY REPORTER.

FLAVORS:
—olate · Neapolitan
—illa · Strawberry · Pe—

TOPPINGS·
—rinkles · Red Hots · Cookie
—chunks · Goobers

DAILY PLANET
SUPERMA—
STOPS
MAGPIE!
By CLARK KENT

DIDN'T I SAY CLARK WAS GONNA DO GREAT THINGS? DIDN'T I? HUH, DIDN'T I?

NO, TOM, DON'T EVER REMEMBER YOU SAYING THAT. THE BOY DID IT ALL BY HIMSELF.

NO OFFENSE, KENT, BUT I THOUGHT IT'D BE ME WHO'D GO OFF TO METROPOLIS AND BECOME A BILLIONAIRE LIKE LEX LUTHOR.

SAY, YOU EVER MEET HIM?

YES. HE PUTS ON HIS PANTS LIKE EVERYBODY ELSE.

ONE LEG AT A TIME.

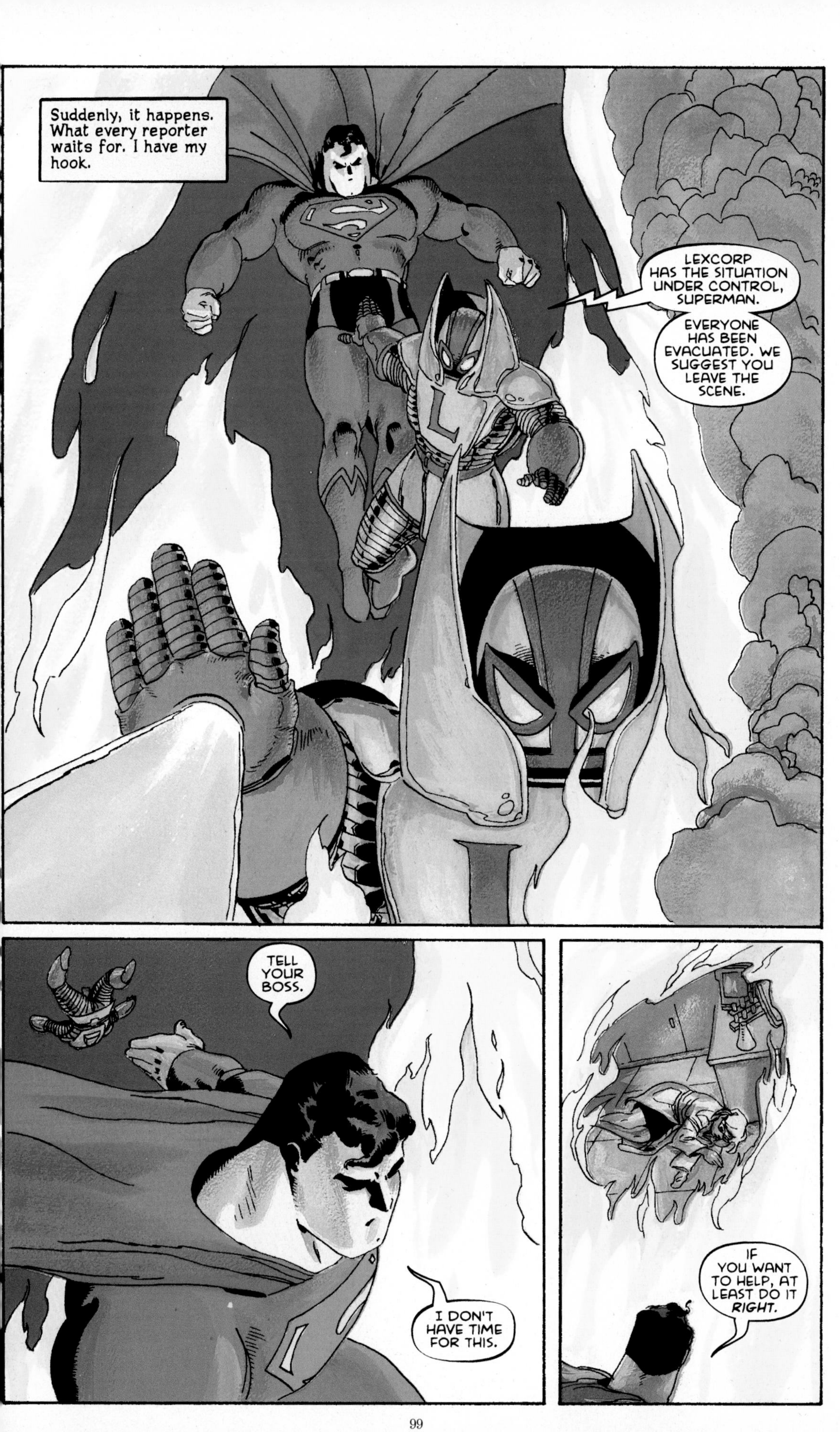
Suddenly, it happens. What every reporter waits for. I have my hook.
LEXCORP HAS THE SITUATION UNDER CONTROL, SUPERMAN.
EVERYONE HAS BEEN EVACUATED. WE SUGGEST YOU LEAVE THE SCENE.
TELL YOUR BOSS.
I DON'T HAVE TIME FOR THIS.
IF YOU WANT TO HELP, AT LEAST DO IT *RIGHT*.

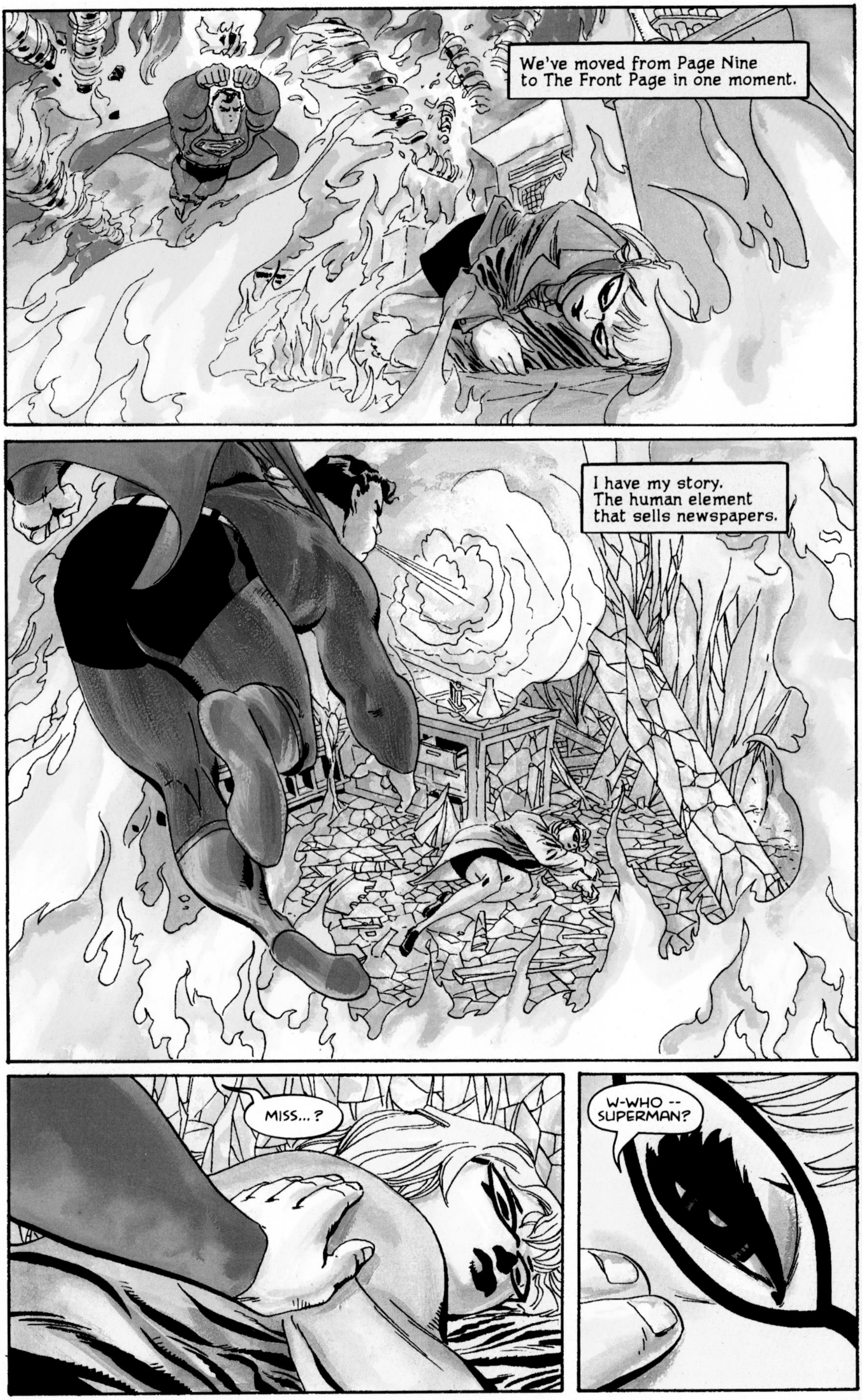
We've moved from Page Nine
to The Front Page in one moment.
I have my story.
The human element
that sells newspapers.
MISS...?
W-WHO --
SUPERMAN?

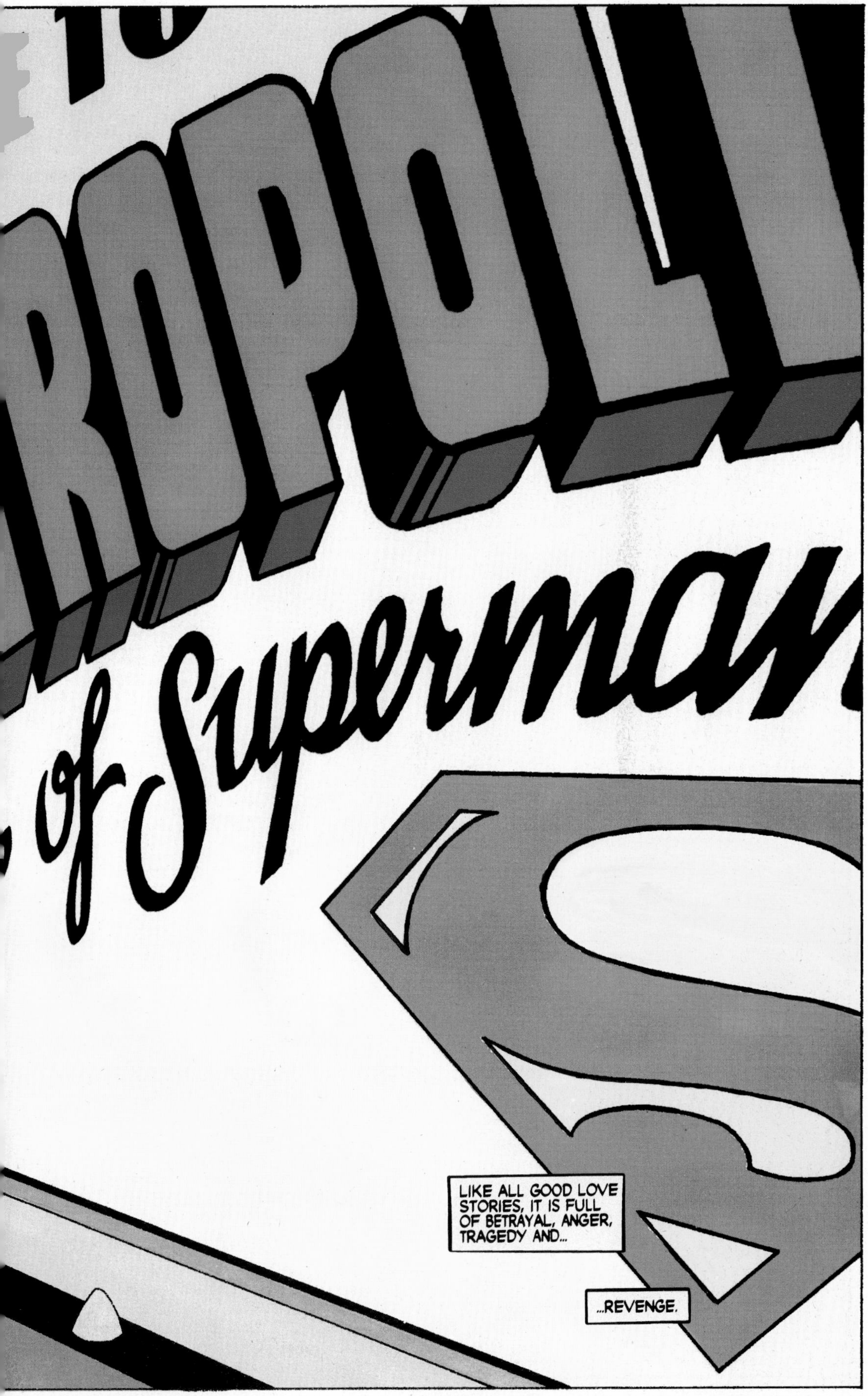
LIKE ALL GOOD LOVE STORIES, IT IS FULL OF BETRAYAL, ANGER, TRAGEDY AND...
...REVENGE.

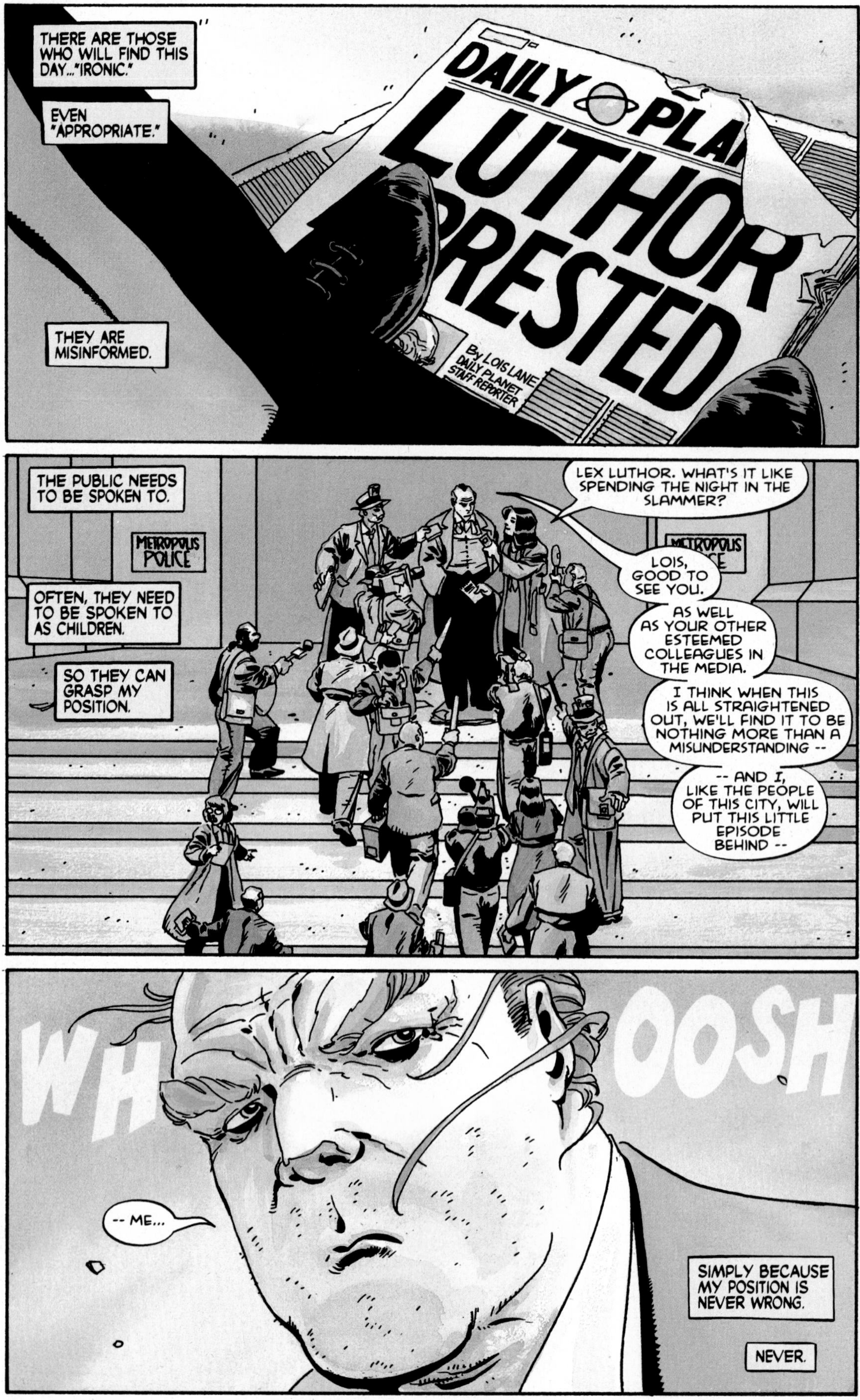
THERE ARE THOSE WHO WILL FIND THIS DAY..."IRONIC."
EVEN "APPROPRIATE."
DAILY PLA
LUTHOR
RESTED
By LOIS LANE
DAILY PLANET STAFF REPORTER
THEY ARE MISINFORMED.
THE PUBLIC NEEDS TO BE SPOKEN TO.
METROPOLIS POLICE
OFTEN, THEY NEED TO BE SPOKEN TO AS CHILDREN.
SO THEY CAN GRASP MY POSITION.
LEX LUTHOR. WHAT'S IT LIKE SPENDING THE NIGHT IN THE SLAMMER?
LOIS, GOOD TO SEE YOU.
AS WELL AS YOUR OTHER ESTEEMED COLLEAGUES IN THE MEDIA.
I THINK WHEN THIS IS ALL STRAIGHTENED OUT, WE'LL FIND IT TO BE NOTHING MORE THAN A MISUNDERSTANDING --
-- AND I, LIKE THE PEOPLE OF THIS CITY, WILL PUT THIS LITTLE EPISODE BEHIND --
WH OOSH
-- ME...
SIMPLY BECAUSE MY POSITION IS NEVER WRONG.
NEVER.

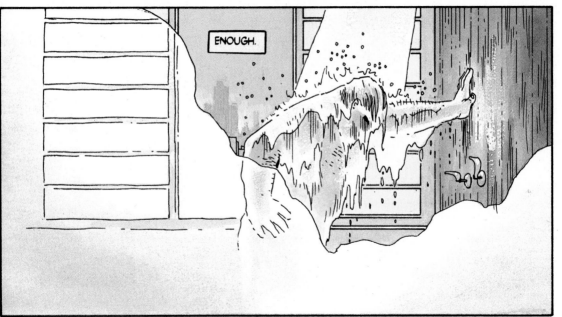

ENOUGH.

SELF-PITY IS FOR LESSER MEN.

EVEN AS A CHILD, I UNDERSTOOD THAT CONCEPT.

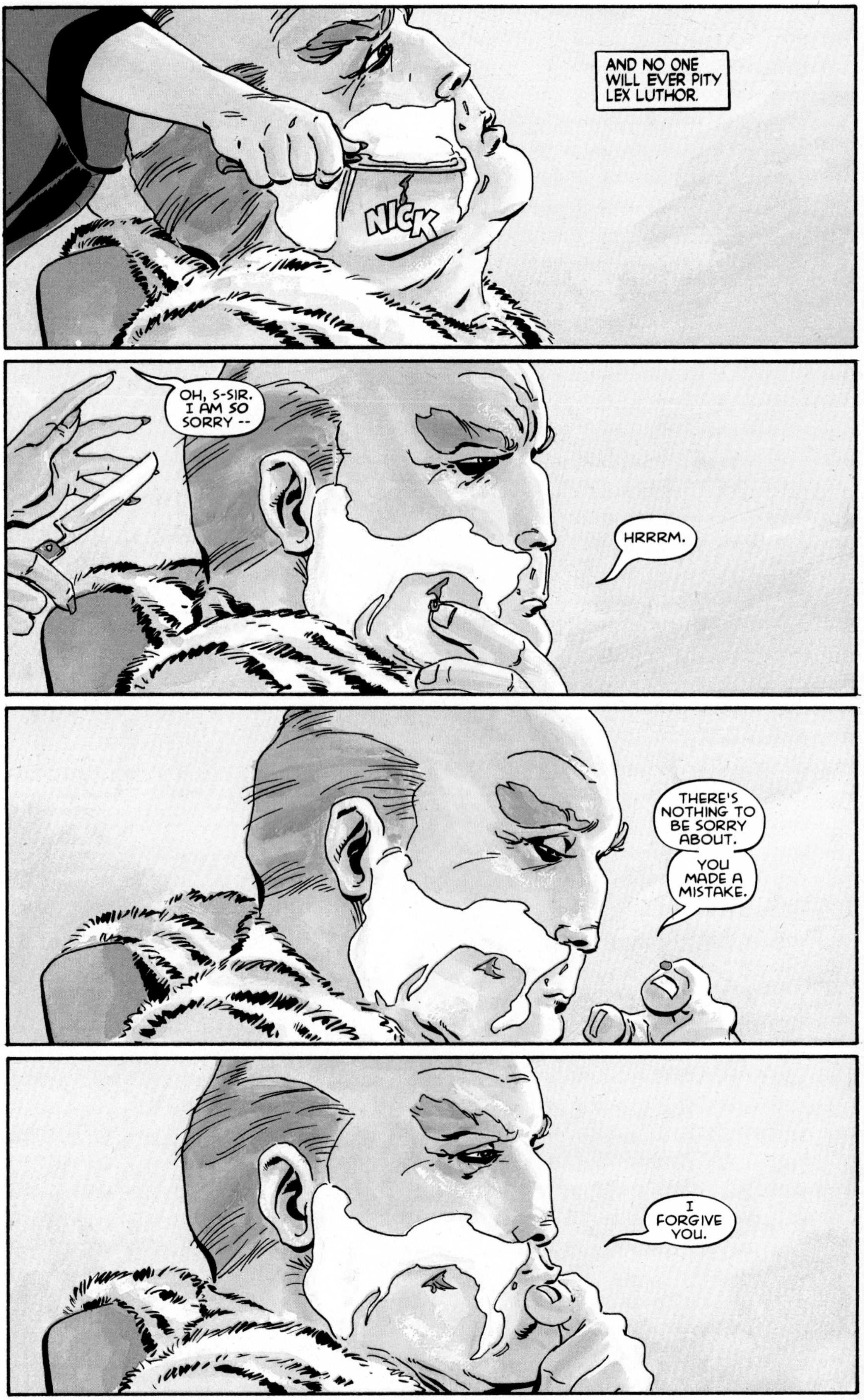
AND NO ONE WILL EVER PITY LEX LUTHOR.
NICK
OH, S-SIR. I AM SO SORRY --
HRRRM.
THERE'S NOTHING TO BE SORRY ABOUT.
YOU MADE A MISTAKE.
I FORGIVE YOU.

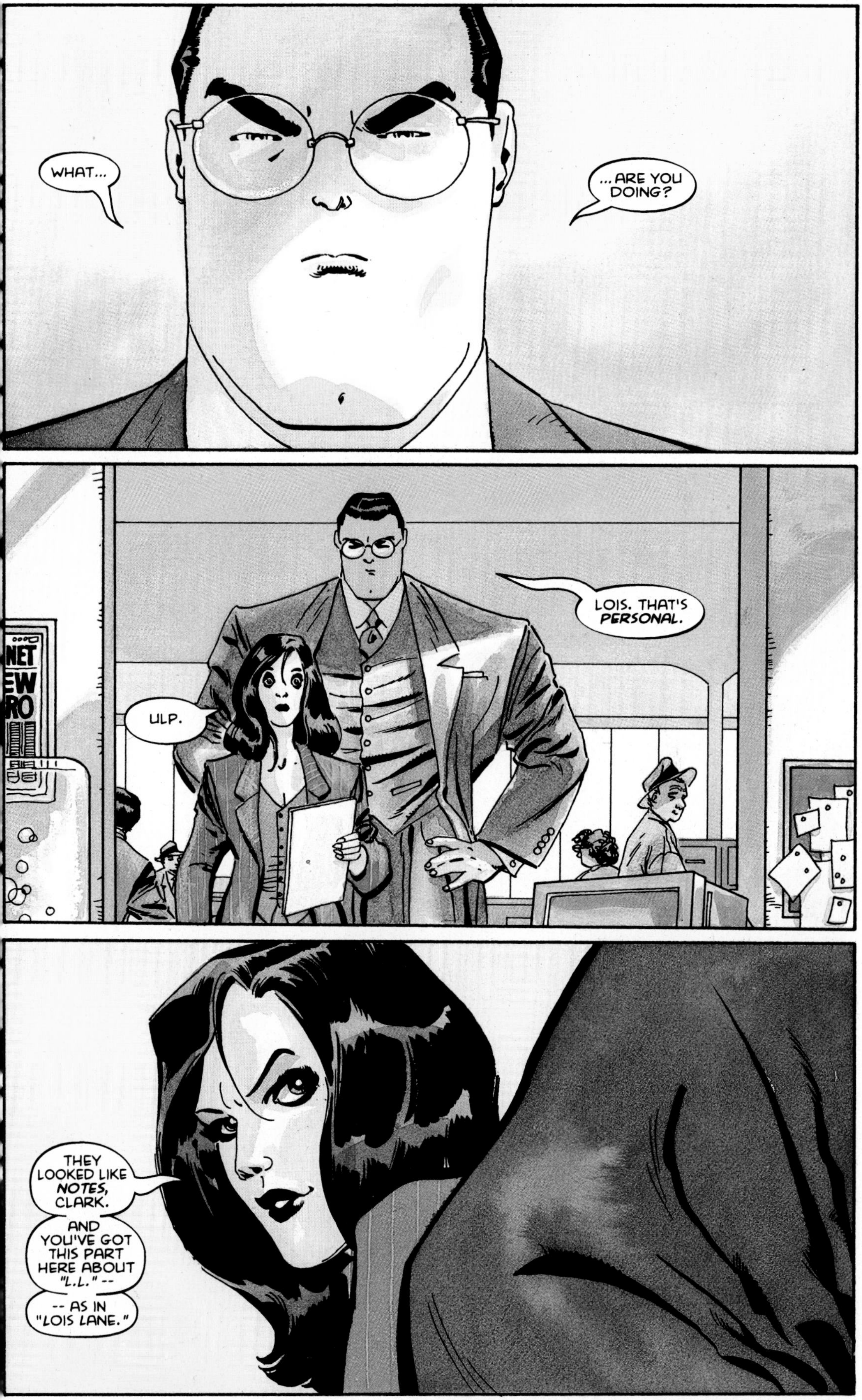
WHAT...
...ARE YOU DOING?
LOIS. THAT'S PERSONAL.
ULP.
THEY LOOKED LIKE NOTES, CLARK.
AND YOU'VE GOT THIS PART HERE ABOUT "L.L." --
-- AS IN "LOIS LANE."

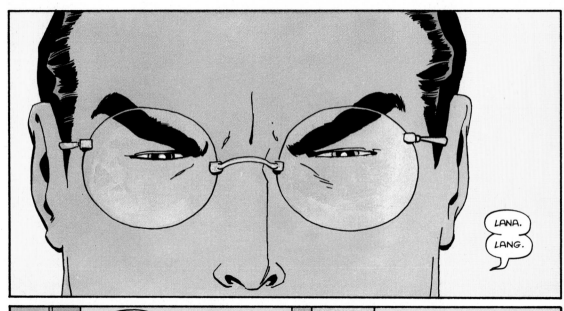

LANA.

LANG.

WELL, THEN, THERE YOU GO.

IT'S THE KIND OF MISTAKE *ANYBODY* COULD MAKE, REALLY.

YOU KNOW HOW COMPETITIVE THIS BUSINESS IS, SMALLVILLE.

HOW MANY PEOPLE DO YOU KNOW THAT HAVE THE *INITIALS* "L.L."?

TRUTH.

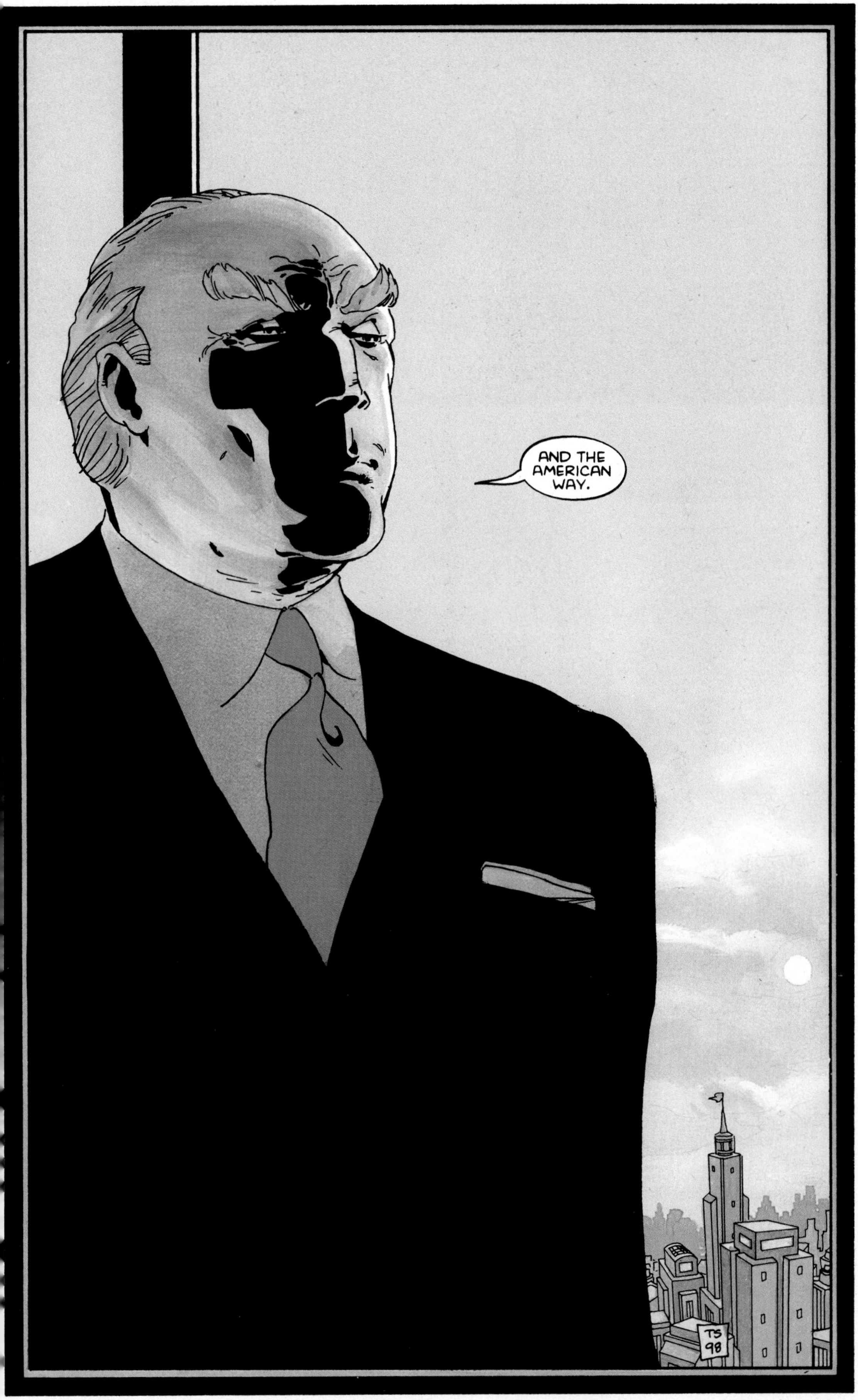
AND THE AMERICAN WAY.
TS 98

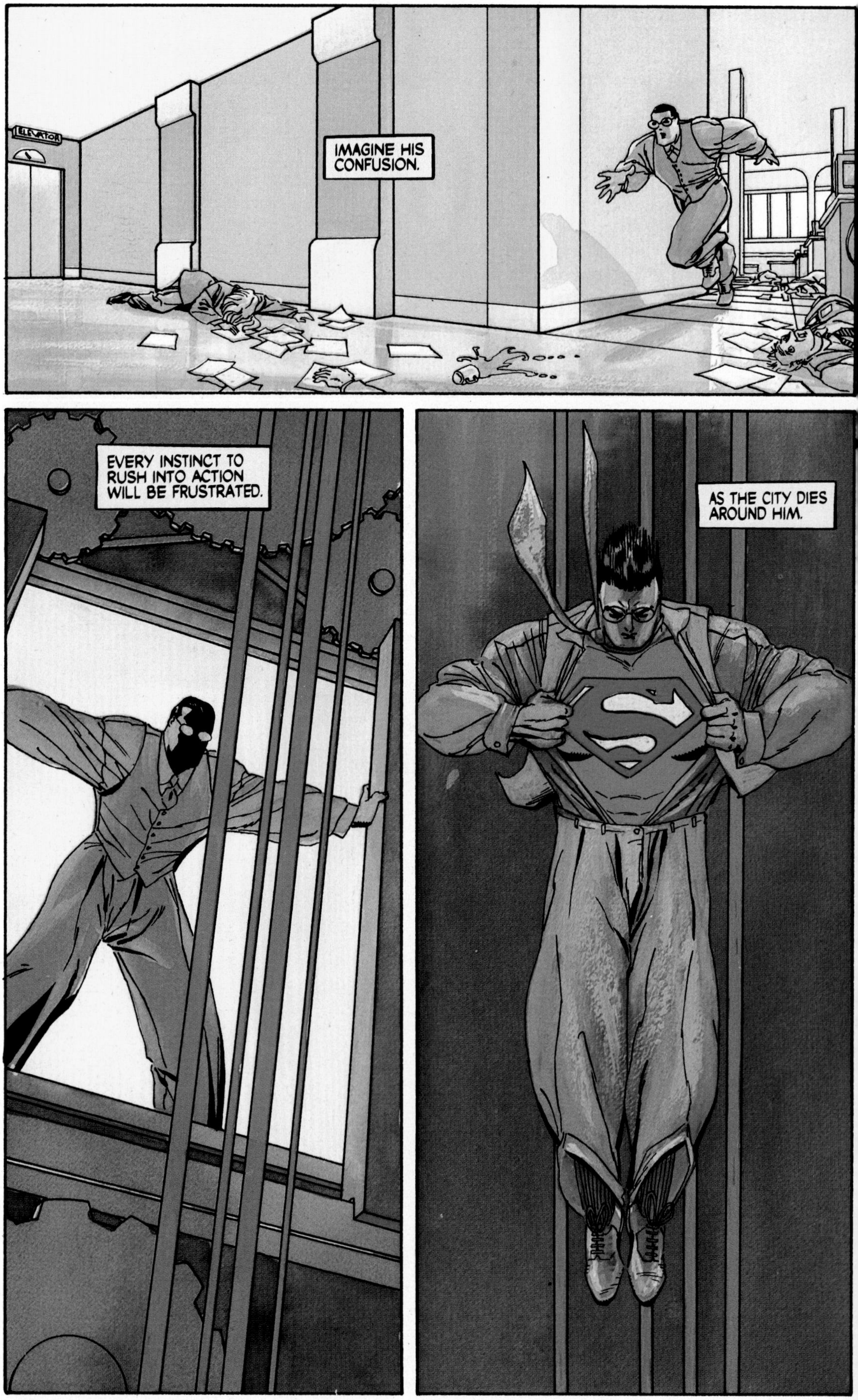
ELEVATOR
IMAGINE HIS CONFUSION.
EVERY INSTINCT TO RUSH INTO ACTION WILL BE FRUSTRATED.
AS THE CITY DIES AROUND HIM.

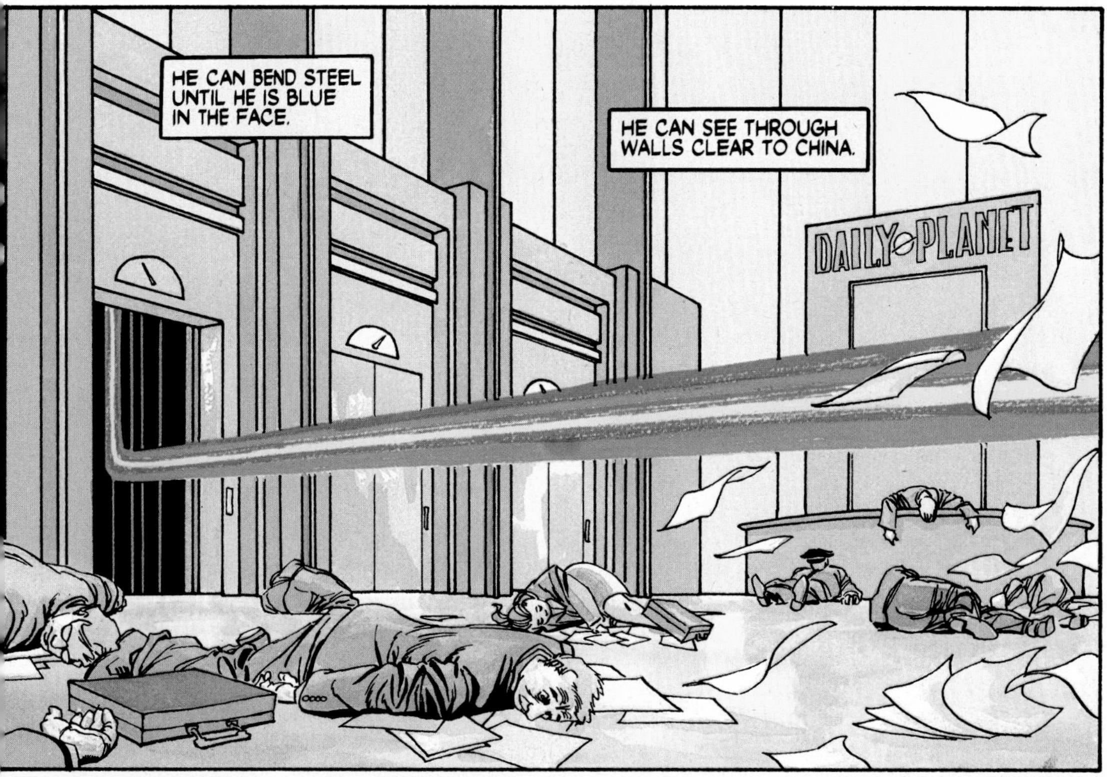
HE CAN BEND STEEL UNTIL HE IS BLUE IN THE FACE.
HE CAN SEE THROUGH WALLS CLEAR TO CHINA.
DAILY PLANET

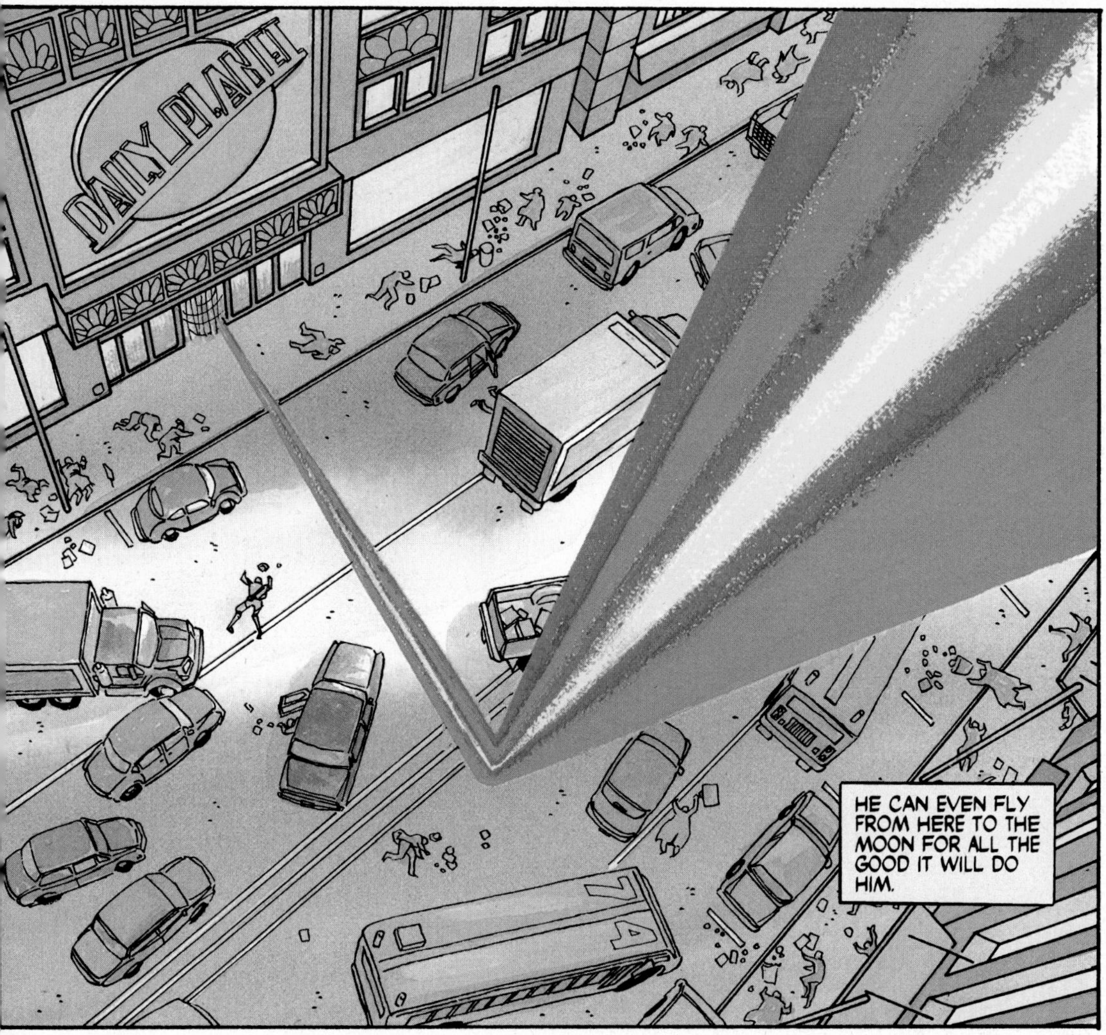
DAILY PLANET
HE CAN EVEN FLY FROM HERE TO THE MOON FOR ALL THE GOOD IT WILL DO HIM.

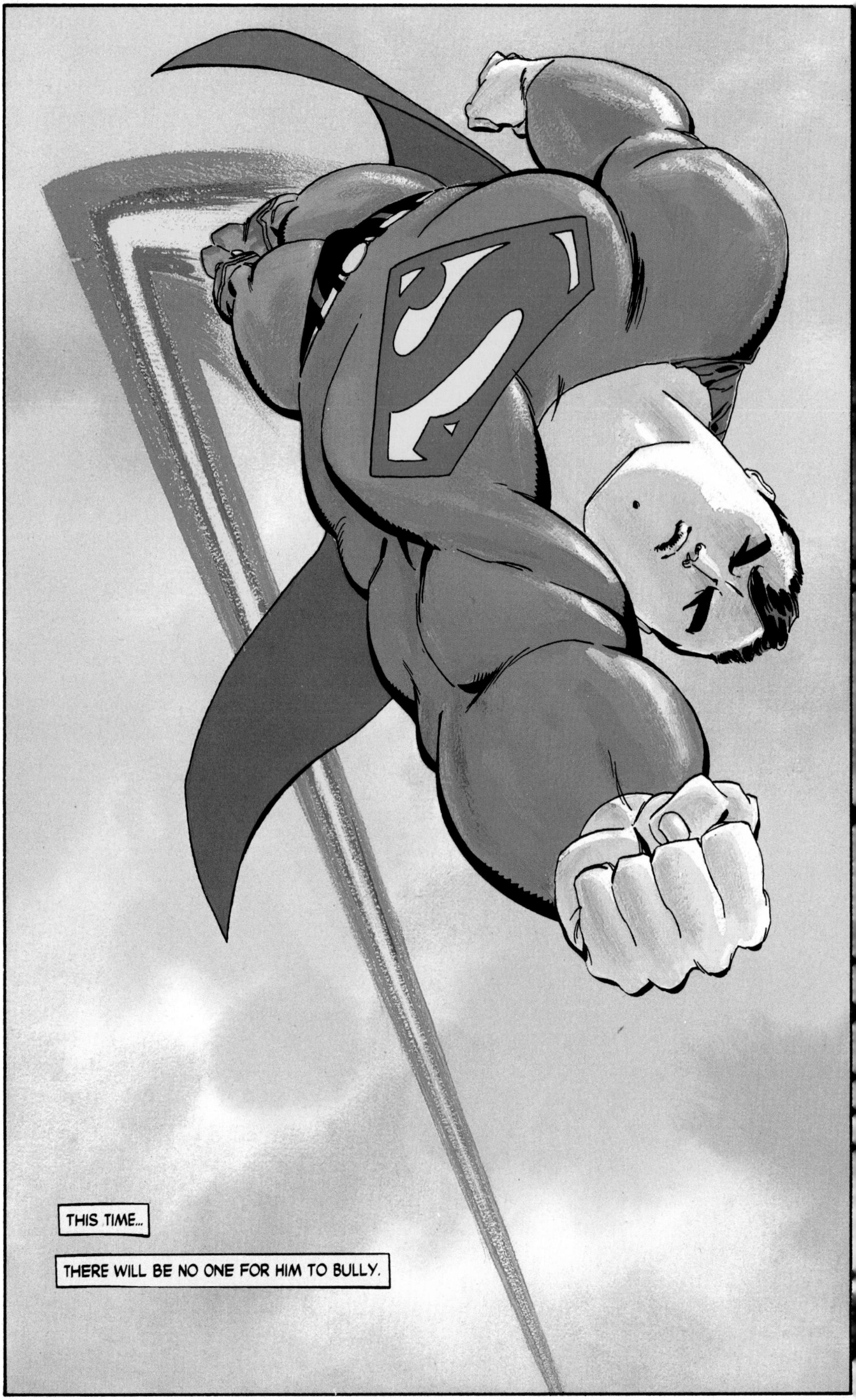
THIS TIME...
THERE WILL BE NO ONE FOR HIM TO BULLY.

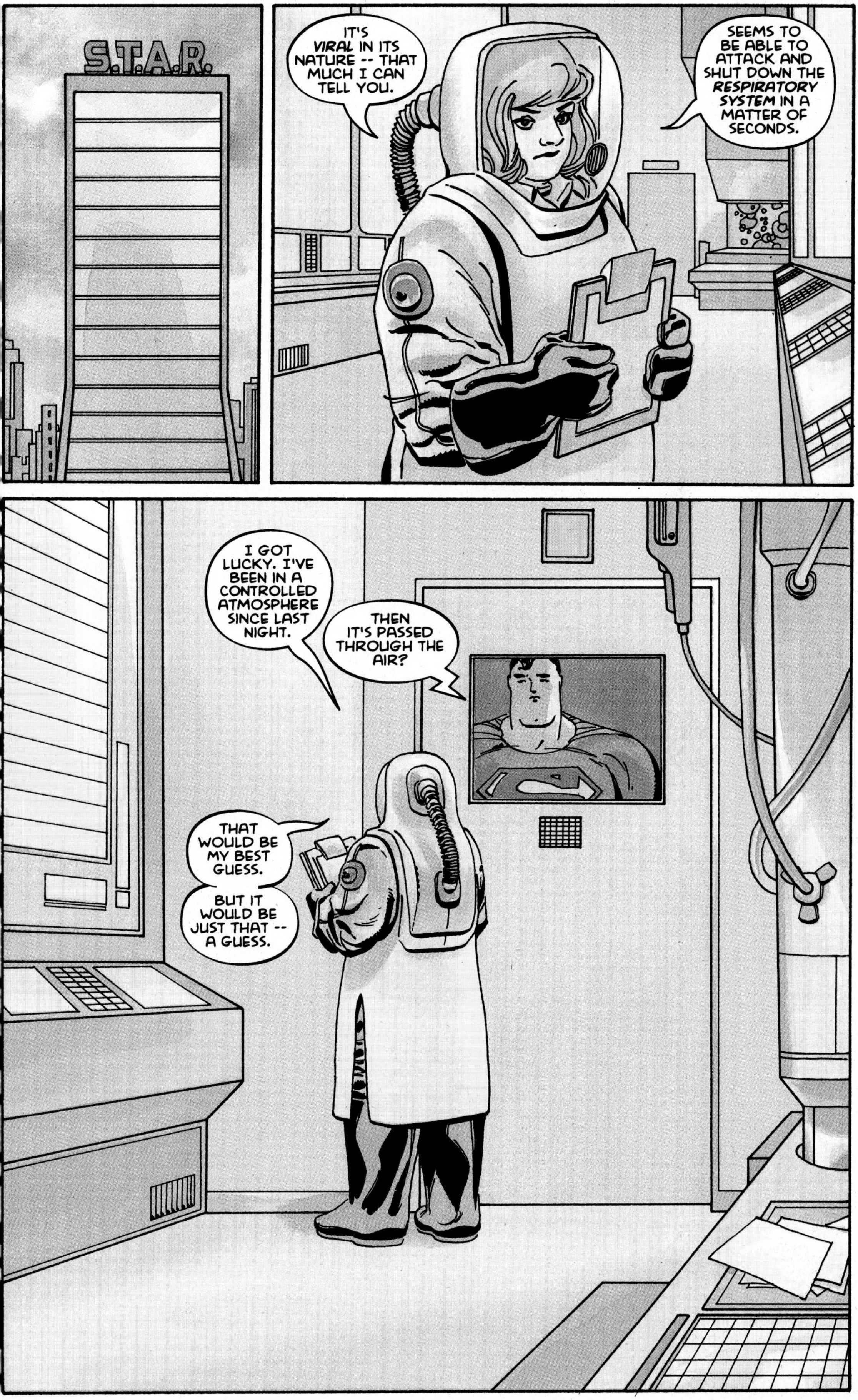
S.T.A.R.
IT'S *VIRAL* IN ITS NATURE -- THAT MUCH I CAN TELL YOU.
SEEMS TO BE ABLE TO ATTACK AND SHUT DOWN THE ***RESPIRATORY SYSTEM*** IN A MATTER OF SECONDS.
I GOT LUCKY. I'VE BEEN IN A CONTROLLED ATMOSPHERE SINCE LAST NIGHT.
THEN IT'S PASSED THROUGH THE AIR?
THAT WOULD BE MY BEST GUESS.
BUT IT WOULD BE JUST THAT -- A GUESS.

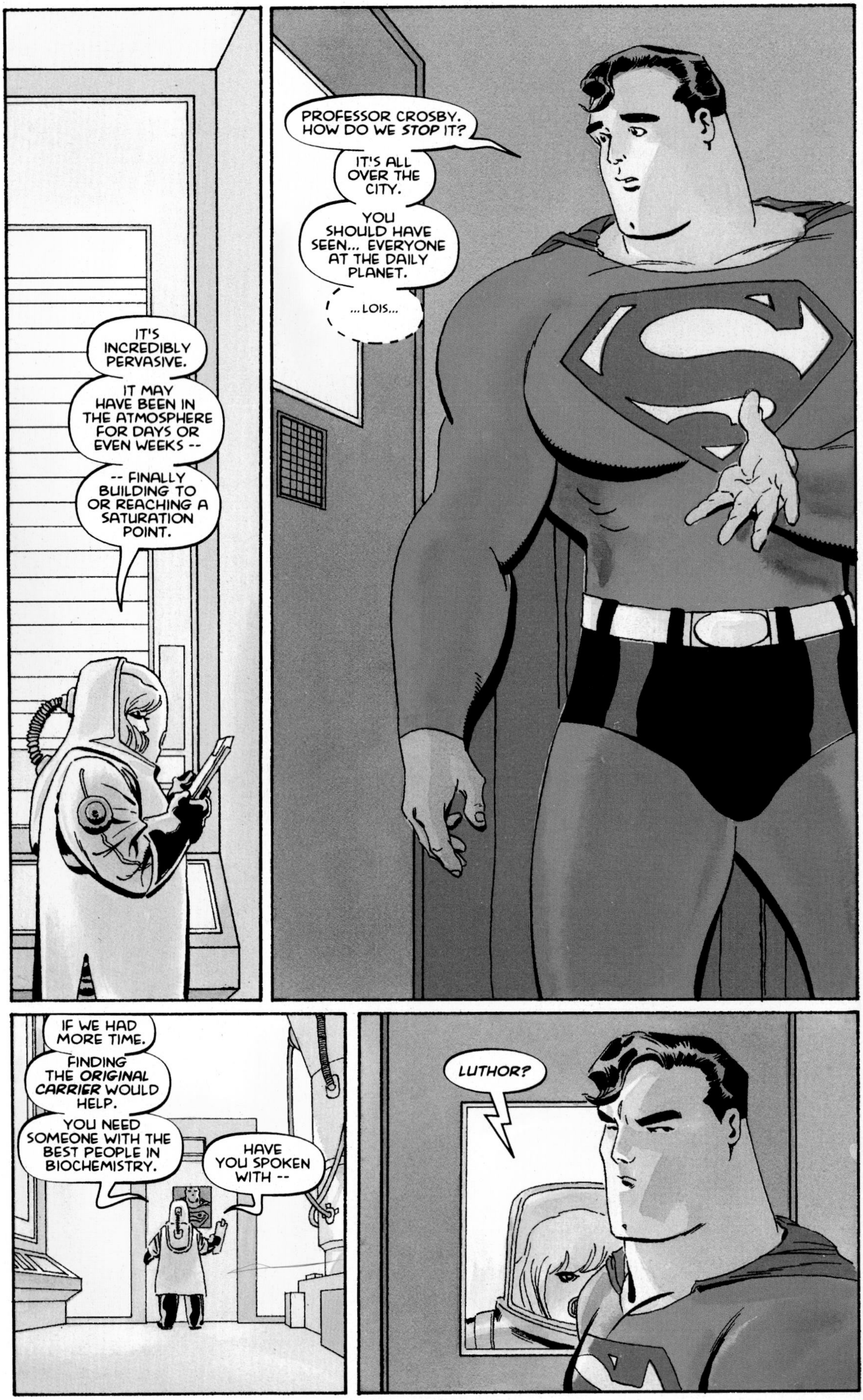
IT'S INCREDIBLY PERVASIVE.
IT MAY HAVE BEEN IN THE ATMOSPHERE FOR DAYS OR EVEN WEEKS --
-- FINALLY BUILDING TO OR REACHING A SATURATION POINT.
PROFESSOR CROSBY. HOW DO WE STOP IT?
IT'S ALL OVER THE CITY.
YOU SHOULD HAVE SEEN... EVERYONE AT THE DAILY PLANET.
...LOIS...
IF WE HAD MORE TIME.
FINDING THE ORIGINAL CARRIER WOULD HELP.
YOU NEED SOMEONE WITH THE BEST PEOPLE IN BIOCHEMISTRY.
HAVE YOU SPOKEN WITH --
LUTHOR?

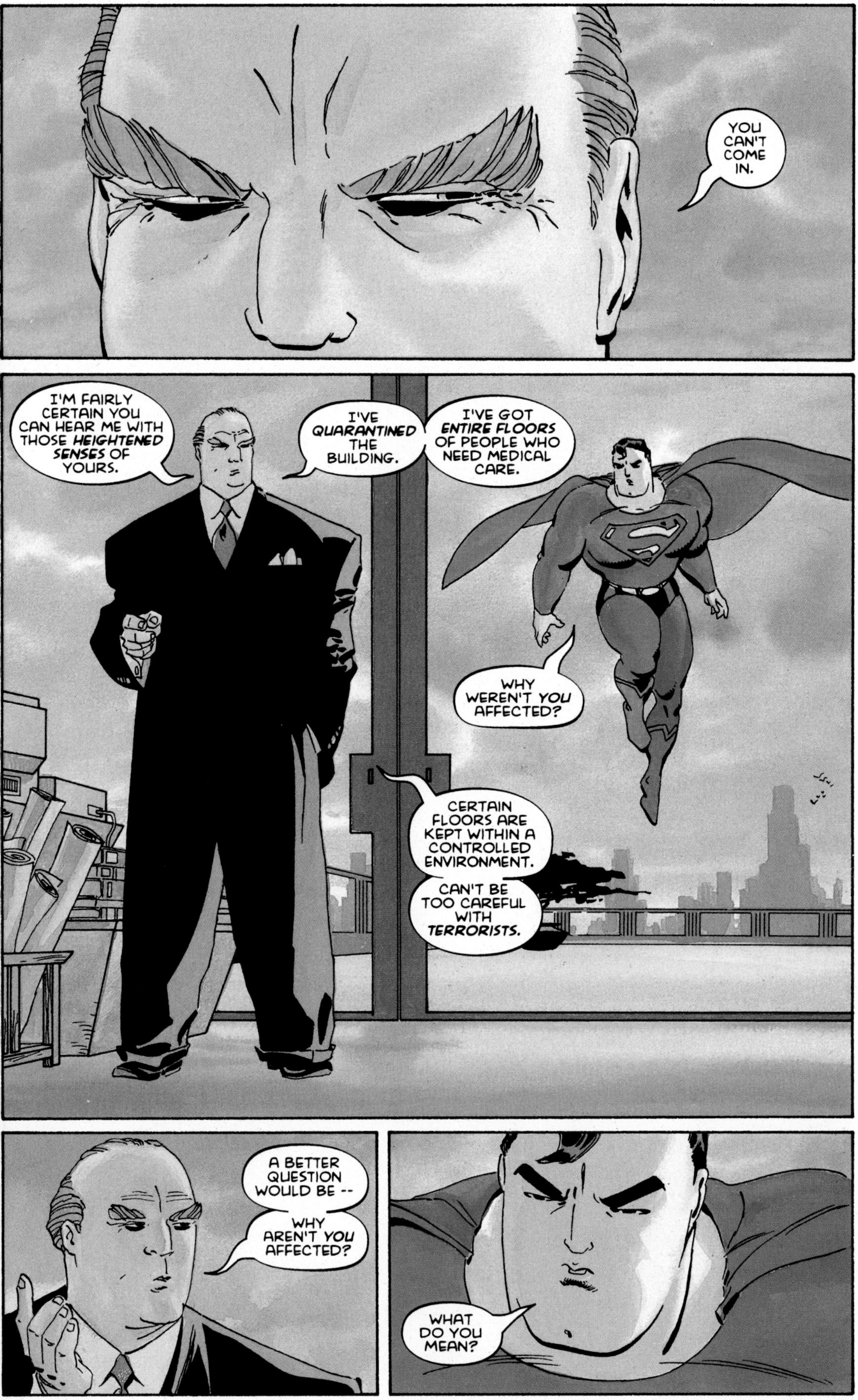
YOU CAN'T COME IN.
I'M FAIRLY CERTAIN YOU CAN HEAR ME WITH THOSE HEIGHTENED SENSES OF YOURS.
I'VE QUARANTINED THE BUILDING.
I'VE GOT ENTIRE FLOORS OF PEOPLE WHO NEED MEDICAL CARE.
WHY WEREN'T YOU AFFECTED?
CERTAIN FLOORS ARE KEPT WITHIN A CONTROLLED ENVIRONMENT.
CAN'T BE TOO CAREFUL WITH TERRORISTS.
A BETTER QUESTION WOULD BE --
WHY AREN'T YOU AFFECTED?
WHAT DO YOU MEAN?

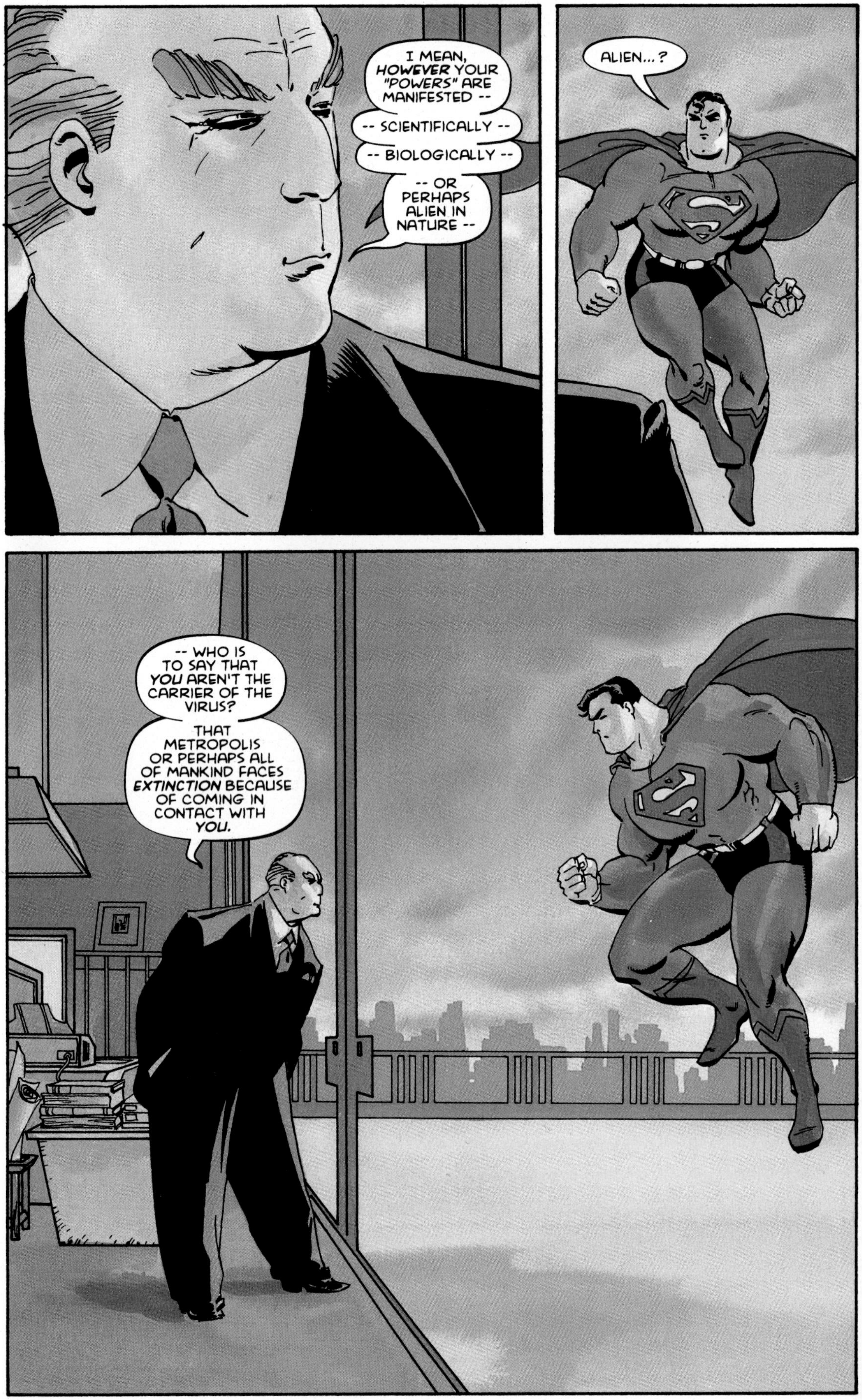
I MEAN, HOWEVER YOUR "POWERS" ARE MANIFESTED --
-- SCIENTIFICALLY --
-- BIOLOGICALLY --
-- OR PERHAPS ALIEN IN NATURE --
ALIEN...?
-- WHO IS TO SAY THAT YOU AREN'T THE CARRIER OF THE VIRUS?
THAT METROPOLIS OR PERHAPS ALL OF MANKIND FACES EXTINCTION BECAUSE OF COMING IN CONTACT WITH YOU.

AND WHO'S TO SAY *YOU* AREN'T THE CAUSE BEHIND ALL THIS MADNESS?

THAT YOU HAVEN'T EXPOSED THIS ENTIRE CITY TO SOME KIND OF MILITARY CHEMICAL WEAPON.

THE PROSPECT OF FAILURE IS TOO OVERWHELMING FOR HIM.

IF I WERE TO *CRASH* THROUGH THE GLASS AND *DRAG* YOU OUT HERE...

HE CANNOT LOSE FAITH IN HIMSELF OR HE IS LOST.

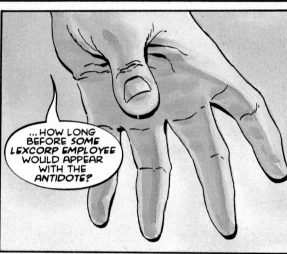

...HOW LONG BEFORE *SOME* LEXCORP EMPLOYEE WOULD APPEAR WITH THE ANTIDOTE?

BUT... I... CAN'T TAKE THAT CHANCE.

I CAN'T BE LIKE *YOU*, LUTHOR.

SO, I'M ASKING YOU --

-- CAN YOU HELP?

AND LOST IS EXACTLY WHERE I WANT HIM TO BE...

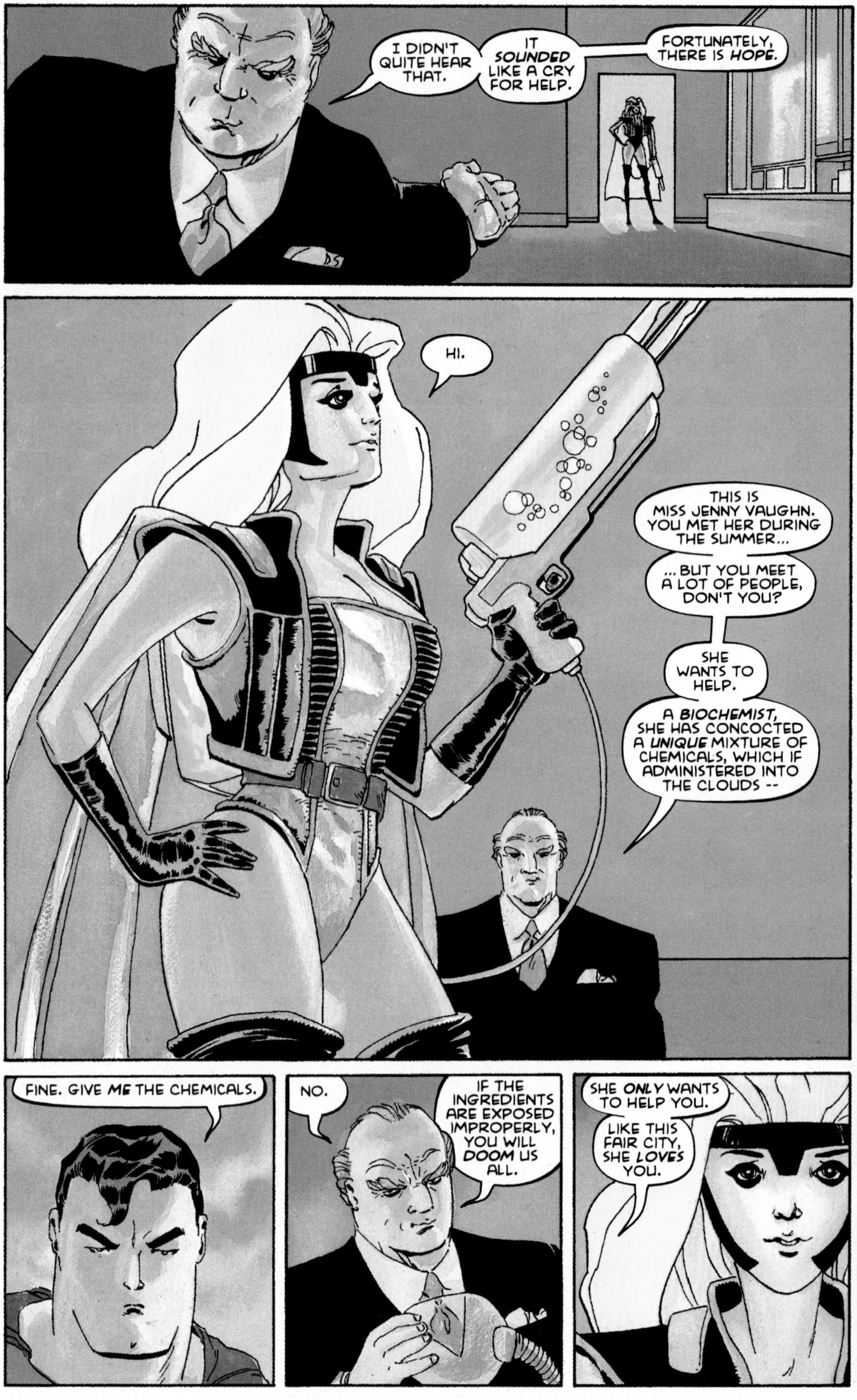
I DIDN'T QUITE HEAR THAT.
IT SOUNDED LIKE A CRY FOR HELP.
FORTUNATELY, THERE IS HOPE.
HI.
THIS IS MISS JENNY VAUGHN. YOU MET HER DURING THE SUMMER...
... BUT YOU MEET A LOT OF PEOPLE, DON'T YOU?
SHE WANTS TO HELP.
A BIOCHEMIST, SHE HAS CONCOCTED A UNIQUE MIXTURE OF CHEMICALS, WHICH IF ADMINISTERED INTO THE CLOUDS --
FINE. GIVE ME THE CHEMICALS.
NO.
IF THE INGREDIENTS ARE EXPOSED IMPROPERLY, YOU WILL DOOM US ALL.
SHE ONLY WANTS TO HELP YOU.
LIKE THIS FAIR CITY, SHE LOVES YOU.

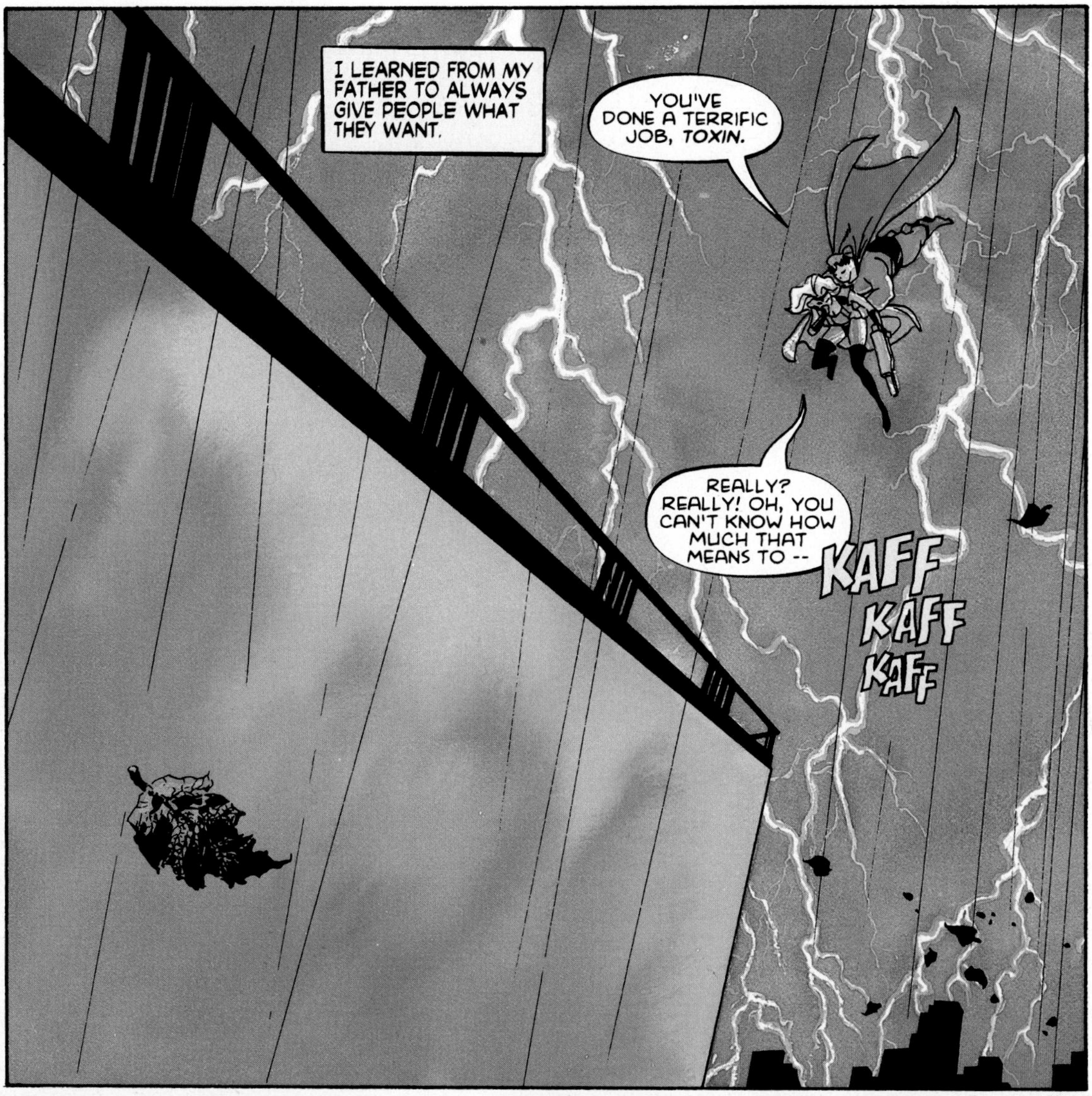
I LEARNED FROM MY FATHER TO ALWAYS GIVE PEOPLE WHAT THEY WANT.
YOU'VE DONE A TERRIFIC JOB, *TOXIN.*
REALLY? REALLY! OH, YOU CAN'T KNOW HOW MUCH THAT MEANS TO --
KAFF
KAFF
KAFF

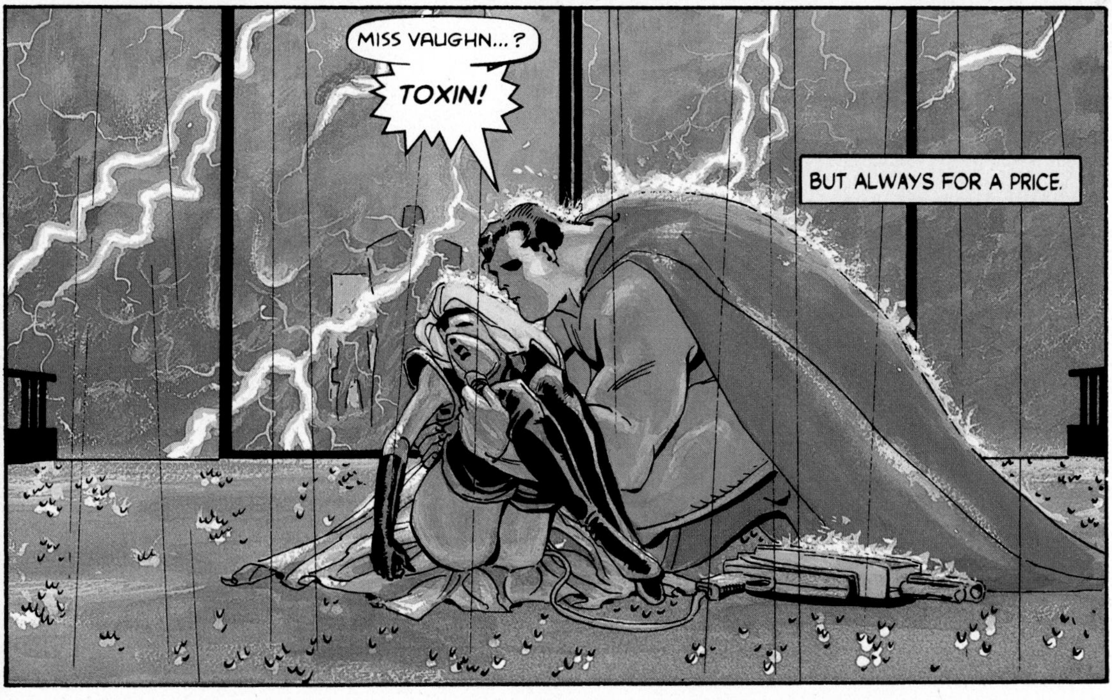
MISS VAUGHN...?
TOXIN!
BUT ALWAYS FOR A PRICE.

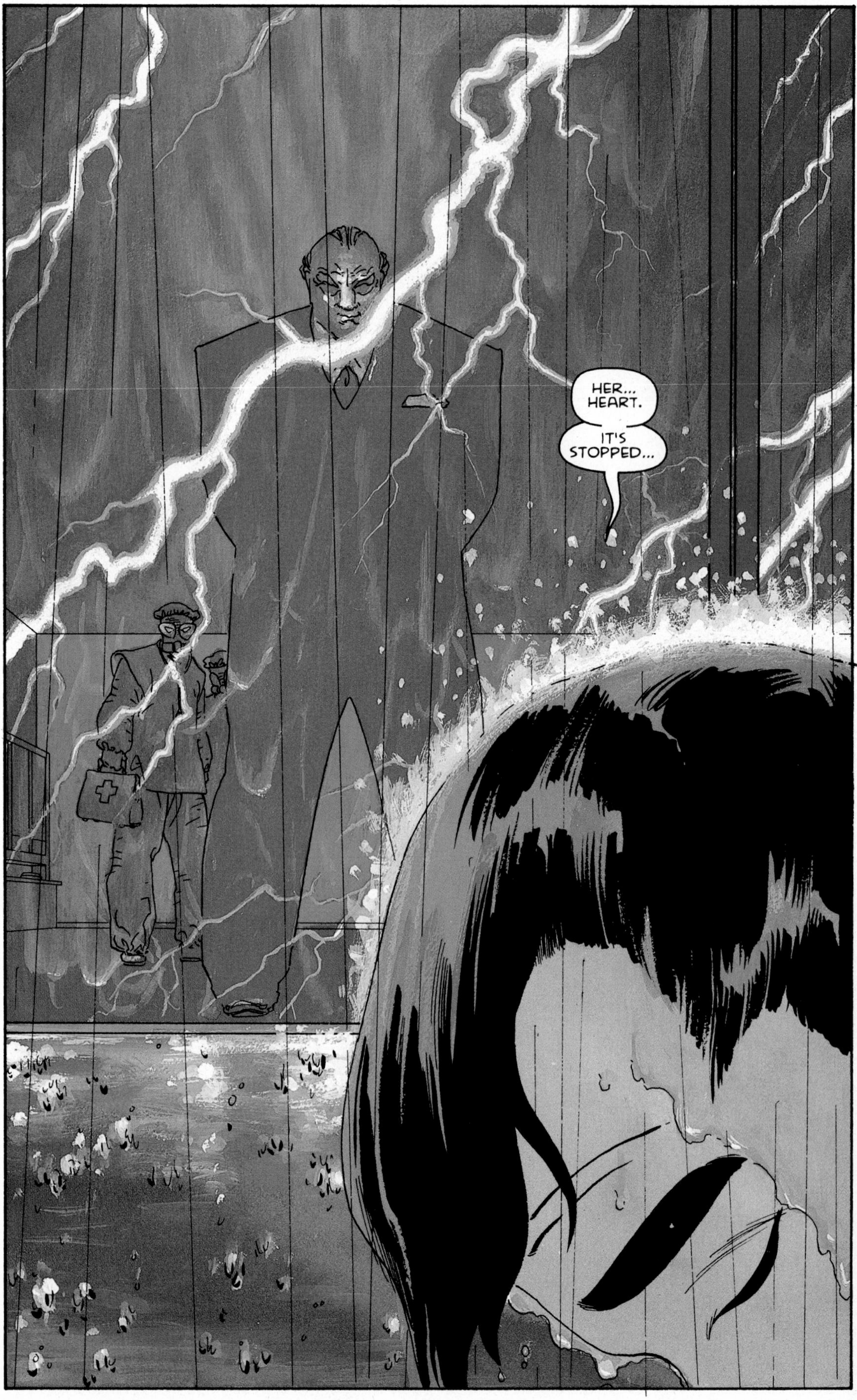
HER... HEART.
IT'S STOPPED...

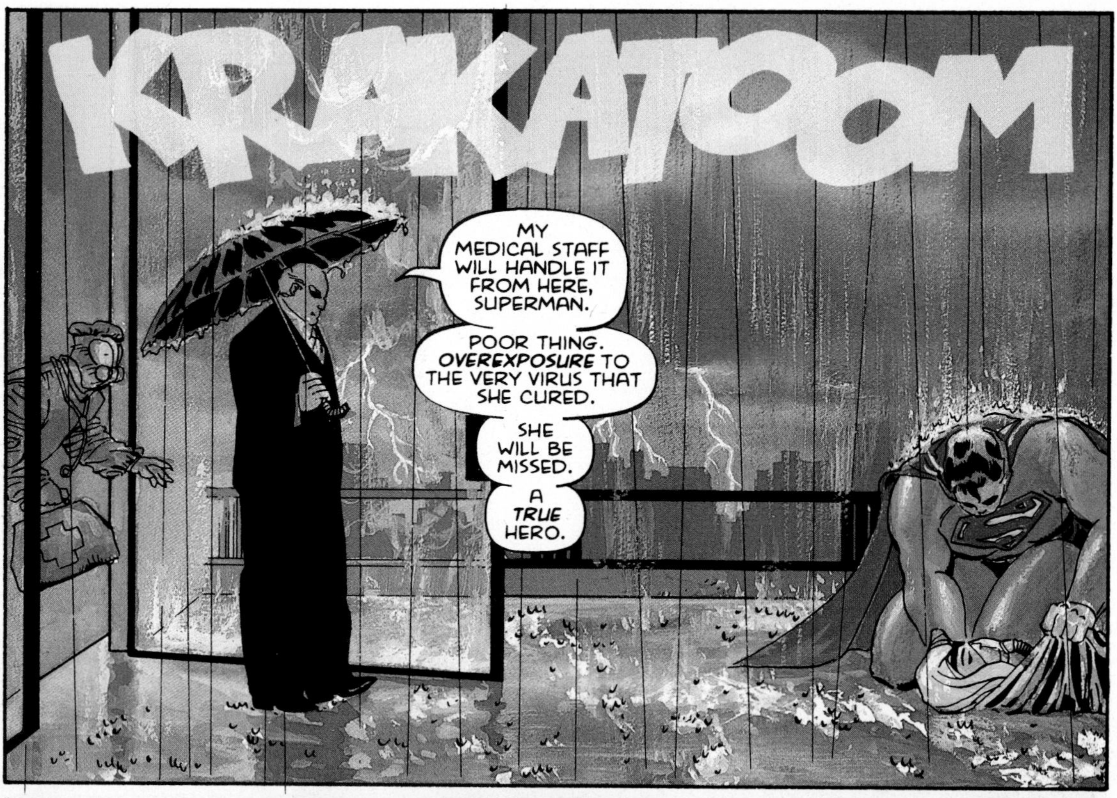
KRAKATOOM
MY MEDICAL STAFF WILL HANDLE IT FROM HERE, SUPERMAN.
POOR THING. OVEREXPOSURE TO THE VERY VIRUS THAT SHE CURED.
SHE WILL BE MISSED.
A TRUE HERO.

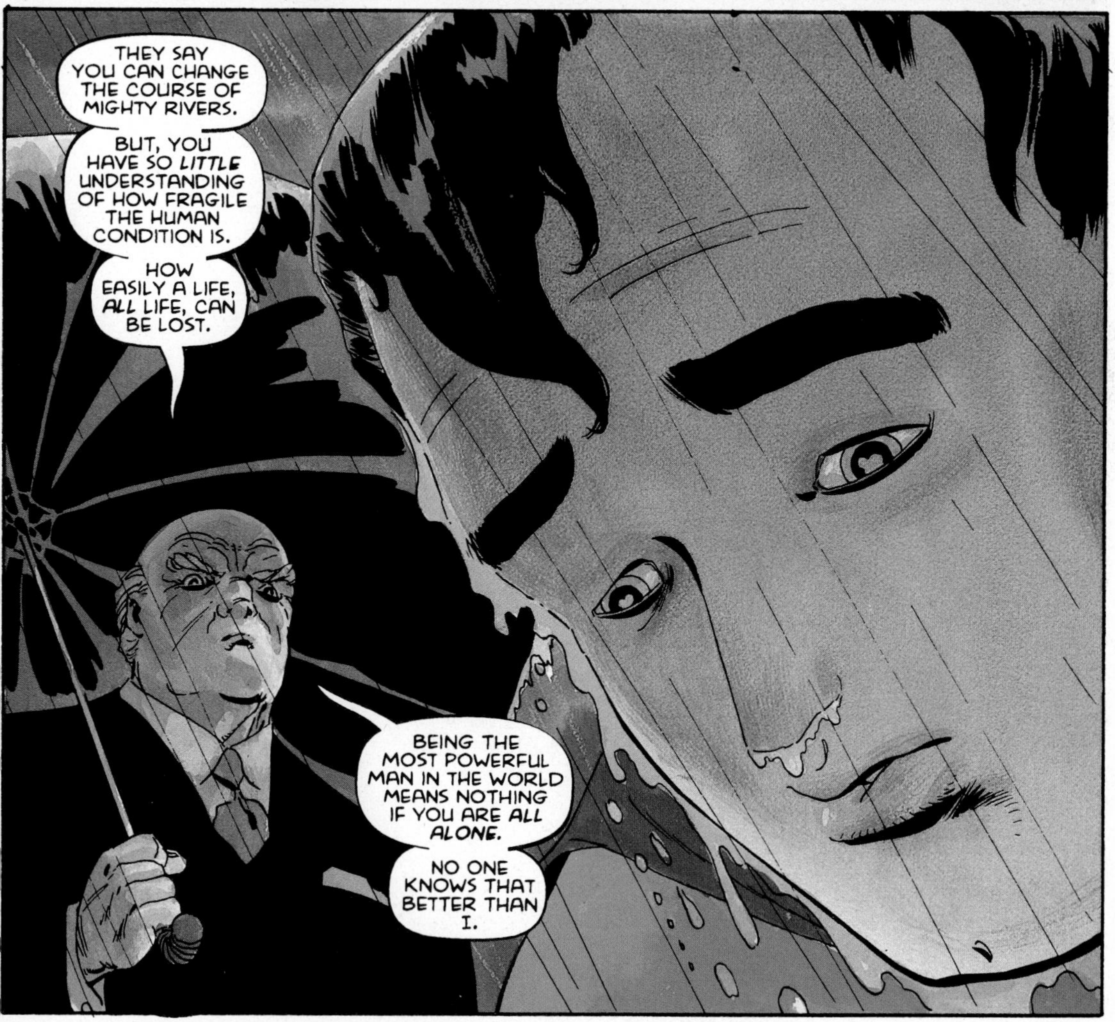
THEY SAY YOU CAN CHANGE THE COURSE OF MIGHTY RIVERS.
BUT, YOU HAVE SO LITTLE UNDERSTANDING OF HOW FRAGILE THE HUMAN CONDITION IS.
HOW EASILY A LIFE, ALL LIFE, CAN BE LOST.
BEING THE MOST POWERFUL MAN IN THE WORLD MEANS NOTHING IF YOU ARE ALL ALONE.
NO ONE KNOWS THAT BETTER THAN I.

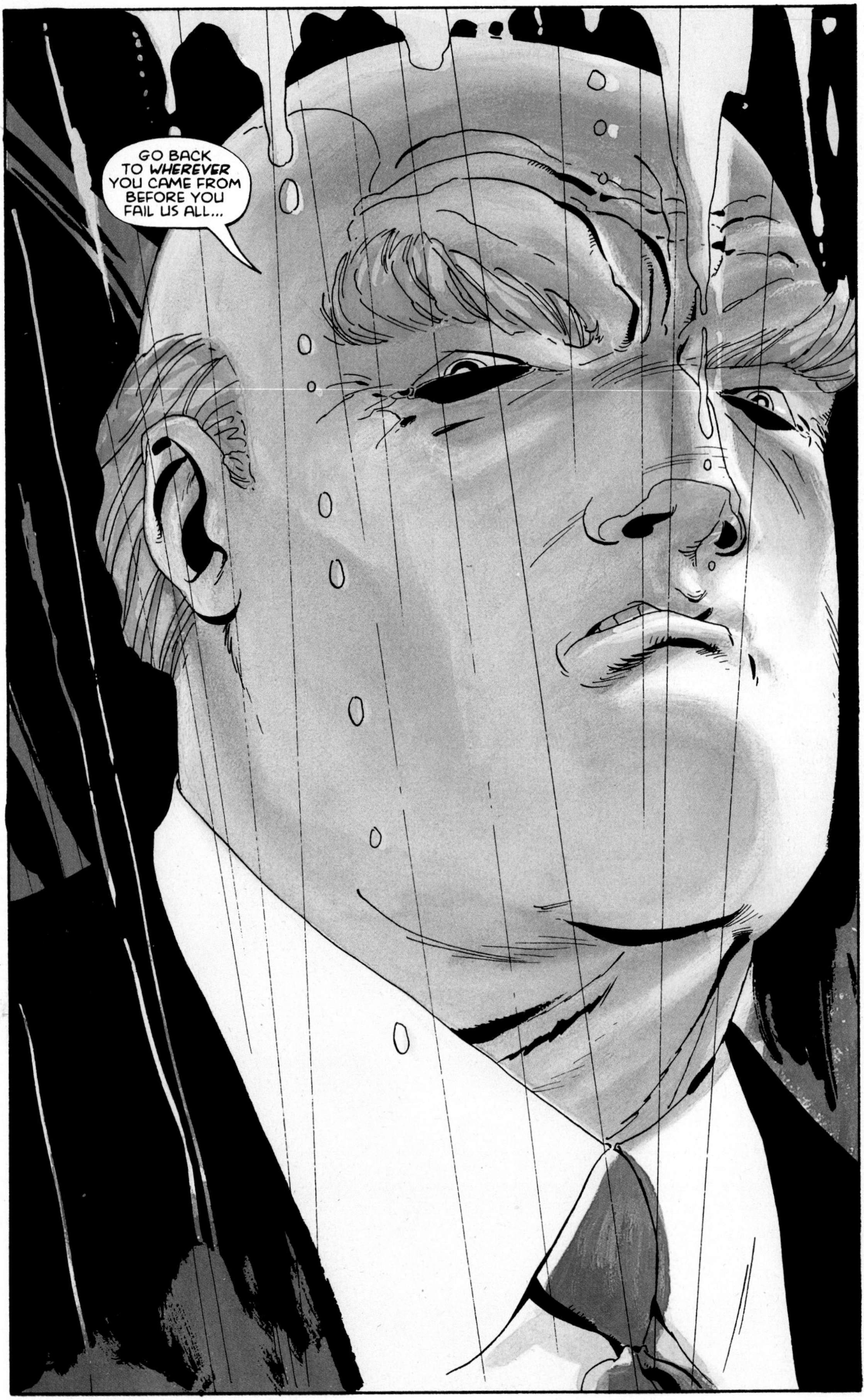
GO BACK TO WHEREVER YOU CAME FROM BEFORE YOU FAIL US ALL...

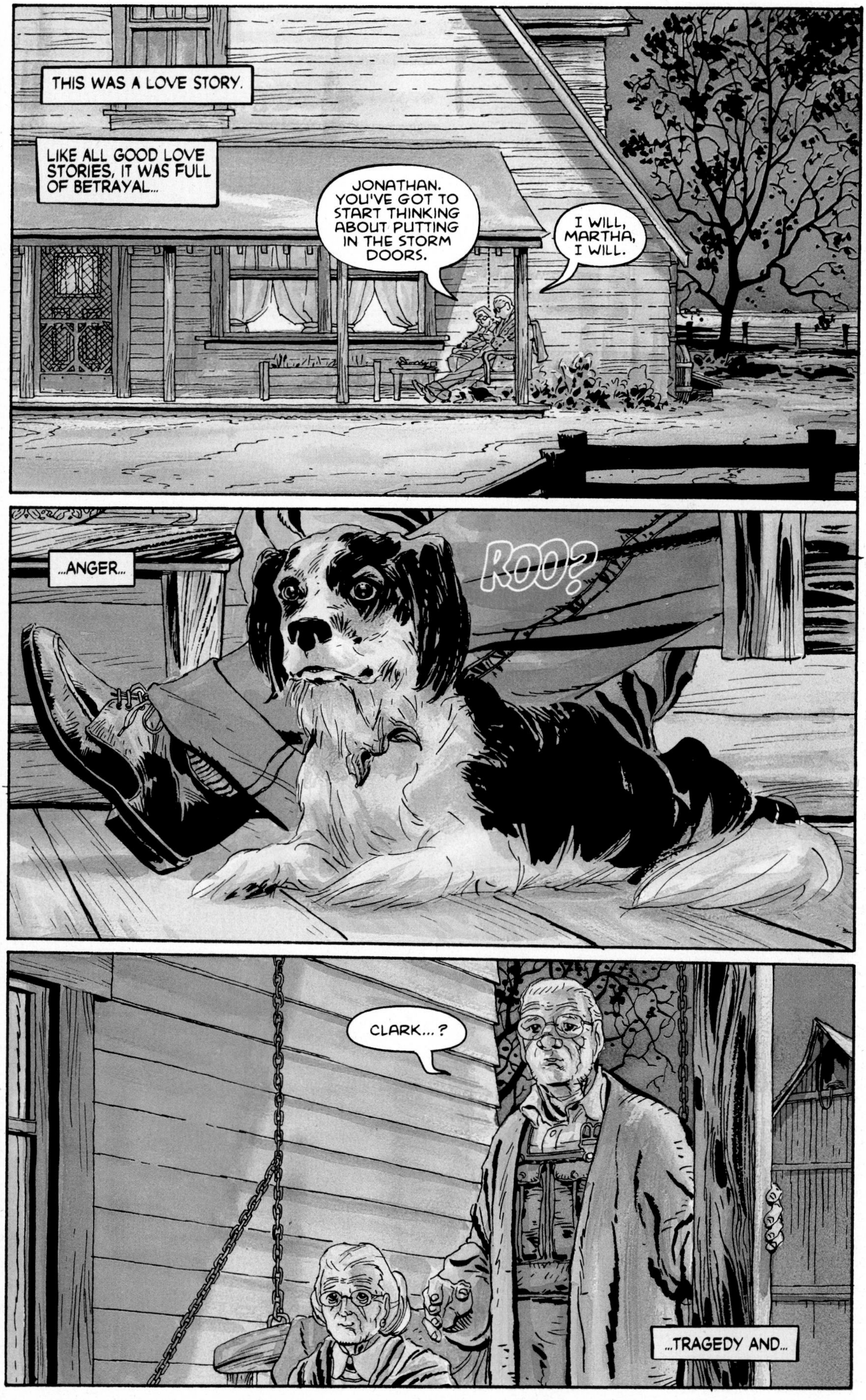

THIS WAS A LOVE STORY.
LIKE ALL GOOD LOVE STORIES, IT WAS FULL OF BETRAYAL...
JONATHAN. YOU'VE GOT TO START THINKING ABOUT PUTTING IN THE STORM DOORS.
I WILL, MARTHA, I WILL.
...ANGER...
ROO?
CLARK...?
...TRAGEDY AND...

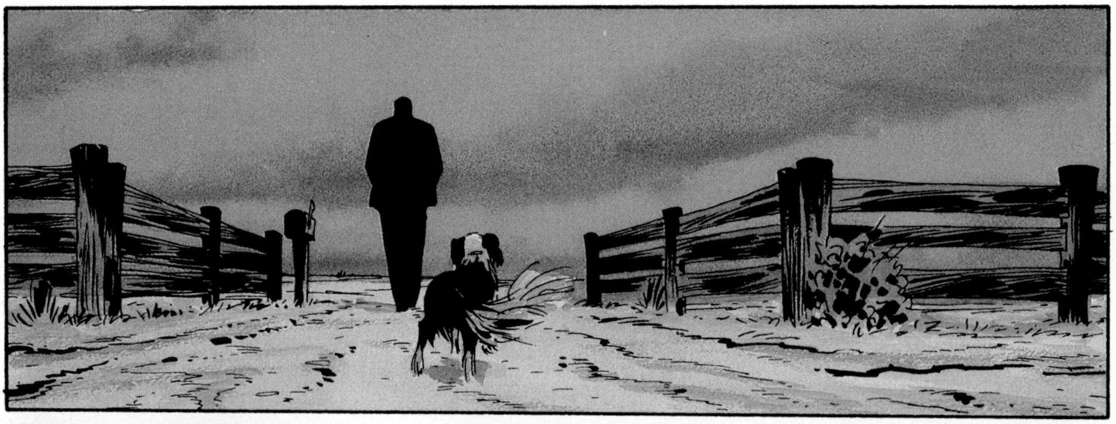

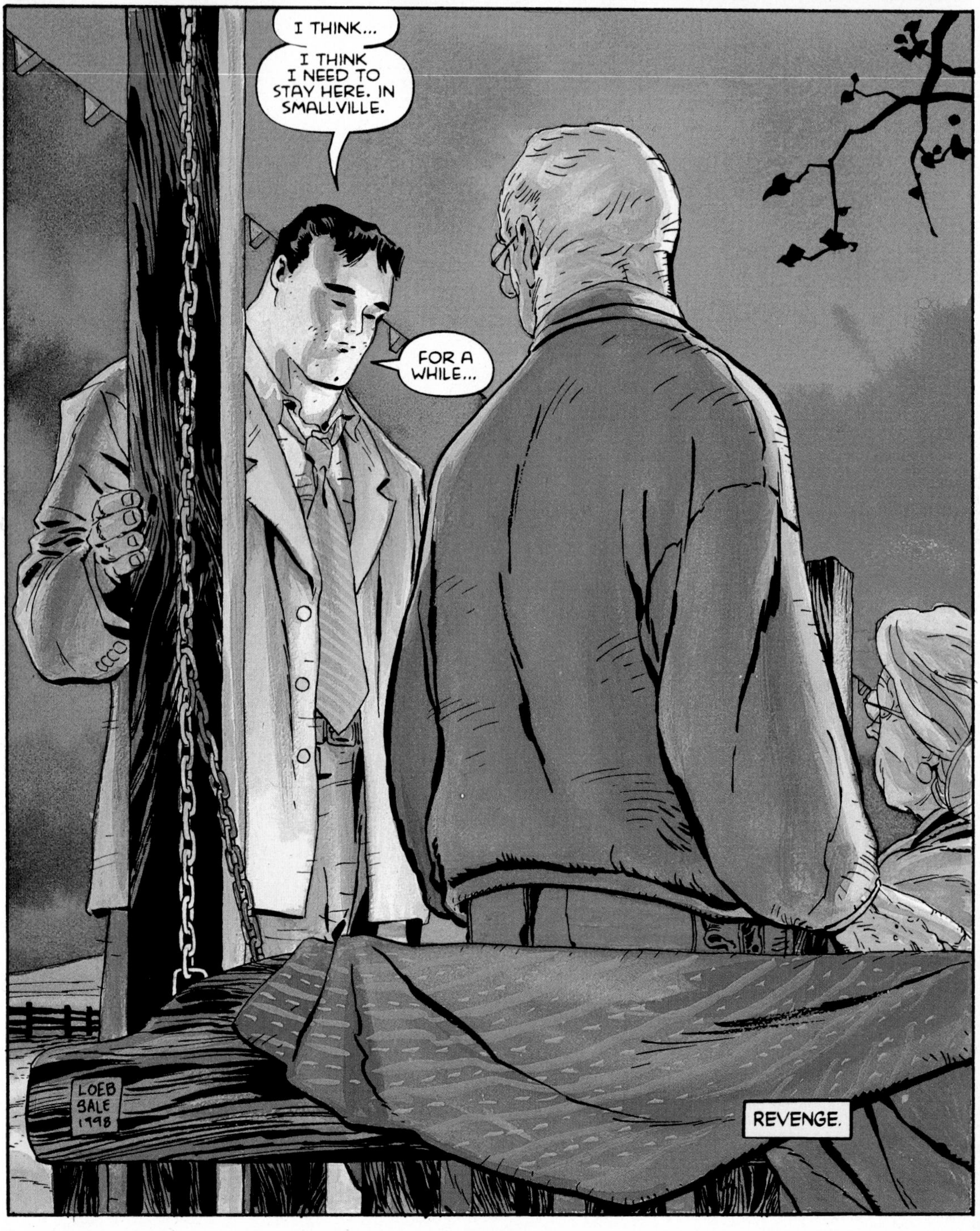
I THINK...
I THINK I NEED TO STAY HERE. IN SMALLVILLE.
FOR A WHILE...
LOEB SALE 1998
REVENGE.

Winter

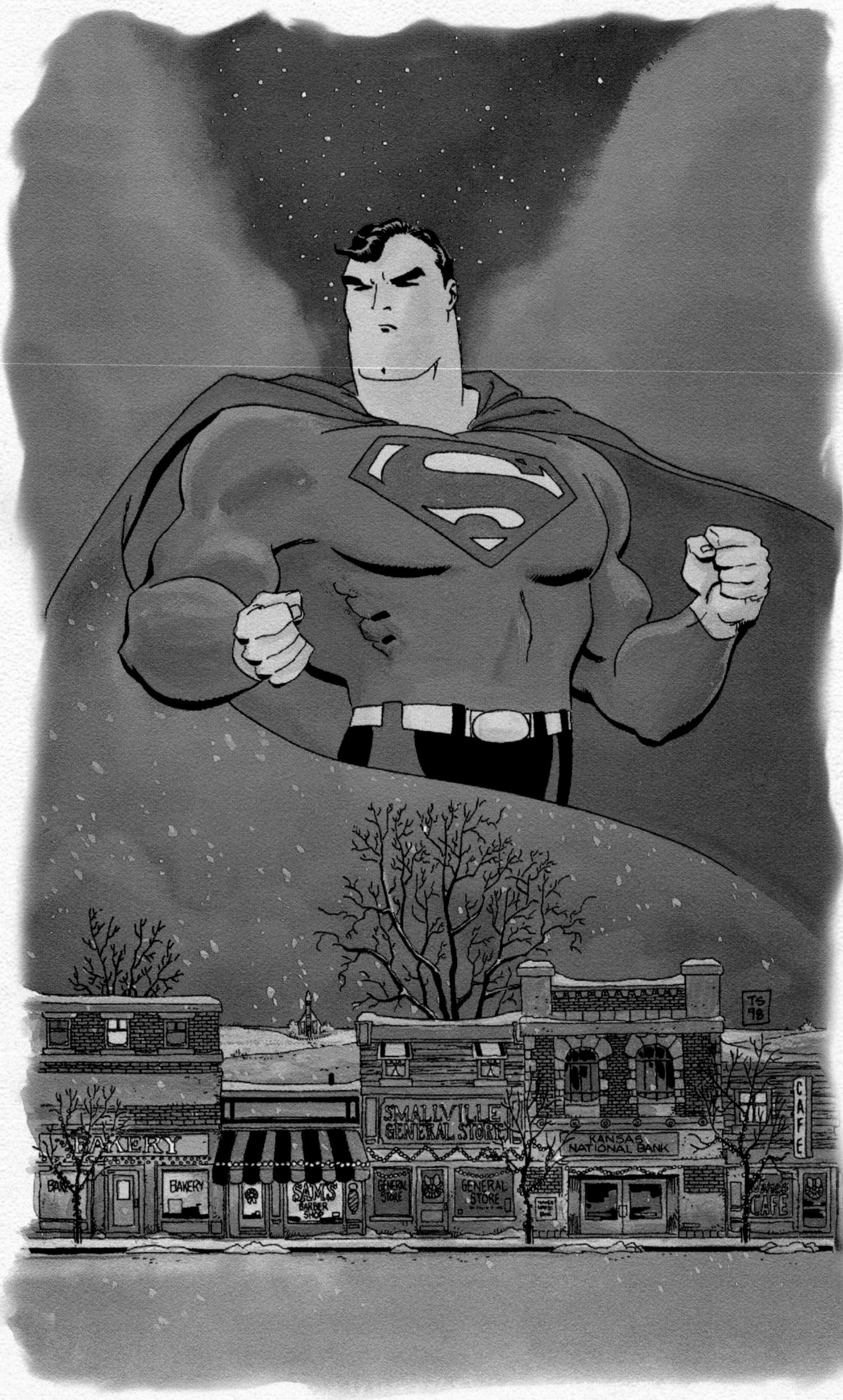
TS
98
BAKERY
BAKERY
SAM'S
BARBER SHOP
SMALLVILLE
GENERAL STORE
GENERAL STORE
GENERAL STORE
KANSAS
NATIONAL BANK
CAFE
CAFE

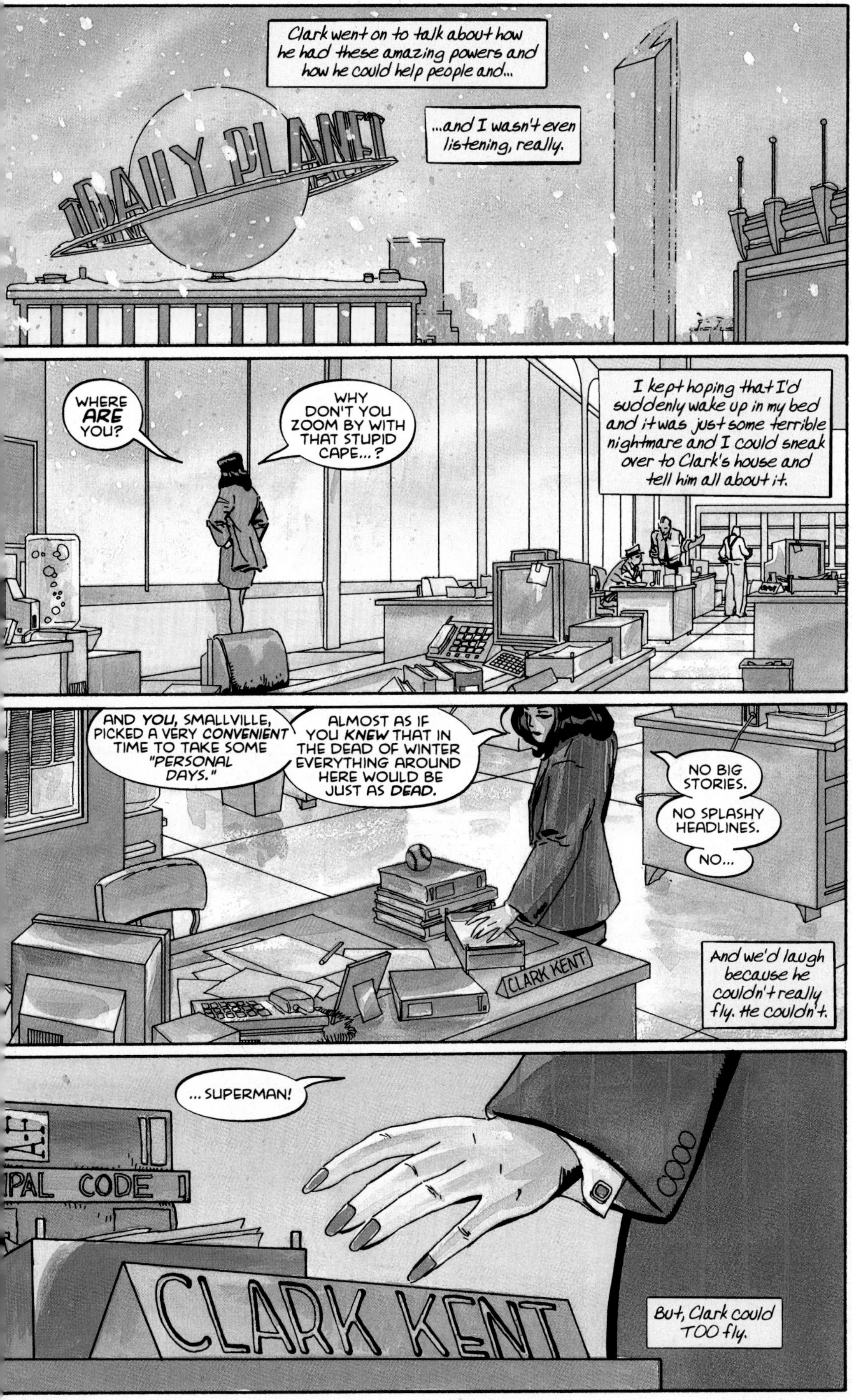
Clark went on to talk about how he had these amazing powers and how he could help people and...
...and I wasn't even listening, really.
DAILY PLANET
WHERE ARE YOU?
WHY DON'T YOU ZOOM BY WITH THAT STUPID CAPE...?
I kept hoping that I'd suddenly wake up in my bed and it was just some terrible nightmare and I could sneak over to Clark's house and tell him all about it.
AND YOU, SMALLVILLE, PICKED A VERY CONVENIENT TIME TO TAKE SOME "PERSONAL DAYS."
ALMOST AS IF YOU KNEW THAT IN THE DEAD OF WINTER EVERYTHING AROUND HERE WOULD BE JUST AS DEAD.
NO BIG STORIES.
NO SPLASHY HEADLINES.
NO...
CLARK KENT
And we'd laugh because he couldn't really fly. He couldn't.
...SUPERMAN!
IPAL CODE
CLARK KENT
But, Clark could TOO fly.

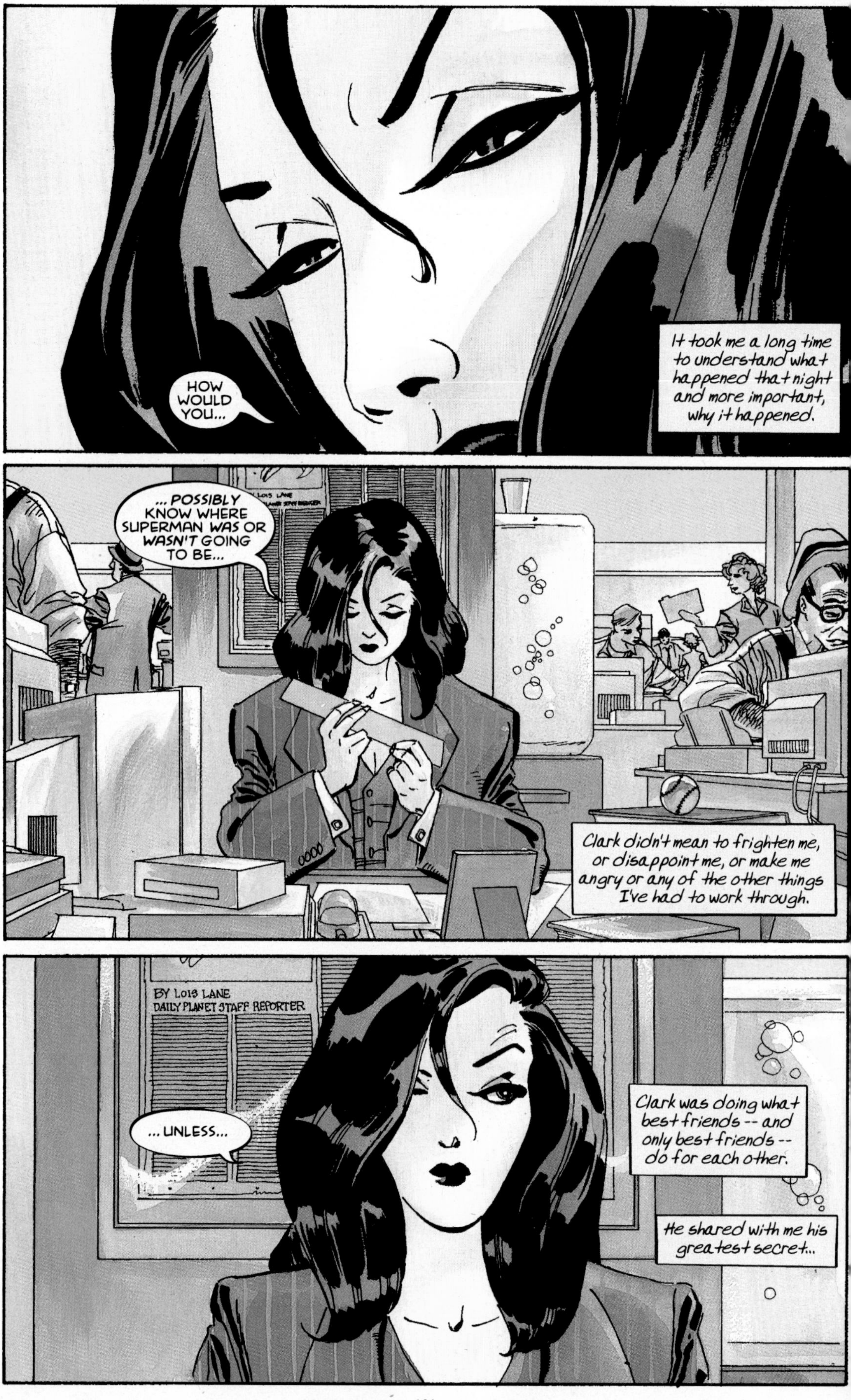
HOW WOULD YOU...
It took me a long time to understand what happened that night and more important, why it happened.
... POSSIBLY KNOW WHERE SUPERMAN WAS OR WASN'T GOING TO BE...
Clark didn't mean to frighten me, or disappoint me, or make me angry or any of the other things I've had to work through.
BY LOIS LANE
DAILY PLANET STAFF REPORTER
... UNLESS...
Clark was doing what best friends -- and only best friends -- do for each other.
He shared with me his greatest secret...

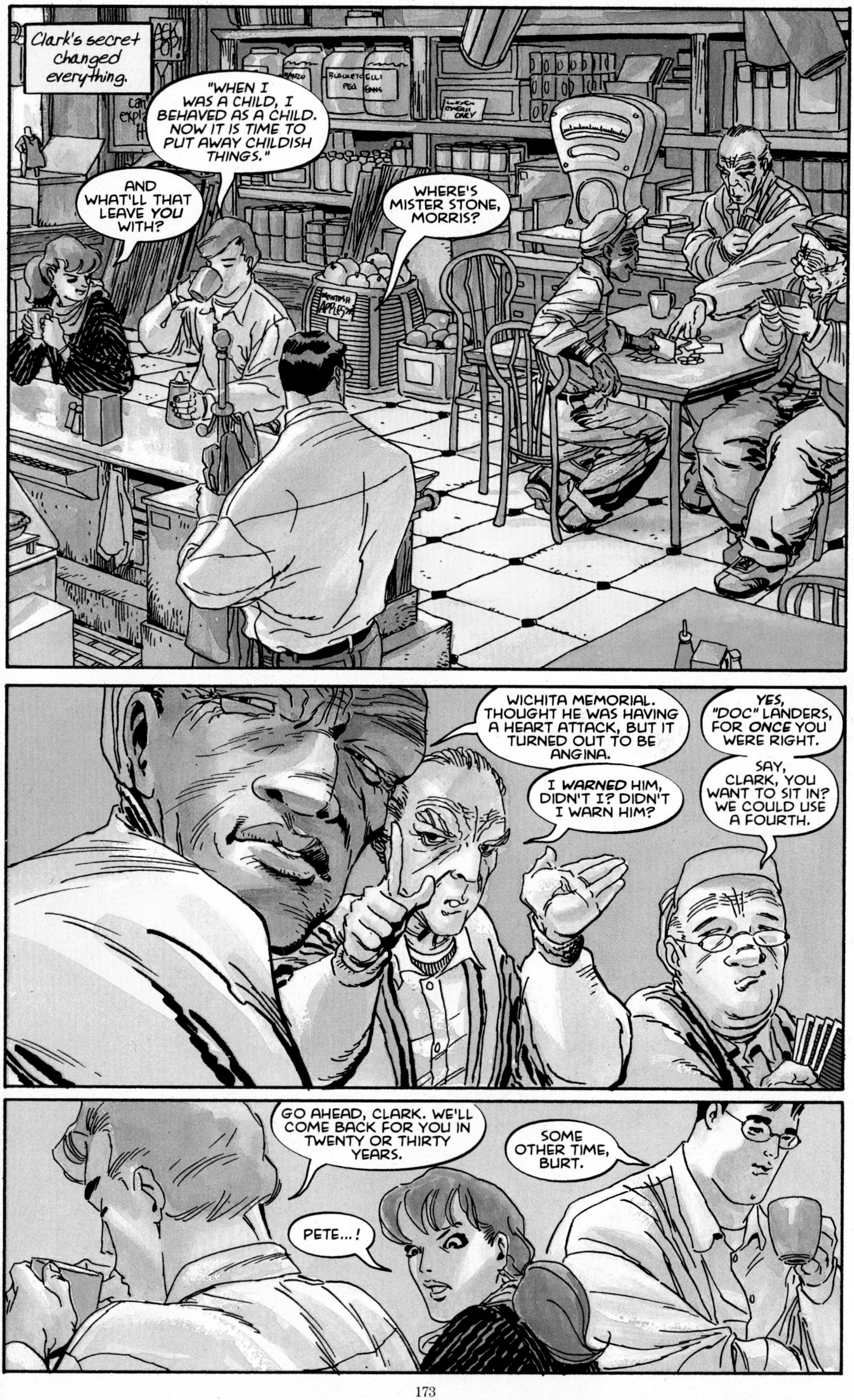
Clark's secret changed everything.
"WHEN I WAS A CHILD, I BEHAVED AS A CHILD. NOW IT IS TIME TO PUT AWAY CHILDISH THINGS."
AND WHAT'LL THAT LEAVE YOU WITH?
WHERE'S MISTER STONE, MORRIS?
MCINTOSH APPLES
WICHITA MEMORIAL. THOUGHT HE WAS HAVING A HEART ATTACK, BUT IT TURNED OUT TO BE ANGINA.
I WARNED HIM, DIDN'T I? DIDN'T I WARN HIM?
YES, "DOC" LANDERS, FOR ONCE YOU WERE RIGHT.
SAY, CLARK, YOU WANT TO SIT IN? WE COULD USE A FOURTH.
GO AHEAD, CLARK. WE'LL COME BACK FOR YOU IN TWENTY OR THIRTY YEARS.
SOME OTHER TIME, BURT.
PETE...!

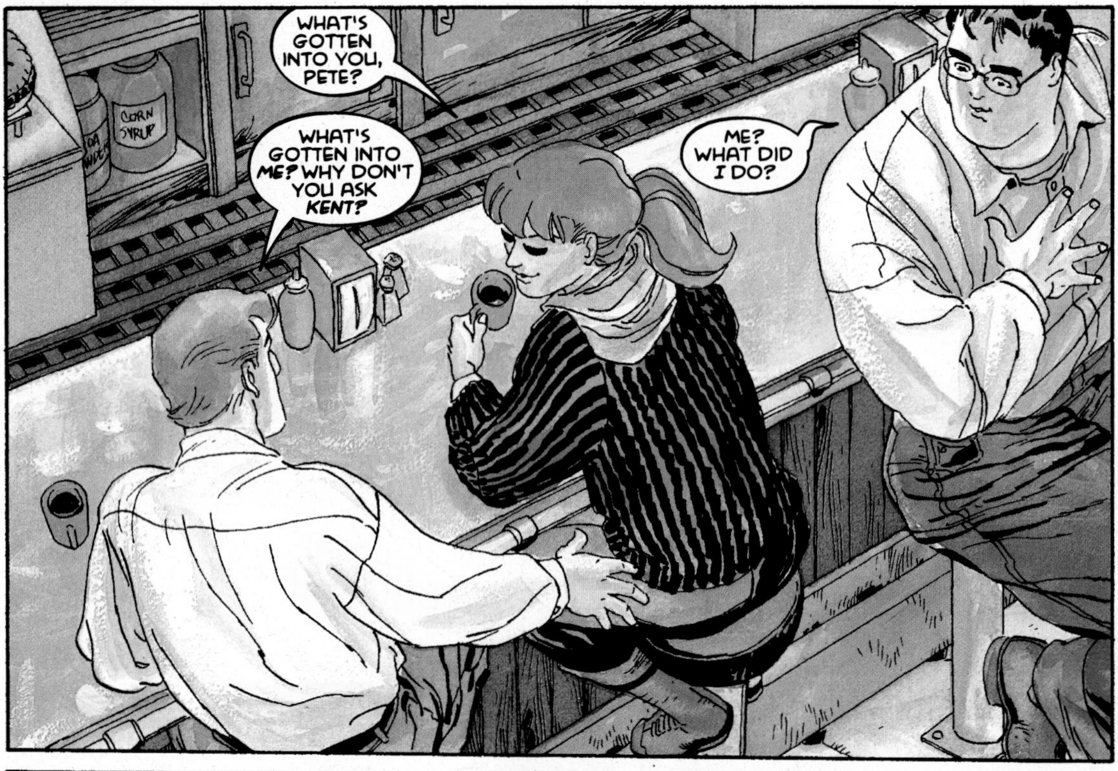
WHAT'S GOTTEN INTO YOU, PETE?
WHAT'S GOTTEN INTO ME? WHY DON'T YOU ASK KENT?
ME? WHAT DID I DO?
CORN SYRUP

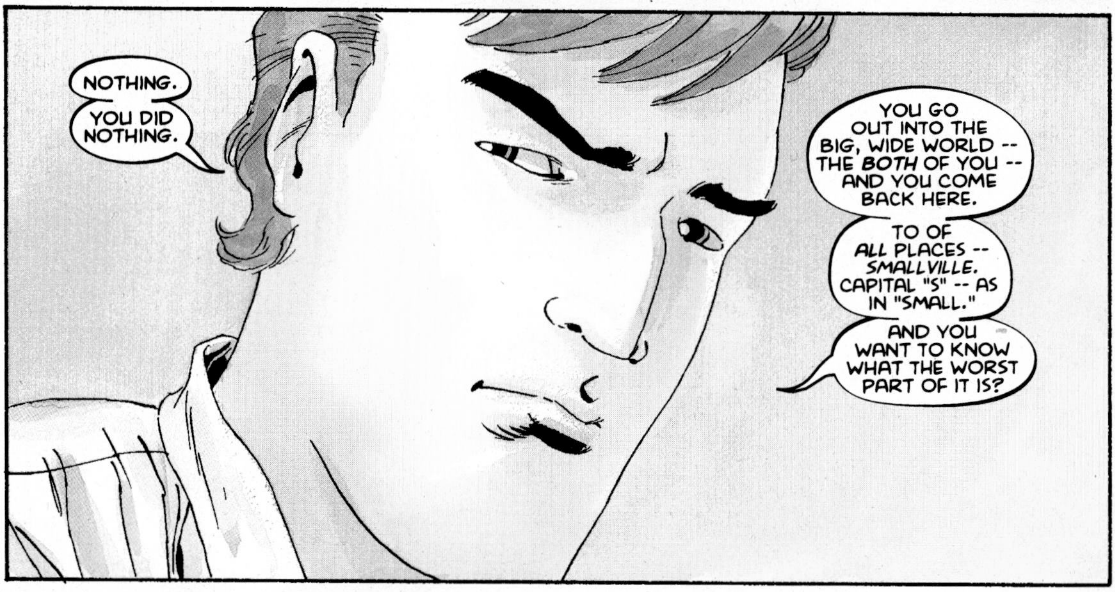
NOTHING.
YOU DID NOTHING.
YOU GO OUT INTO THE BIG, WIDE WORLD -- THE BOTH OF YOU -- AND YOU COME BACK HERE.
TO OF ALL PLACES -- SMALLVILLE. CAPITAL "S" -- AS IN "SMALL."
AND YOU WANT TO KNOW WHAT THE WORST PART OF IT IS?

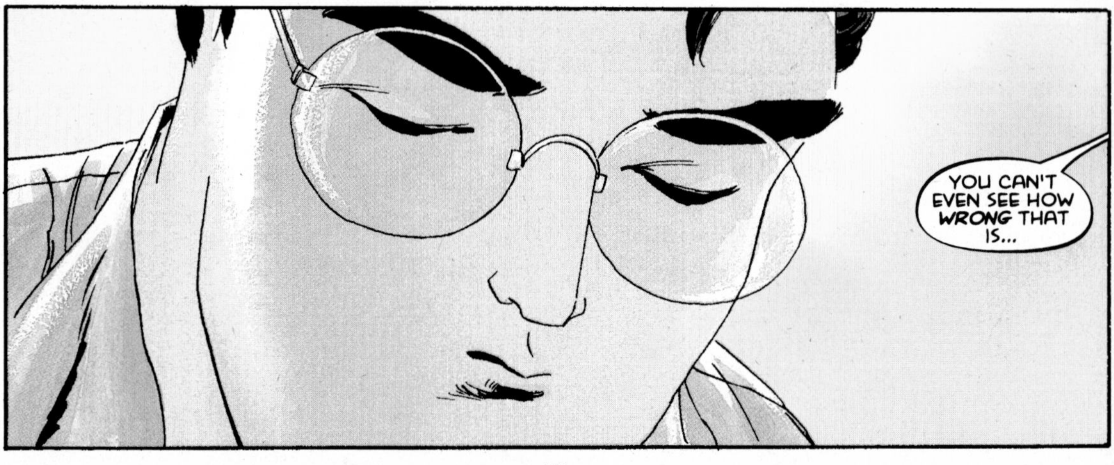
YOU CAN'T EVEN SEE HOW WRONG THAT IS...

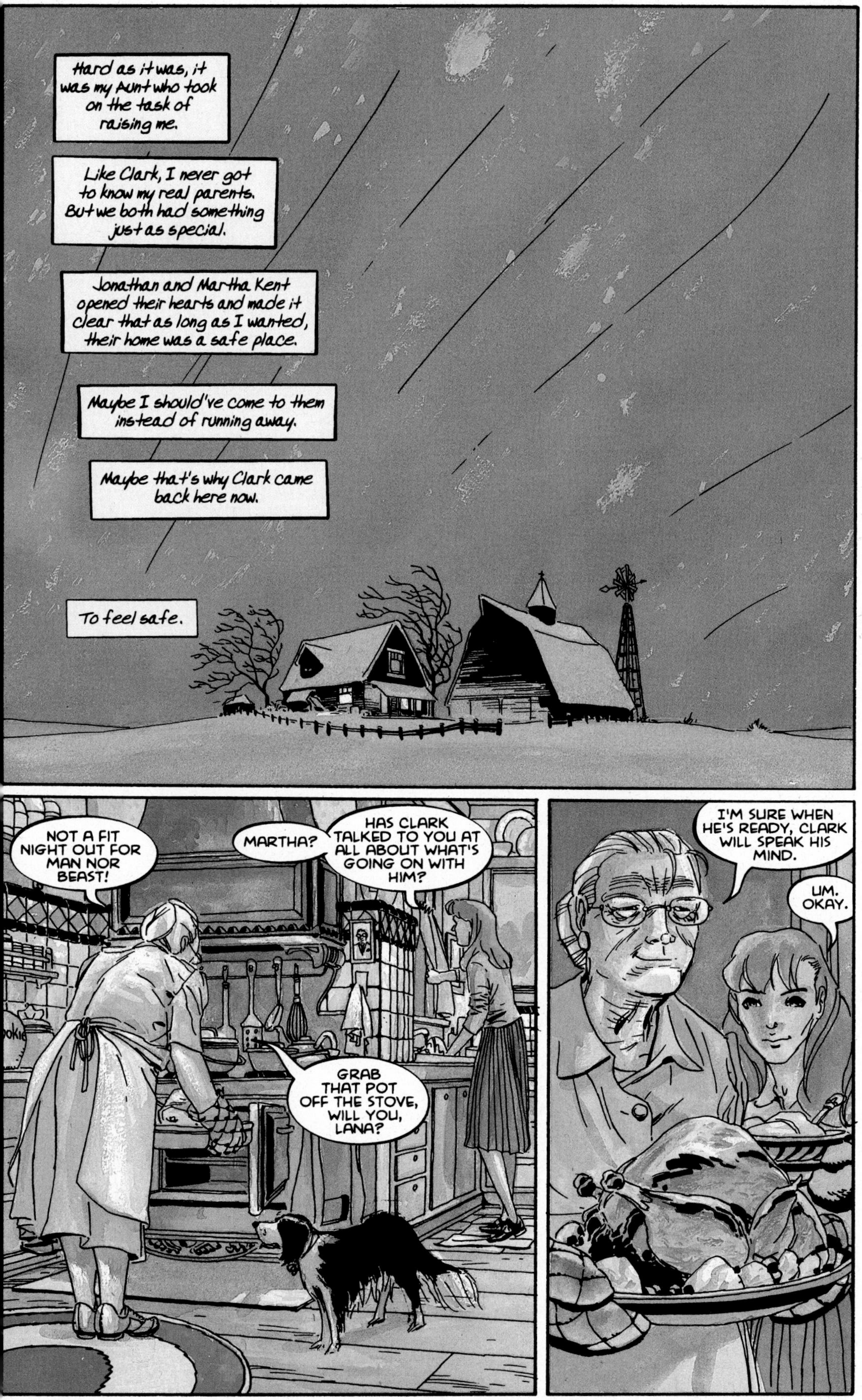
Hard as it was, it was my Aunt who took on the task of raising me.
Like Clark, I never got to know my real parents. But we both had something just as special.
Jonathan and Martha Kent opened their hearts and made it clear that as long as I wanted, their home was a safe place.
Maybe I should've come to them instead of running away.
Maybe that's why Clark came back here now.
To feel safe.
NOT A FIT NIGHT OUT FOR MAN NOR BEAST!
MARTHA?
HAS CLARK TALKED TO YOU AT ALL ABOUT WHAT'S GOING ON WITH HIM?
GRAB THAT POT OFF THE STOVE, WILL YOU, LANA?
I'M SURE WHEN HE'S READY, CLARK WILL SPEAK HIS MIND.
UM. OKAY.

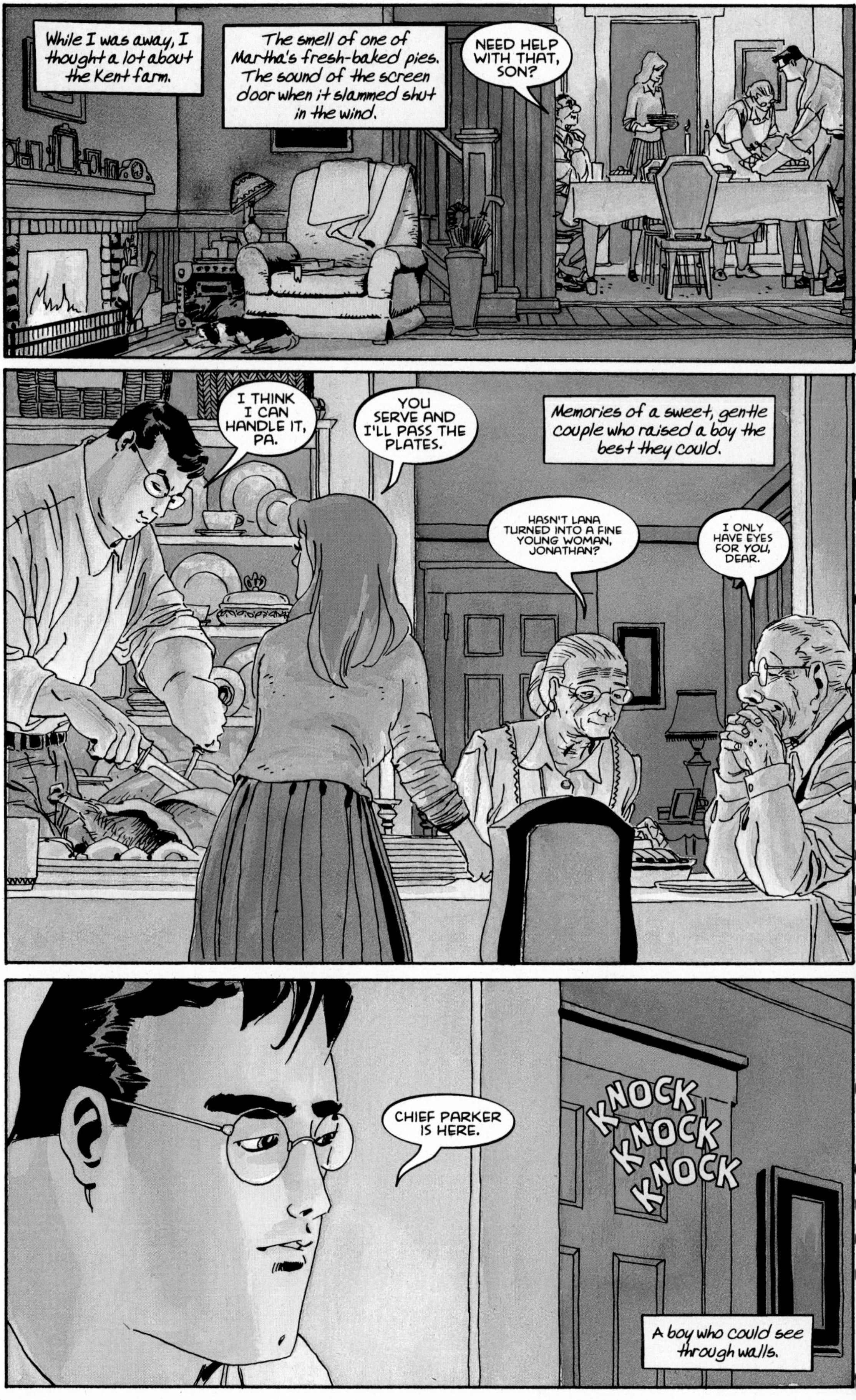
While I was away, I thought a lot about the Kent farm.
The smell of one of Martha's fresh-baked pies. The sound of the screen door when it slammed shut in the wind.
NEED HELP WITH THAT, SON?
I THINK I CAN HANDLE IT, PA.
YOU SERVE AND I'LL PASS THE PLATES.
Memories of a sweet, gentle couple who raised a boy the best they could.
HASN'T LANA TURNED INTO A FINE YOUNG WOMAN, JONATHAN?
I ONLY HAVE EYES FOR YOU, DEAR.
CHIEF PARKER IS HERE.
KNOCK KNOCK KNOCK
A boy who could see through walls.

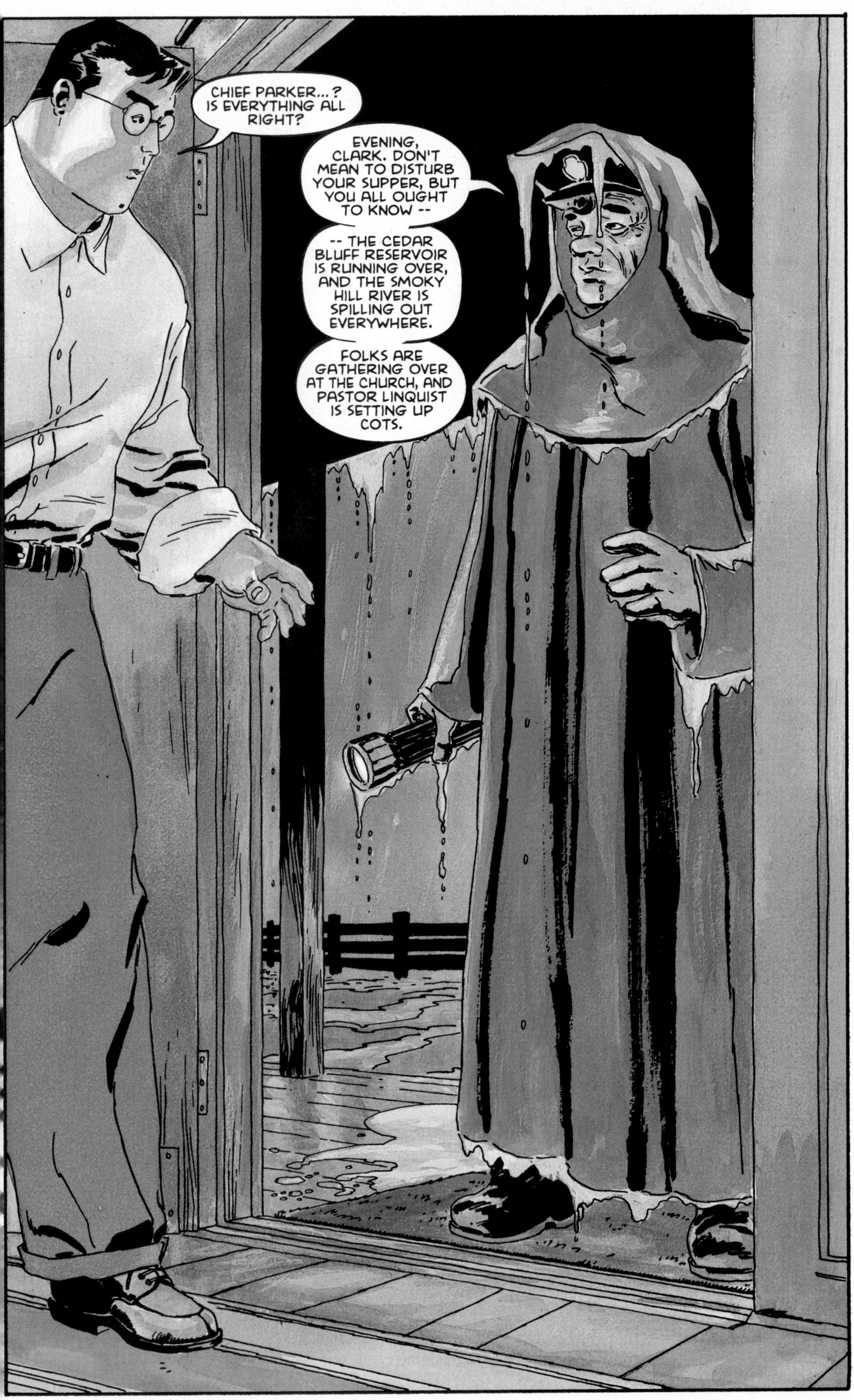
CHIEF PARKER...? IS EVERYTHING ALL RIGHT?
EVENING, CLARK. DON'T MEAN TO DISTURB YOUR SUPPER, BUT YOU ALL OUGHT TO KNOW --
-- THE CEDAR BLUFF RESERVOIR IS RUNNING OVER, AND THE SMOKY HILL RIVER IS SPILLING OUT EVERYWHERE.
FOLKS ARE GATHERING OVER AT THE CHURCH, AND PASTOR LINQUIST IS SETTING UP COTS.

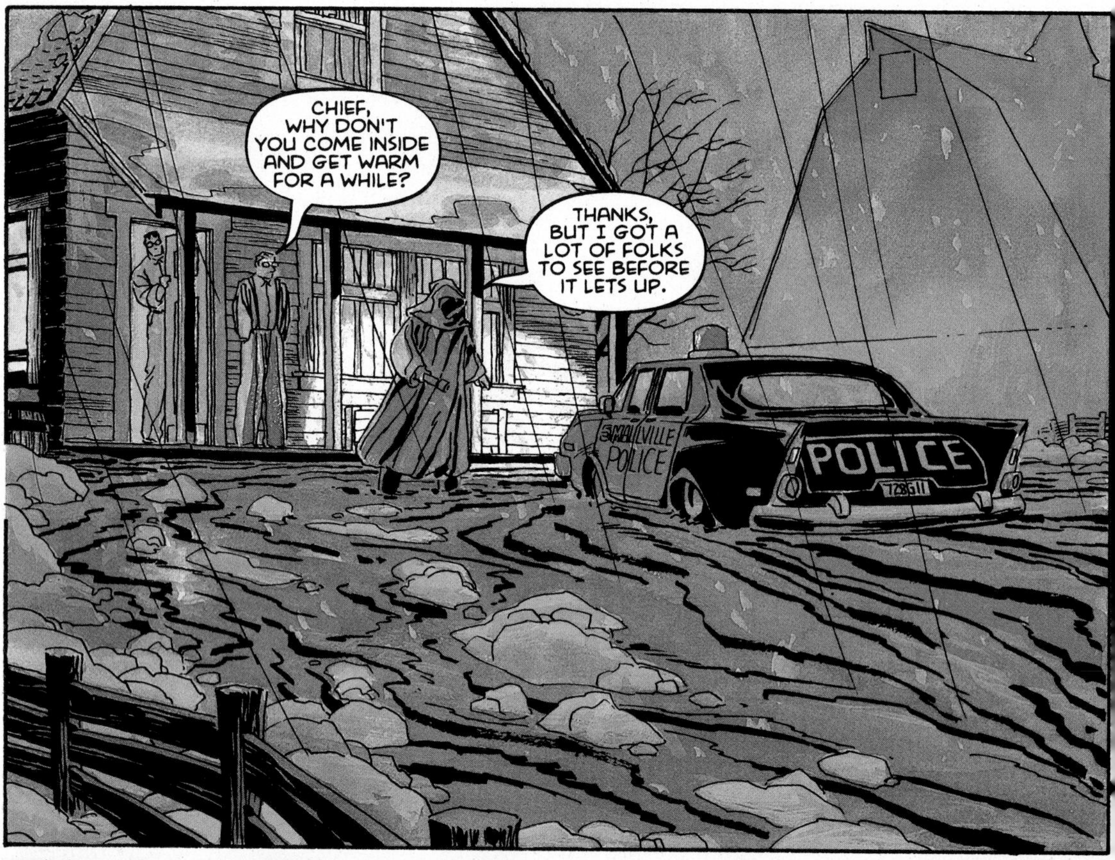
CHIEF, WHY DON'T YOU COME INSIDE AND GET WARM FOR A WHILE?
THANKS, BUT I GOT A LOT OF FOLKS TO SEE BEFORE IT LETS UP.
SMALLVILLE POLICE
POLICE

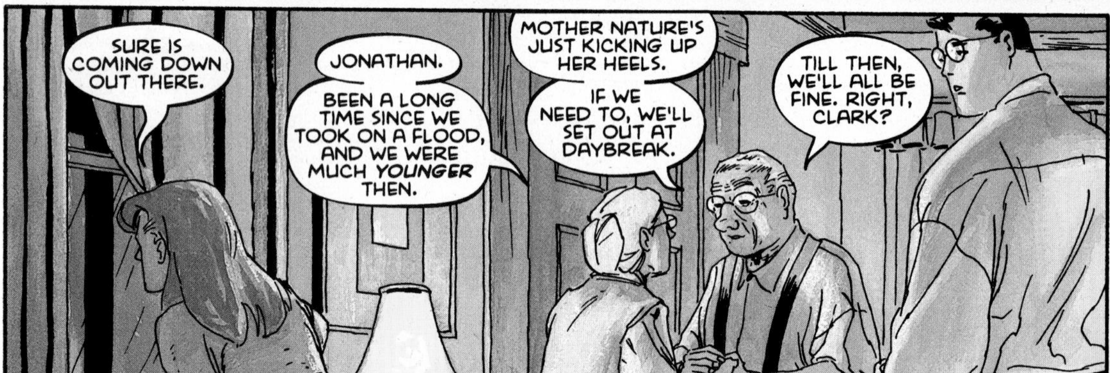
SURE IS COMING DOWN OUT THERE.
JONATHAN.
BEEN A LONG TIME SINCE WE TOOK ON A FLOOD, AND WE WERE MUCH *YOUNGER* THEN.
MOTHER NATURE'S JUST KICKING UP HER HEELS.
IF WE NEED TO, WE'LL SET OUT AT DAYBREAK.
TILL THEN, WE'LL ALL BE FINE. RIGHT, CLARK?

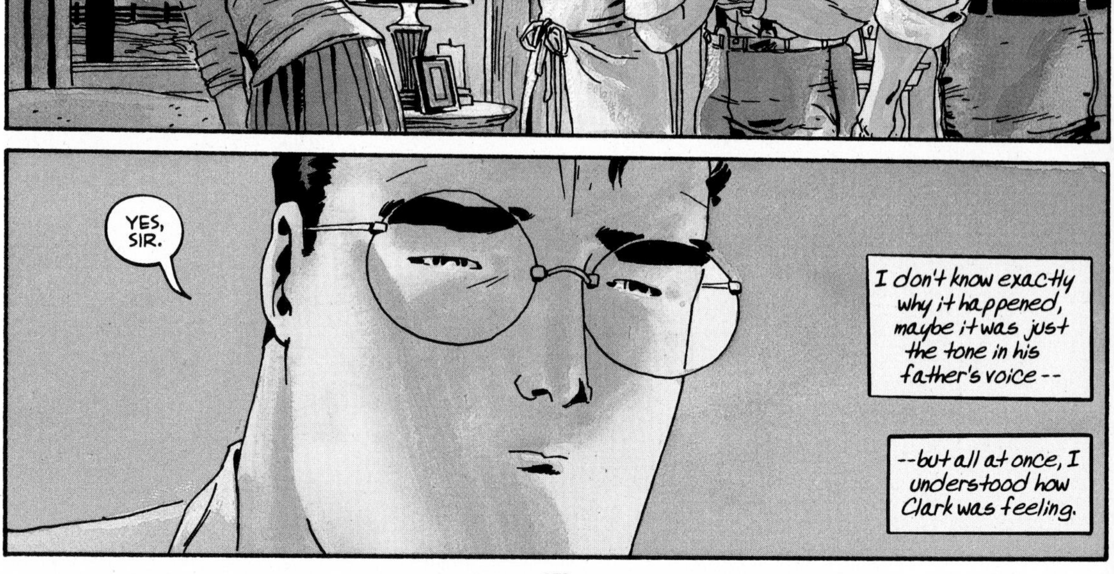
YES, SIR.
I don't know exactly why it happened, maybe it was just the tone in his father's voice --
--but all at once, I understood how Clark was feeling.

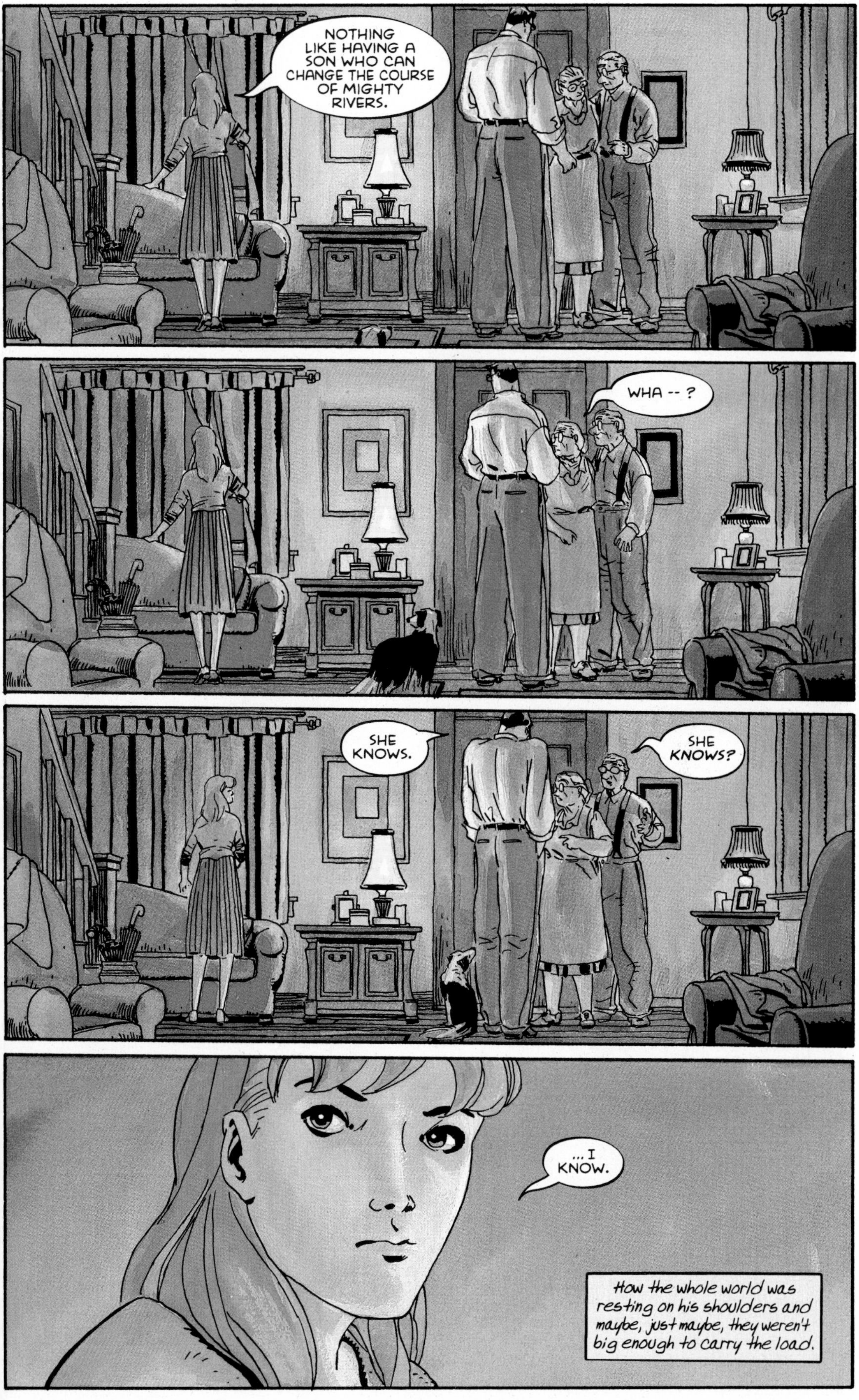
NOTHING LIKE HAVING A SON WHO CAN CHANGE THE COURSE OF MIGHTY RIVERS.
WHA -- ?
SHE KNOWS.
SHE KNOWS?
...I KNOW.
How the whole world was resting on his shoulders and maybe, just maybe, they weren't big enough to carry the load.

Maybe standing in that field that night, telling me how, with all his special powers, he would help as many people as he could --

-- maybe it wasn't such a good idea or, at least, not nearly as easy as that boy who could fly thought.

PA. I BEGAN TO THINK THAT I COULD DO *ANYTHING.*

AND I CAN'T.

C.K.

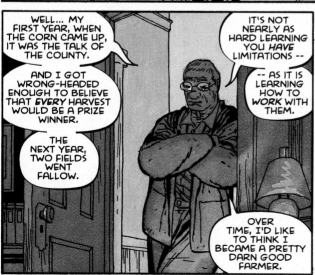

WELL... MY FIRST YEAR, WHEN THE CORN CAME UP, IT WAS THE TALK OF THE COUNTY.

AND I GOT WRONG-HEADED ENOUGH TO BELIEVE THAT *EVERY* HARVEST WOULD BE A PRIZE WINNER.

THE NEXT YEAR, TWO FIELDS WENT FALLOW.

IT'S NOT NEARLY AS HARD LEARNING YOU *HAVE* LIMITATIONS --

-- AS IT IS LEARNING HOW TO WORK WITH THEM.

OVER TIME, I'D LIKE TO THINK I BECAME A PRETTY DARN GOOD FARMER.

OVER TIME, SON.

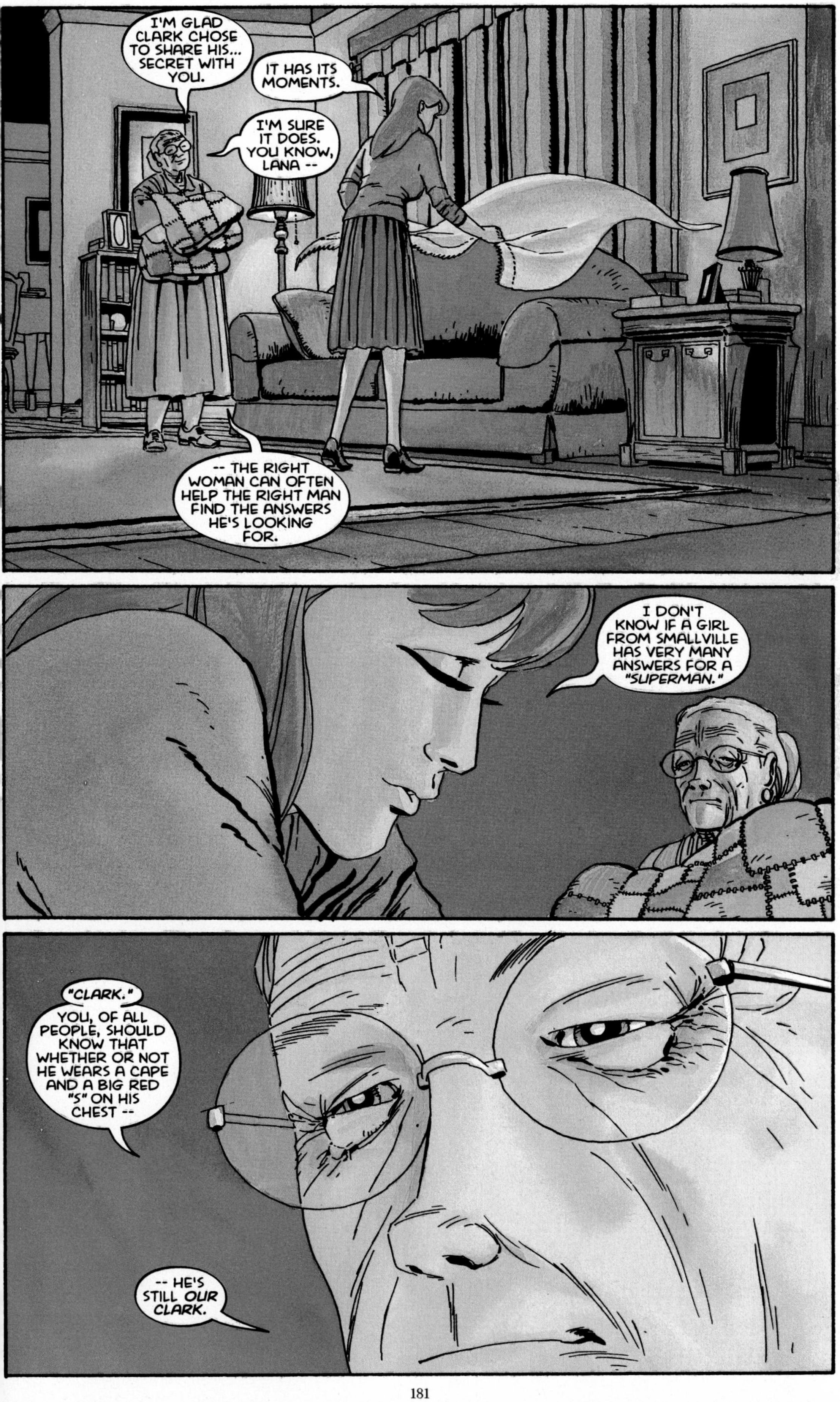
I'M GLAD CLARK CHOSE TO SHARE HIS... SECRET WITH YOU.
IT HAS ITS MOMENTS.
I'M SURE IT DOES. YOU KNOW, LANA --
-- THE RIGHT WOMAN CAN OFTEN HELP THE RIGHT MAN FIND THE ANSWERS HE'S LOOKING FOR.
I DON'T KNOW IF A GIRL FROM SMALLVILLE HAS VERY MANY ANSWERS FOR A "SUPERMAN."
"CLARK." YOU, OF ALL PEOPLE, SHOULD KNOW THAT WHETHER OR NOT HE WEARS A CAPE AND A BIG RED "S" ON HIS CHEST --
-- HE'S STILL OUR CLARK.

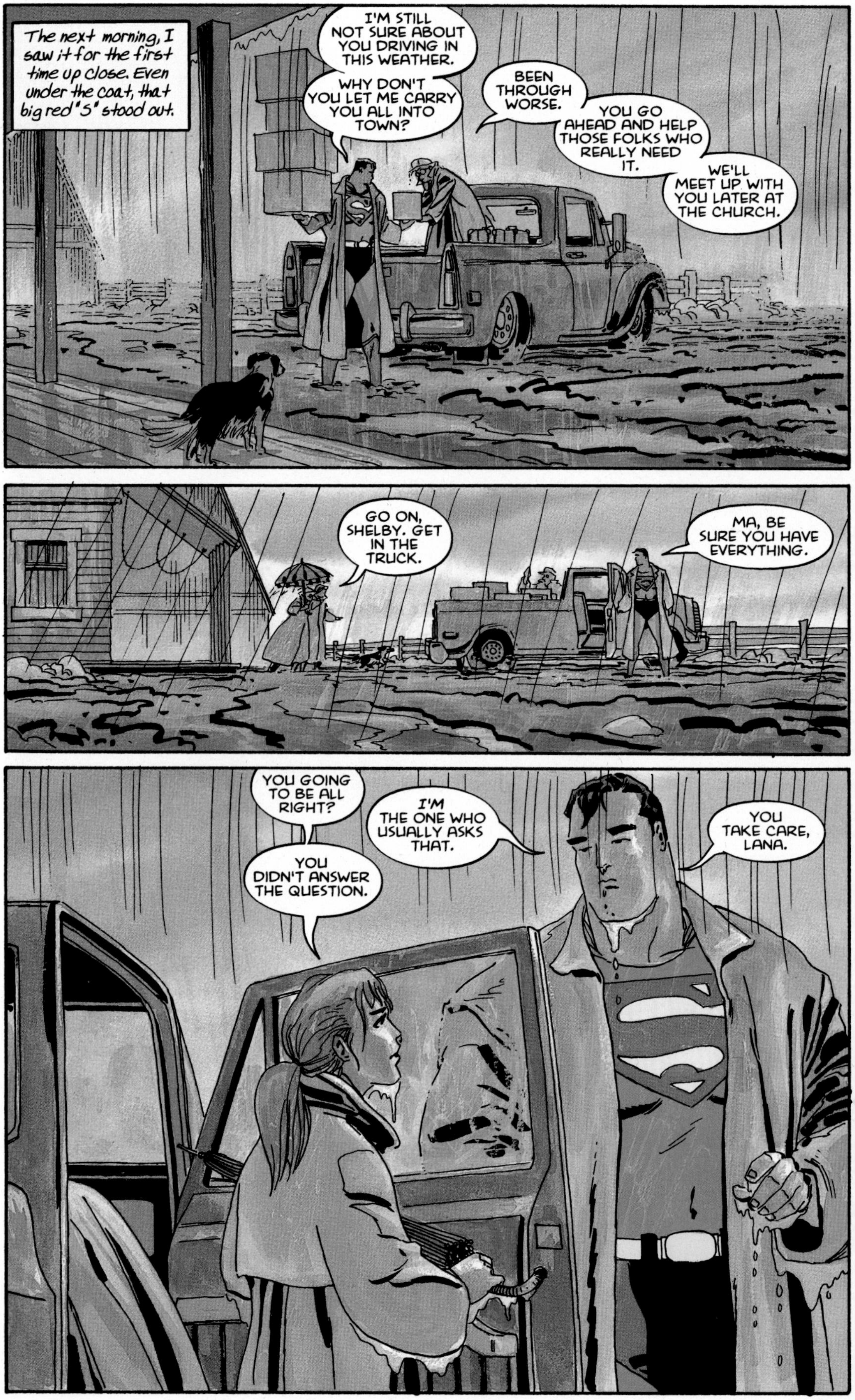
The next morning, I saw it for the first time up close. Even under the coat, that big red "S" stood out.
I'M STILL NOT SURE ABOUT YOU DRIVING IN THIS WEATHER.
WHY DON'T YOU LET ME CARRY YOU ALL INTO TOWN?
BEEN THROUGH WORSE.
YOU GO AHEAD AND HELP THOSE FOLKS WHO REALLY NEED IT.
WE'LL MEET UP WITH YOU LATER AT THE CHURCH.
GO ON, SHELBY. GET IN THE TRUCK.
MA, BE SURE YOU HAVE EVERYTHING.
YOU GOING TO BE ALL RIGHT?
YOU DIDN'T ANSWER THE QUESTION.
I'M THE ONE WHO USUALLY ASKS THAT.
YOU TAKE CARE, LANA.

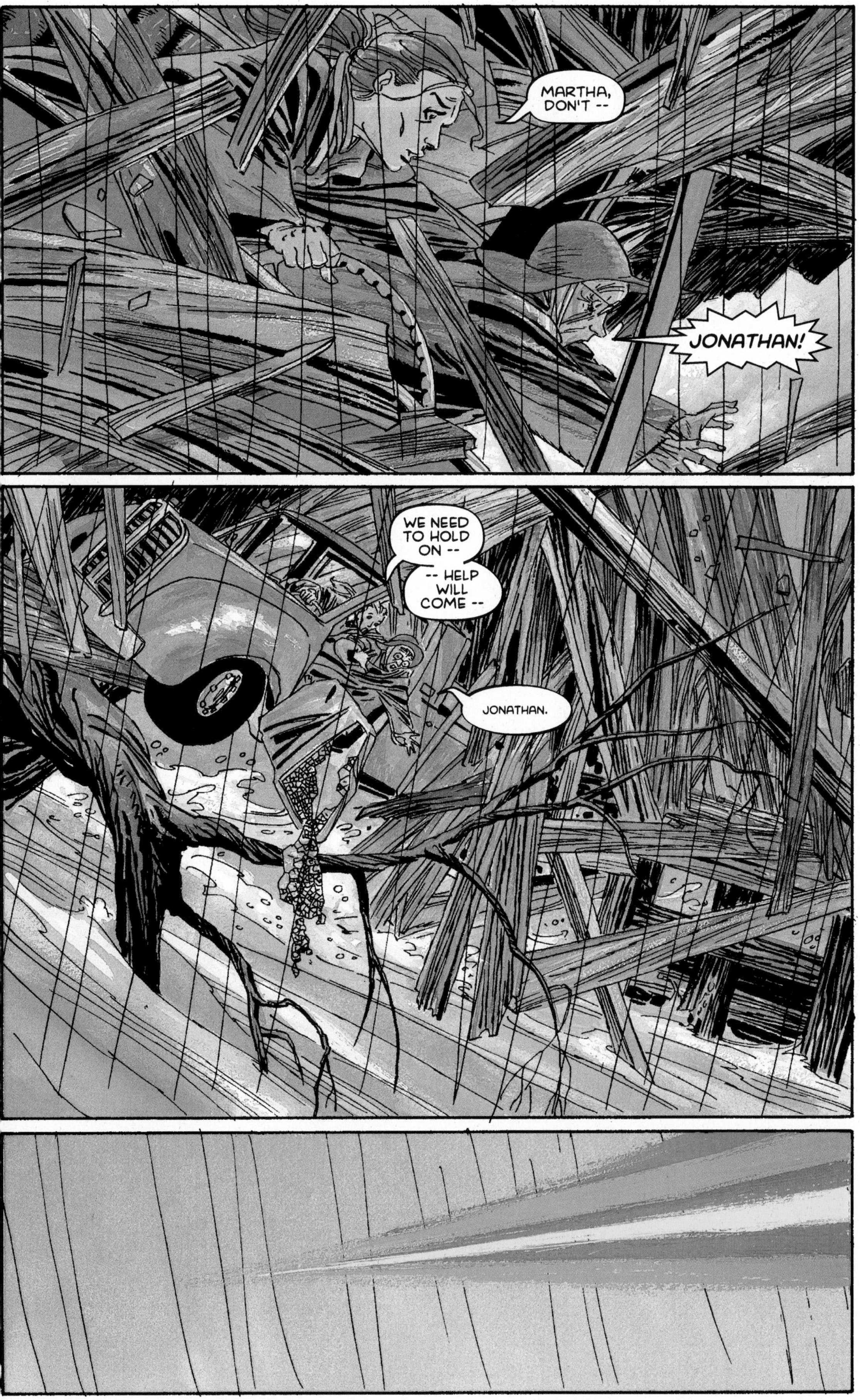
MARTHA, DON'T --
JONATHAN!
WE NEED TO HOLD ON --
-- HELP WILL COME --
JONATHAN.

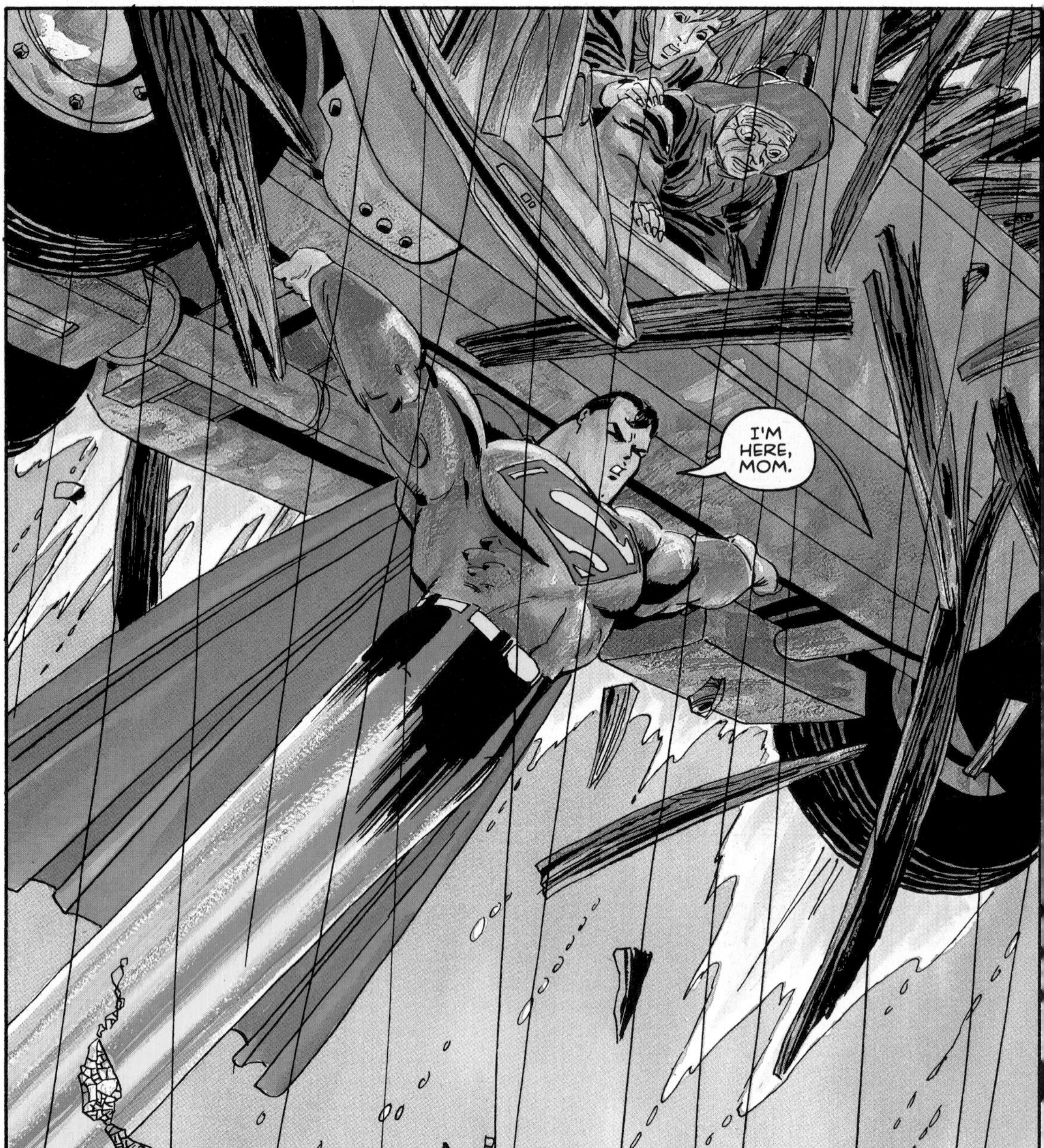
I'M HERE, MOM.

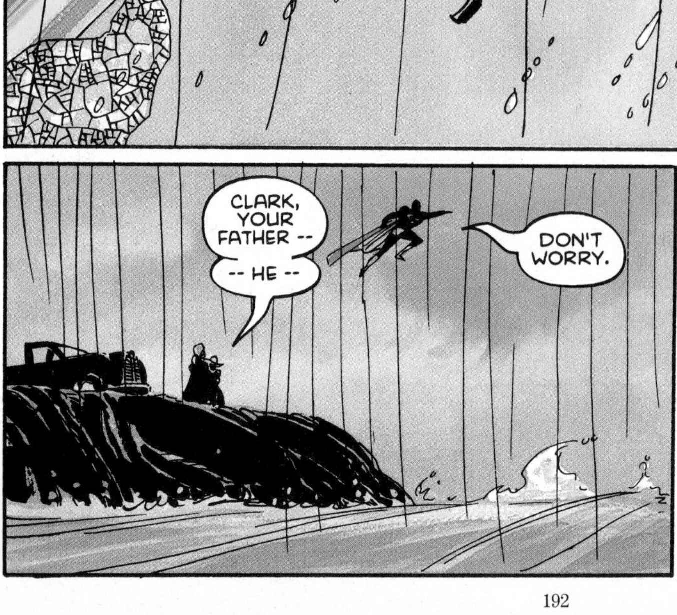
CLARK, YOUR FATHER --
-- HE --
DON'T WORRY.

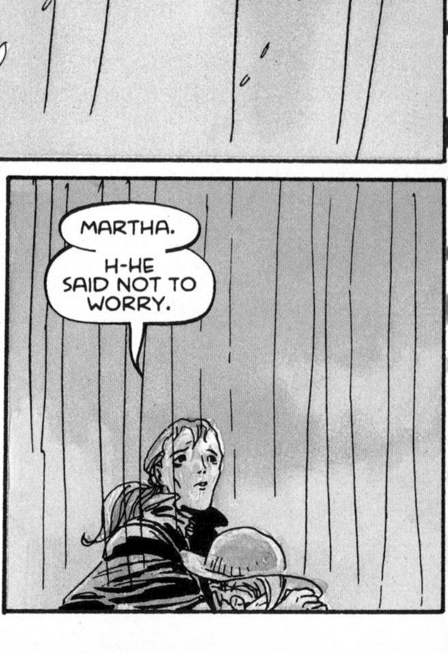
MARTHA.
H-HE SAID NOT TO WORRY.

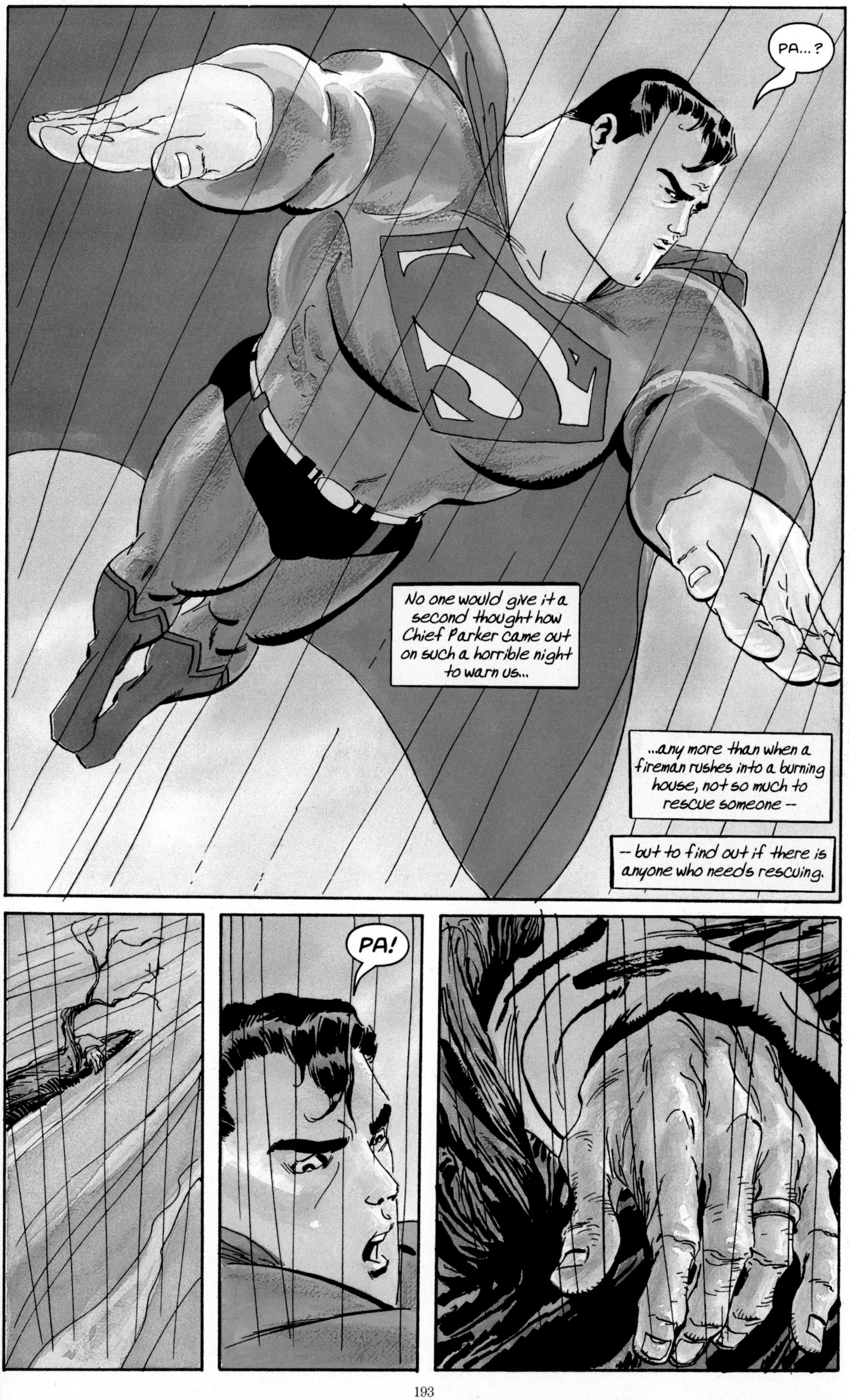
PA...?
No one would give it a second thought how Chief Parker came out on such a horrible night to warn us...
...any more than when a fireman rushes into a burning house, not so much to rescue someone --
-- but to find out if there is anyone who needs rescuing.
PA!

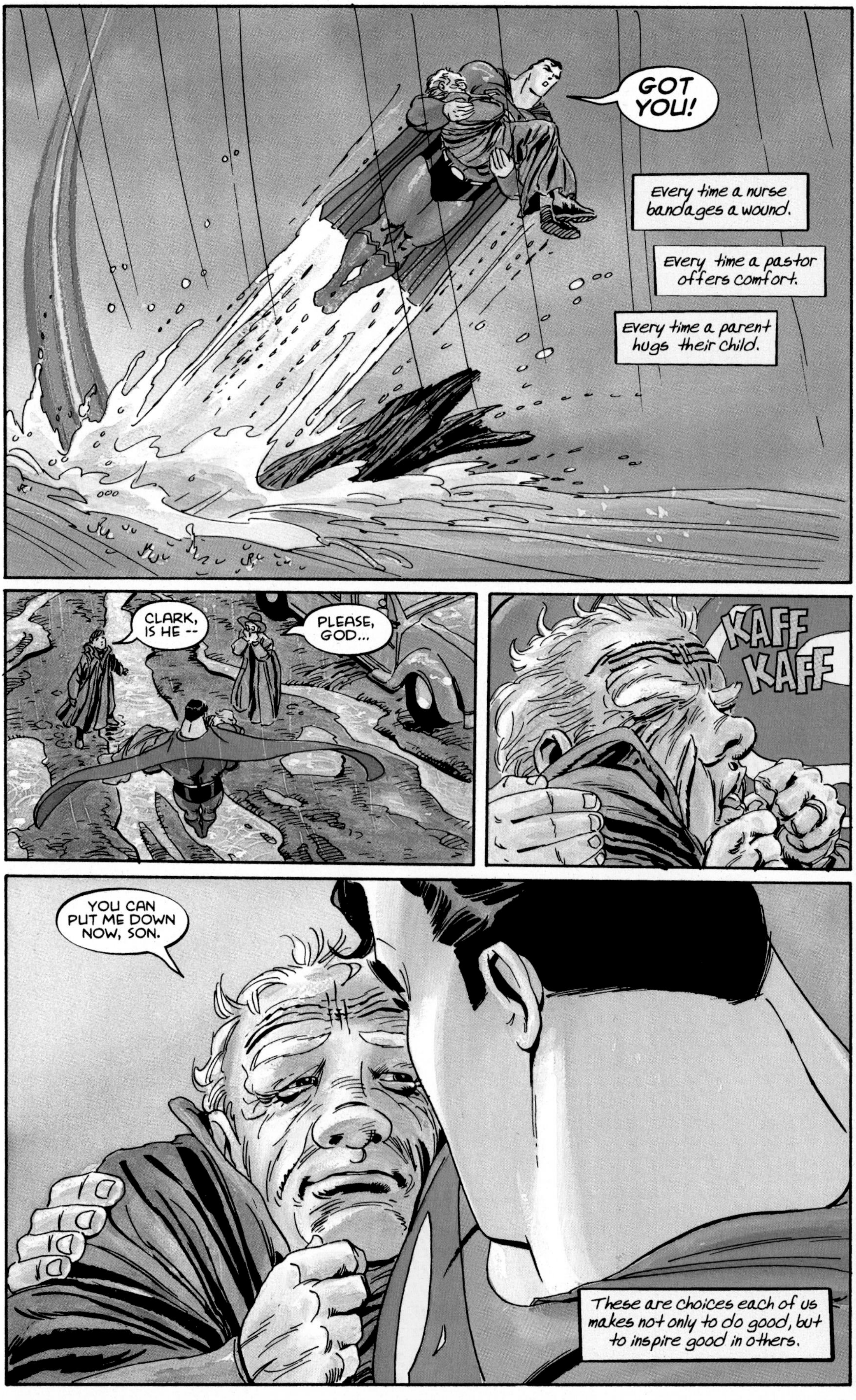
GOT YOU!
Every time a nurse bandages a wound.
Every time a pastor offers comfort.
Every time a parent hugs their child.
CLARK, IS HE --
PLEASE, GOD...
KAFF KAFF
YOU CAN PUT ME DOWN NOW, SON.
These are choices each of us makes not only to do good, but to inspire good in others.

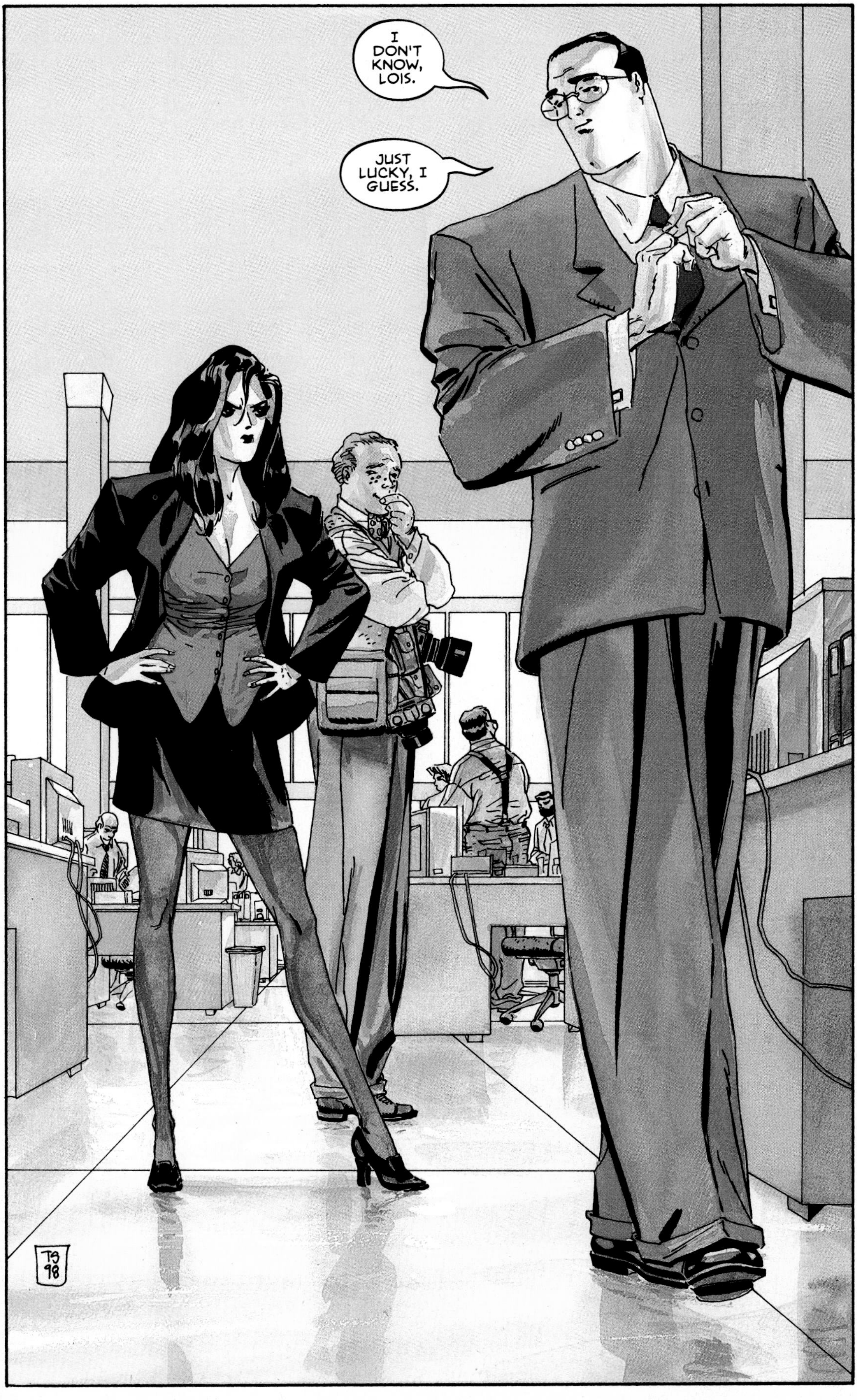
I DON'T KNOW, LOIS.
JUST LUCKY, I GUESS.
TS 98

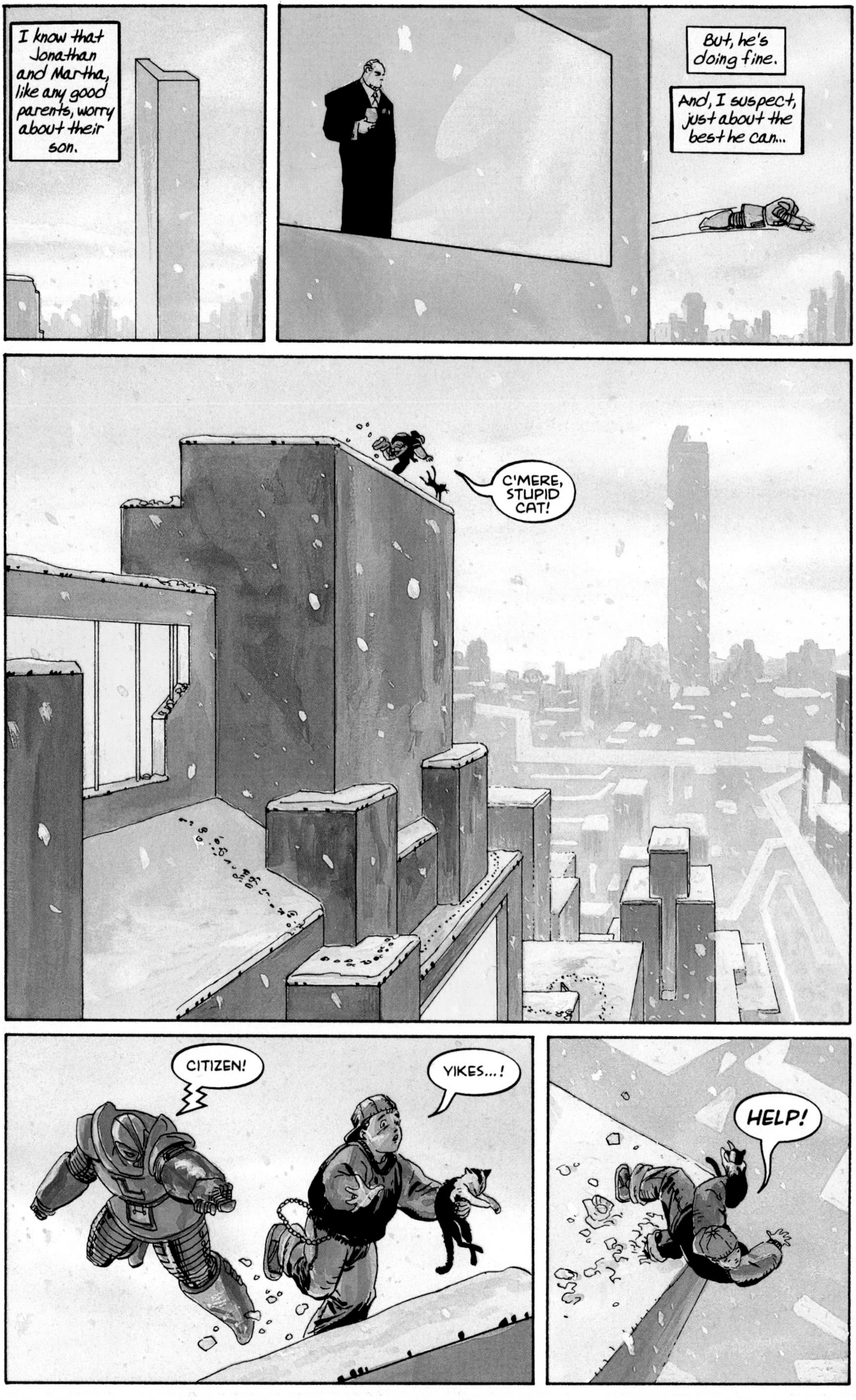
I know that Jonathan and Martha, like any good parents, worry about their son.
But, he's doing fine.
And, I suspect, just about the best he can...
C'MERE, STUPID CAT!
CITIZEN!
YIKES...!
HELP!

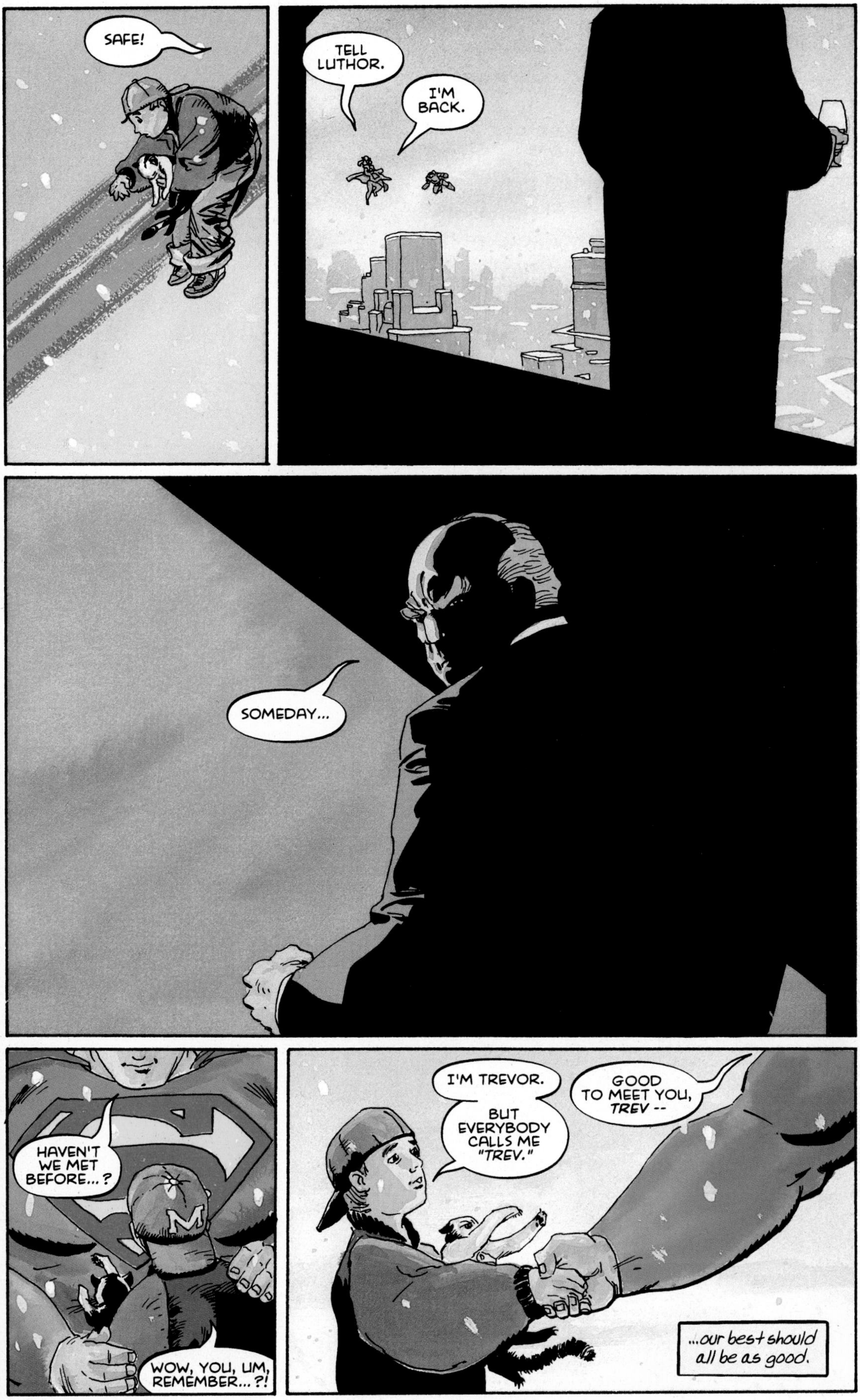
SAFE!
TELL LUTHOR.
I'M BACK.
SOMEDAY...
HAVEN'T WE MET BEFORE...?
WOW, YOU, UM, REMEMBER...?!
I'M TREVOR.
BUT EVERYBODY CALLS ME "TREV."
GOOD TO MEET YOU, TREV --
...our best should all be as good.

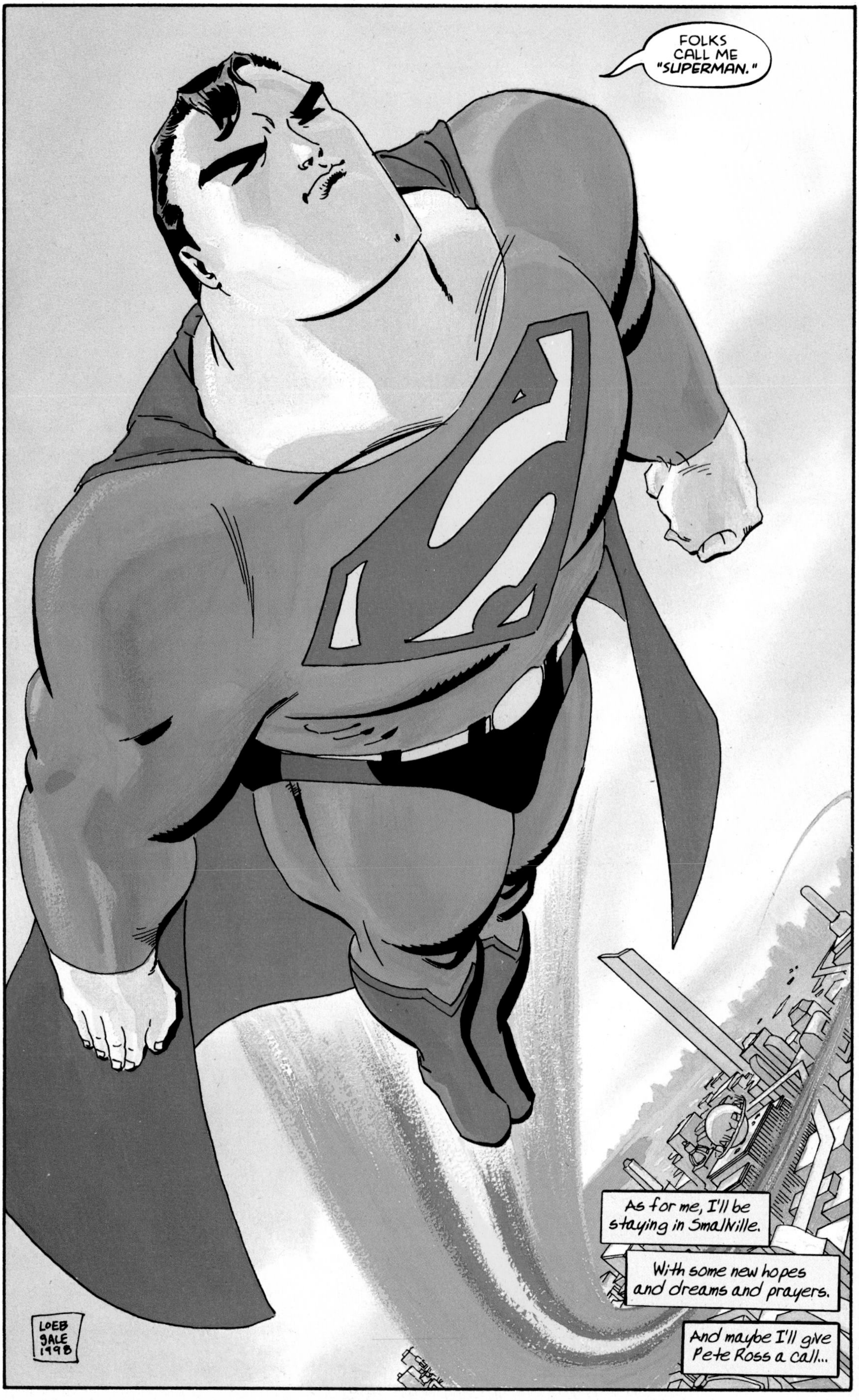
FOLKS CALL ME "SUPERMAN."
As for me, I'll be staying in Smallville.
With some new hopes and dreams and prayers.
And maybe I'll give Pete Ross a call...
LOEB GALE 1998

Jeph Loeb is the author of BATMAN: THE LONG HALLOWEEN, BATMAN: DARK VICTORY, *Daredevil: Yellow* and *Spider-Man: Blue*. A writer/producer living in Los Angeles, his credits include *Teen Wolf, Commando, Buffy: The Animated Series* and *Smallville*.

Tim Sale lives in Seattle with his two dogs, Hotspur and Shelby. He is the artist of BATMAN: DARK VICTORY, BATMAN: THE LONG HALLOWEEN, *Daredevil: Yellow, Spider-Man: Blue, Billi 99, The Amazon,* DEATHBLOW and *Grendel*.

Bjarne Hansen lives in Denmark, working as an illustrator and commercial artist. He earned praise far and wide for his work on Vertigo's HOUSE OF SECRETS.

Richard Starkings is best known for his work on BATMAN: THE KILLING JOKE, BATTLE CHASERS, *The Fantastic Four* and BATMAN: THE LONG HALLOWEEN. He lives in Santa Monica with his wife, Youshka, and their boys, Hunter and Jet.

BOOKS BY JEPH LOEB AND TIM SALE

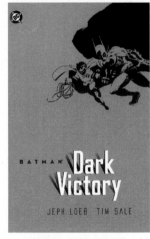

BATMAN: HAUNTED KNIGHT

BATMAN: THE LONG HALLOWEEN

BATMAN: DARK VICTORY

"THREE OF THE TOP 100 TRADE PAPERBACKS OF ALL TIME!" — *Wizard*

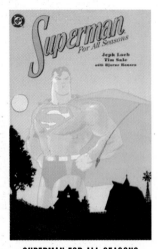

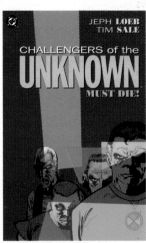

SUPERMAN FOR ALL SEASONS

CHALLENGERS OF THE UNKNOWN
MUST DIE

BATMAN: ARKHAM ASYLUM
Grant Morrison/Dave McKean

BATMAN: THE DARK KNIGHT RETURNS
Frank Miller/Klaus Janson/
Lynn Varley

**BATMAN: THE DARK KNIGHT
STRIKES AGAIN**
Frank Miller/Lynn Varley

BATMAN: HUSH Vols. 1-2
Jeph Loeb/Jim Lee/Scott Williams

BATMAN: THE KILLING JOKE
Alan Moore/Brian Bolland

BATMAN: YEAR ONE
Frank Miller/David Mazzucchelli

CRISIS ON INFINITE EARTHS
Marv Wolfman/George Pérez/
various

GREEN ARROW Vols. 1-4
Kevin Smith/Brad Meltzer/Judd Winick/
Phil Hester/Ande Parks

JLA Vols. 1-14
Grant Morrison/Mark Waid/Joe Kelly/
Howard Porter/John Dell/Bryan Hitch/
Paul Neary/Doug Mahnke/ various

JLA: EARTH 2
Grant Morrison/Frank Quitely

JSA Vols. 1-5
David Goyer/Geoff Johns/James Robinson/
Stephen Sadowski/Rags Morales/
Leonard Kirk/various

JSA ALL STARS
David Goyer/Geoff Johns/Darwyn Cooke/
Tim Sale/Tony Harris/Michael Lark/
Phil Winslade/various

JSA: THE LIBERTY FILES
Dan Jolley/Tony Harris/Ray Snyder

KINGDOM COME
Mark Waid/Alex Ross

RONIN
Frank Miller

SON OF SUPERMAN
Howard Chaykin/David Tischman/
J.H. Williams III/Mick Gray

STARMAN Vols. 1-10
James Robinson/Tony Harris/
Wade von Grawbadger/Peter Snjebjerg/
Phil Jimenez/various

SUPERMAN: THE MAN OF STEEL Vols. 1-3
John Byrne/Marv Wolfman/
Dick Giordano/Jerry Ordway

WATCHMEN
Alan Moore/Dave Gibbons